KEARNEY, Robert N. The politics of Ceylon (Sri Lanka). Cornell,
1973. 249p map tab bibl 73-8702. 13.50.   ISBN 0-8014-
0798-2.   C.I.P.
A basic introduction to the contemporary national politics and society
of Ceylon, now called Sri Lanka since the adoption of the new constitution in 1972. Primarily descriptive in nature, the volume examines the
fundamentals of Ceylonese social and political history, structure of
governmental institutions, religious and ethnic composition of political
parties, some major economic and political problems, and group politics in Ceylon. Simple and lucid in its exposition, it would serve as
an excellent textbook for an undergraduate course on Ceylon. Index
and a brief bibliography are included.

SOUTH ASIAN
POLITICAL SYSTEMS

General Editor
RICHARD L. PARK

The Politics of Nepal: Persistence and
Change in an Asian Monarchy
by Leo E. Rose *and* Margaret W. Fisher

The Politics of Pakistan:
A Constitutional Quest
by Richard S. Wheeler

The Politics of Afghanistan
by Richard S. Newell

The Politics of Ceylon
(Sri Lanka)
by Robert N. Kearney

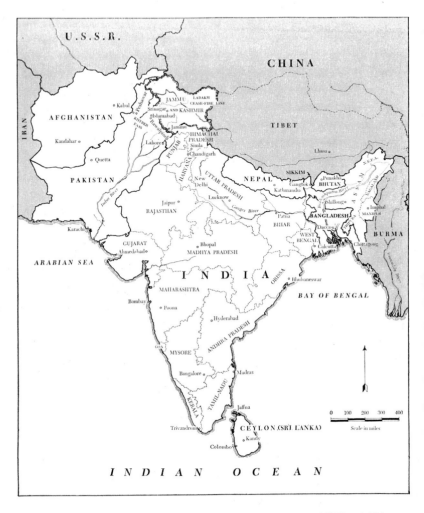

SOUTH ASIA

The Politics of Ceylon (Sri Lanka)

ROBERT N. KEARNEY

Cornell University Press

ITHACA AND LONDON

First published 1973 by Cornell University Press.
Published in the United Kingdom by Cornell University Press Ltd., 2-4 Brook Street, London W1Y 1AA.

International Standard Book Number 0-8014-0798-2
Library of Congress Catalog Card Number 73-8702

Printed in the United States of America by York Composition Co., Inc.

Librarians: Library of Congress cataloging information appears on the last page of the book.

Foreword

Serious study of modern South Asia is a relatively recent development in the United States. It began shortly after World War II, and was made possible by opportunities for language study and research in the region. Scholarly work on current South Asian themes, however, rests upon older academic traditions that emphasized principally the philosophy, religion, and classical literature of these ancient civilizations. This series, "South Asian Political Systems," is addressed to contemporary political problems, but is presented in the context of institutions and value systems that were centuries in the making.

Over the past quarter century, humanists and social scientists in Asia, Europe, the United States, and elsewhere throughout the world have worked together to study modern South Asian cultures. Their efforts have been encouraged by a recognition of the importance of the rapid rise of nationalism in Asia in the twentieth century, by the decline, hastened by the war, of Western imperial systems, and by the appearance of dozens of independent states since the founding of the United Nations. Scholars were made increasingly aware that the South Asian peoples were not anonymous masses or abstract representatives of distant traditions. They were, like us, concerned with their own political affairs, with raising families, building houses, constructing industries, educating the young, and creating better societies. They were nourished by their heritage, but they also struggled to devise political institutions, economic processes, and social organizations that were responsive to modern needs. And their needs were, and continue to be, great.

It was an awareness of these realities that encouraged private foundations and agencies of government to sponsor intensive field work in South Asia, including firsthand observation of day-to-day life and opportunities to discover and use rare source material. India has received the most attention, in part because of its size and intrinsic importance, in part because scholars have concentrated on teaching Indian languages, and research tends to be done where the languages are understood. More and more the other countries of South Asia—Pakistan, Nepal, Ceylon, Afghanistan, and Bangladesh—have begun to attract scholarly attention. Whereas in the late 1940's one was hard pressed to find literature about the region, except in journalistic accounts or in British imperial histories, in the 1970's competent monographs and reliable periodicals are abundantly available. Today one can draw from an impressive bibliography on South Asia, including a commendable list of political works.

It remains true, however, that recent South Asian studies have been largely monographic—books that examine narrow themes in detail and that appeal to a small group of specialists who happen to be concerned with these themes. There are few broad guides to the politics of the countries of South Asia. This series has been designed to fill part of the need.

One of the problems in writing introductory works is that learning about a foreign culture is never a simple process. Experience tells us that each political system is imbedded in a broader social system, which in turn has roots in a particular history and a unique set of values. Language transmits culture, so one way to approach an unfamiliar culture is through the close study of language and literature. Knowledge of history, or of the arts, or of social organization offers another path to understanding.

The focus of this series is on political systems. Each author starts with a common organizational framework—brief history, political dynamics, political structure, continuing problems—and weaves in unique factors. For India, a complex federal organization of government and a varied and changing political party system require emphasis. For Pakistan, the constitutional dilemma is the most crucial issue. For Nepal and Afghanistan, monarchical traditions in conflict with pressures to modernize necessitate treatments that are more historically oriented. Ceylon, too, has political problems, especially ethnic and religious, not readily comparable with others. Used together the books should provide excellent opportunities for comparison and contrast.

Professor Robert N. Kearney has studied Ceylonese politics and society since 1960 and has lived in or visited Ceylon more than a half dozen times in the intervening years. A recurrent theme of his research—encompassing political parties, trade unions, communal groups, and the public service in the Ceylonese political system—has been the changes and adaptations of political structures and practices in response to modernization. Ceylon, recently redesignated the Republic of Sri Lanka, has enjoyed constitutional stability and popularly elected civilian government. It also has experienced the tensions and problems of a communally divided, economically underdeveloped society undergoing profound social changes. His book presents an analysis of the contemporary Ceylonese political system, including discussion of the insurrection which erupted in 1971 and the constitution adopted in 1972, and brings out the problems of slow economic growth, of rising popular aspirations and demands, and of lingering social cleavages, along with the areas of political stability and sophistication.

RICHARD L. PARK

Ann Arbor, Michigan

Preface

It is suggestive of the nature of contemporary Ceylonese politics that during the slightly more than two years this work was in progress, a stunning election landslide brought to power a rival political leadership with a markedly different ideological perspective, an insurrection of unprecedented magnitude and violence rocked the island, and a new constitution was drafted and promulgated. Breathtaking change has been a pervasive feature of Ceylonese politics and society in recent decades. Significant elements of continuity are also apparent, however, and no abrupt and shattering upheaval of the political order has occurred in modern times. Political institutions have displayed considerable resilience, although they have been required to adjust to rapidly changing styles and patterns of political activity. Few contemporary trends cannot be traced to the 1950's or before, but few observers two decades ago could have foreseen the pace and extent of adaptation and change which were to occur by the early 1970's.

Political change in modern Ceylon can be conceived as occurring in a series of stages: (1) social change and the growth of elite political consciousness, ca. 1880–1915; (2) elite politics and constitutional evolution, ca. 1916–1930; (3) the emergence of popular elections and the prelude to mass politics, ca. 1931–1947; (4) rising mass participation, electoral competition, and the popularization of politics, ca. 1948–1959; and (5) the consolidation and institutionalization of mass politics, ca. 1960–1972.

Space and other limitations prevent the tracing of each of these stages in the present work, which is primarily concerned with the character, functioning, and development of the political system in the fourth and, particularly, the fifth of these stages, when mass popular participation had become firmly established and major adjustments to the new environment had been made by the island's political institutions. Although much in this study might be labeled "mere description," this seemed unavoidable and not without usefulness, since Ceylon's political structures and processes have been subjected to relatively little scholarly examination, even of the merely descriptive variety.

The names of political parties and other organizations appear in this work in the form in which the organizations cite their names in English. Some organizations employ English translations of their Sinhalese or Tamil names; others, particularly those more recently founded, use transliterations of their Sinhalese or Tamil names in English, but without diacritical marks distinguishing long from short vowels and retroflex from dental consonants. Thus, for example, the name used in English for the United National Party is a translation of its Sinhalese name, Eksath Jathika Pakshaya, whereas the Mahajana Eksath Peramuna (which could be translated as the People's United Front) has employed its Sinhalese name in English speech and writing. English translations of the Sinhalese names of some organizations have been provided parenthetically for descriptive purposes, but in subsequent references the organizations have been cited by their Sinhalese or Tamil names. Following common practice in Ceylon and in order to avoid the use of diacritical marks or symbols, the sibilant pronounced "sh," which in scholarly works is generally reproduced as *ş*, has been transliterated as *sh*. Similarly, the dental *t* has been transliterated as *th* (the aspirate *t* rarely appears in Sinhalese) and the retroflex *t* simply as *t*.

It is regrettably impossible to mention individually the scores of persons who have made generous and substantial contributions to my work on Ceylonese politics over a dozen years. I am, nonetheless, deeply grateful to each of these many individuals, whose aid and cooperation made this volume possible. Among those from whom I have repeatedly received invaluable information and assistance of many kinds are E. F. Dias Abeyesinghe, Hector Abhayavardhana, S. J. V. Chelvanayakam, Joseph A. L. Cooray, Doric de Souza, Leslie Goonewardene, Godfrey Gunatilleke, Kumari Jayawardena, J. R. Jayewardene, Pieter Keuneman, S. Rajaratnam, T. B. Subasinghe, Bala Tampoe, M. J. Tissainayagam, H. S. Wanasinghe, Sydney Wanasinghe, and D. G. William. In addition, the manuscript has profited greatly from the thoughtful comments and suggestions of James W. Gair, James E. Leader, and Ronald H. McDonald. Richard L. Park not only read the entire manuscript but originally proposed the volume and offered many valuable suggestions for its organization and content. Of course, none of the persons mentioned here is in any way responsible for the errors and omissions or for the interpretations and conclusions contained in this work, the responsibility for which rests entirely with the author.

ROBERT N. KEARNEY

Syracuse, New York

Contents

Tables

Figures

Maps

Abbreviations for Political Parties and Other Organizations

CP	Ceylon Communist Party
CWC	Ceylon Workers' Congress
DMK	Dravida Munnetra Kazhagam
DWC	Democratic Workers' Congress
EBP	Eksath Bhikkhu Peramuna
FP	Federal Party
JVP	Janatha Vimukthi Peramuna
LSSP	Lanka Sama Samaja Party
LSSP(R)	Lanka Sama Samaja Party (Revolutionary)
MEP	Mahajana Eksath Peramuna
SLFP	Sri Lanka Freedom Party
SLFSP	Sri Lanka Freedom Socialist Party
SMP	Sinhala Mahajana Pakshaya
TC	Tamil Congress
UNP	United National Party
VLSSP	Viplavakari Lanka Sama Samaja Party

The Politics of

Ceylon (Sri Lanka)

1. Ceylonese Society
and History

Ceylon, a tropical island nation separated by a narrow strait from the southern tip of India, was formally designated the Republic of Sri Lanka by a new constitution adopted in 1972. This constitution combined a commitment to an egalitarian socialist society with the adoption of the traditional Sinhalese name for the island,[1] symbolizing the nation's recent political and social trends toward increasing responsiveness to the aspirations of the masses of the people.

Ceylon emerged from four centuries of Western colonial rule in February 1948. In the intervening quarter of a century, a sophisticated and highly competitive political system has evolved, accompanied by a "participation revolution" as political awareness spread rapidly through the society. In the creation and institutionalization of political parties, representative institutions, and administrative agencies, and in the rising level of purposeful mass participation in politics, Ceylon must be categorized as among the most politically "modernized" of the newly independent

---

[1] As the nation is still known to the outside world as Ceylon, this name has been retained in the present work. Also, in Ceylon it has become increasingly common to refer in English to the majority ethnic group and its language by the indigenous form "Sinhala" rather than by the anglicized "Sinhalese." As "Sinhala" has not yet become standard English usage outside Ceylon, the form "Sinhalese" is used in this work except, of course, in quotations, where "Sinhala" frequently appears.

1

states. These impressive political and social achievements have not, however, been matched by economic performance. Lagging economic advancement, with a rapid growth in population and an explosive rise in education and aspirations, threatens to place heavy stresses on the political system.

Like other "developing" or "modernizing" societies, Ceylon is undergoing profound and relatively rapid social, economic, political, and ideological changes involving the dislocation of traditional patterns and relationships, the erosion of old values and attitudes, a widening of social and political awareness, and an expansion of effective participation in the political process to include new and broader social groups. With the rapid transformations have come not only new freedoms and opportunities but also new uncertainties, stresses, and frustrations. The changes often proceed unevenly, leaving some geographic regions or social groups lagging behind others, resulting in regional or communal grievances and tensions. Or, to cite a major recent crisis of Ceylon, a swift expansion in secondary and university education may occur without any substantial increase in the employment opportunities for educated persons. It is in an environment of change and transition, accompanied by the erosion of the old familiar patterns and values and the incomplete emergence of the new, that the political system of Ceylon must function.

Society and People of Ceylon

The island of Ceylon is a southern extension of the Indian peninsula, separated from the mainland by a strait thirty to fifty miles in width. Relative to its massive northern neighbor, Ceylon is a small country in population and area. Its population of 13 million is about the same as that of Australia and the Netherlands, its area of 25,332 square miles approximately the same as that of Ireland and the Benelux countries. The maximum distance from north to south is about 270 miles and from east to west 140 miles. Its small size has allowed the country to be bound together by single and well-developed networks of transportation and communications and has facilitated the development of uniform and centralized government administration. Few villages are beyond easy access to a road, a school, a dispensary, a market, and a route of the ubiquitous state-operated bus service.

Ethnically, linguistically, and culturally, the Ceylonese are closely related to the peoples of India. Most of the peoples of Ceylon migrated to the island from India over a period of at least 2,500 years, and the island's languages, religions, and forms of social organization are largely Indian in origin. Theravada Buddhism, brought from India but preserved in Ceylon after its decline on the subcontinent, has acted as a powerful force for differentiation of the majority of the Ceylonese who remain Buddhists from the Hindus of India and has produced some sense of ties with the Theravada Buddhist peoples of Southeast Asia. Other influences have come to Ceylon by sea, notably those brought with the Western incursions of the last five centuries, producing in Ceylon a unique culture and society. Nonetheless, the affinity with India in culture and in social ethos and organization remains close.

The inhabitants of Ceylon are divided by ethnic, linguistic, religious, and caste cleavages. The Sinhalese form the largest ethnic and linguistic community, 71 per cent of the total population (see Table 1). Migrations from North India 2,500 years ago brought the Sinhalese to the island. They speak the Sinhalese language, an Indo-European language related to the languages of North India, and are predominantly Buddhists. The Sinhalese people are divided into low-country and Kandyan branches, a distinction of regional origin. The low-country Sinhalese, comprising three-fifths of the community, are concentrated on the

Table 1. Ethnic communities of Ceylon, 1963

Community	Number	Per cent of total population
Sinhalese		
Low-country	4,470,276	42.2
Kandyan	3,042,639	28.8
Total	7,512,915	71.0
Ceylon Tamils	1,164,689	11.0
Indian Tamils	1,122,961	10.6
Ceylon Moors	626,803	5.9
Indian Moors	55,413	0.5
Burghers and Eurasians	45,944	0.4
Malays	33,428	0.3
Others	19,911	0.2
Total	10,582,064	100.0[a]

[a] Does not add to 100.0 per cent due to rounding.

Source: Ceylon, Department of Census and Statistics, *Statistical Abstract of Ceylon, 1967–1968* (Colombo: Department of Government Printing, 1970), Tables 17–18, pp. 32–33.

densely populated western and southern coastal plains. The Kandyan Sinhalese inhabit the interior hill country and the north-central "dry zone."

The Ceylon Tamils, whose ancestors migrated from South India perhaps 1,000 years ago, speak the Tamil language, one of the Dravidian languages of South India, and are primarily Saivite Hindus. They are concentrated on and near the Jaffna Peninsula at the northern tip of the island and on the east coast. The Ceylon Moors are Muslims resident in Ceylon for several centuries who claim Arabic ancestry but probably are also descended from Indian Muslims. The small Indian Moor community is composed of Muslims recently migrated from India, many of whom are engaged in trade and commerce. The name Moor was applied to the Muslims encountered in Ceylon by the Portuguese in the sixteenth century and has remained in use. The Burghers are of Portuguese or Dutch or, more commonly, of mixed European and Ceylonese extraction. They are largely urban, English-speaking, and Christian. The Malays form a very small Muslim community whose ancestors were brought to Ceylon from the East Indies as soldiers by the Dutch.

The Indian Tamils are a second Tamil-speaking, predominately Hindu minority. They are migrants or the descendants of migrants from South India who came to Ceylon over the past century in search of employment, primarily as estate laborers, and they remain concentrated in the estate areas of the south-central hill country. Shortly after independence, Ceylonese citizenship was defined to exclude most of the Indian Tamils, who were commonly viewed as foreigners without roots or permanent ties on the island. An agreement negotiated between the governments of Ceylon and India in 1964 provided for the repatriation to India of 525,000 noncitizen Indian Tamils and the granting of Ceylonese citizenship to 300,000 over a fifteen-year period, with the disposition of a remaining 150,000 left for later decision. Implementation of the pact has been extremely slow and surrounded by partisan controversy, leaving the Indian Tamil community a precariously situated minority facing an uncertain future on the island.

The introduction of Christianity and the English language during colonial rule blurred only slightly the congruence of ethnic community, religion, and language. Two-thirds of the population of Ceylon are Buddhists, almost one-fifth are Hindus, 8 per cent are Christians, and 7 per cent are Muslims. The Buddhists are almost entirely Sinhalese, the Hindus are Ceylon and Indian Tamils, and the Muslims are Moors and Malays. The Christians are primarily low-country Sinhalese, Ceylon Tamils, and Burghers. While some bilingualism and trilingualism exists, most of the island's people speak only one language (Table 2). English became established early in the nineteenth century as the language of government, higher education, the professions, and large-scale commerce and industry. A rapid growth of education in Sinhalese and Tamil led by independence to insistent demands

Table 2. Languages spoken by persons three years of age and over, 1953

Language(s) spoken	Per cent of population
Sinhalese only	58.9
Tamil only	21.6
English only	0.2
Sinhalese and Tamil	9.9
Sinhalese and English	4.2
Tamil and English	2.0
Sinhalese, Tamil, and English	3.2

Source: Ceylon, Department of Census and Statistics, *Census of Ceylon, 1953,* Vol. III, Part I (Colombo: Government Press, 1960), Table 17, p. 604.

for improved opportunities for those educated in the indigenous languages. Sinhalese was declared to be the sole official language in 1956, and its use in administration, education, and public affairs has subsequently increased considerably.

The Sinhalese and Tamil societies are internally segmented by caste systems. Castes, particularly among the Sinhalese, have largely lost their traditional occupational functions, and hierarchical ranking has declined in effective significance with the appearance of new occupations and new forms of social stratification based on wealth, education, and profession rather than on ascribed status. Castes have, nonetheless, retained importance as endogamous and solidary social groups. The Goyigama (cultivator) caste is the largest in size and generally considered the highest in status of the Sinhalese castes. Other relatively large and prominent Sinhalese castes include the low-country Karāva (fishermen), Salāgama (cinnamon peeler), and Durāva (toddy tapper) castes. The ubiquitous Vahumpura (jaggery maker) and the Batgam (traditional function uncertain) of the interior Kandyan districts are among the larger Sinhalese castes of relatively low traditional status. In Ceylon Tamil society, the Vellala (cultivator) caste has been socially and economically dominant. Next to the Vellala in traditional status is the Koviyar (domestic servant) caste. The Karayar caste is numerous along the northern coast and the Mukkuvar caste is found on the east coast. Both are traditionally associated with fishing. Among the other Ceylon Tamil castes are the Palla (agricultural laborer), Valava (toddy tapper), Ambattar (barber), and Paraya (scavenger) castes. "Untouchable" castes constitute a considerable section of Ceylon Tamil society. The Indian Tamils represent the castes of Madras, a large proportion being from those of low status.

The lingering influences of an ascriptive, rigidly hierarchical, feudal society are evident in contemporary Ceylonese social attitudes and practices, despite modern egalitarian, universalistic, and secular trends. Strong consciousness of status and rank and tenacious attachment to particularistic identifications have persisted in contemporary society. While caste is of declining significance in many social circumstances, the caste background and ethos probably has contributed to the compartmentalization of society and has tended to perpetuate and reinforce concern with relative status and hierarchical position. The recent spread of egalitarian political doctrines, rather than contradicting the importance attributed to status, may be a consequence of the pervasiveness and prominence of hierarchy and privilege in the society. A tendency for the wealthy and powerful to surround themselves with retainers and supporters who extend personal loyalty and deference in exchange for protection and preference, which is exhibited in politics as well as in many other areas of modern life, appears to be rooted in the patron-client relationships of the premodern society. The persistence of particularistic attitudes and identifications probably has inhibited the development of a broadly inclusive civic consciousness and notion of social responsibility, and presumably also has contributed to the fragmentation, rivalries, and schismatic tendencies evident among political parties and other organizations. A common expectation seems to be that a person holding a public office or other position of power will use his position for the near-exclusive benefit of his "own people," defined by kinship, caste, ethnic community, or personal loyalty.

About two-thirds of the Ceylonese population lives in the southwestern quarter of the island, nearly 40 per cent in the four districts of Colombo, Kalutara, Galle, and Matara on the southwest coast (see Map 1). The Colombo district alone includes about one-fifth of the total population although it constitutes only about 3 per cent of the island's area. Population density in Ceylon averages 423 persons per square mile. Density varies, however, from 2,787 persons per square mile in the Colombo district to 48 in the Vavuniya and Monaragala districts. Five of the six districts with the highest population density, all above 900 persons per square mile, are in the southwest corner of the island.[2] The population has been growing very rapidly. The 1963 census enumerated a population of 10,582,064, double the population of 1931. From 1953 to 1963, the population increased by about

[2] Ceylon, Department of Census and Statistics, *Statistical Abstract of Ceylon, 1967–1968* (Colombo: Department of Government Printing, 1970), Table 15, p. 30.

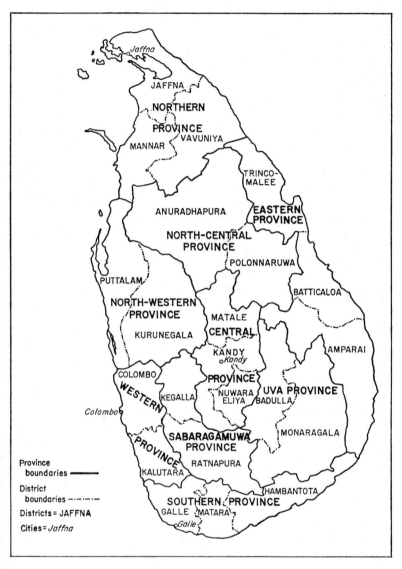

Map 1. Ceylon, showing provinces and administrative districts

30 per cent. By the late 1960's, however, the annual growth rate had declined to about 2.2 per cent.

The Ceylonese are primarily rural villagers. In the 1963 census, 81 per cent of the population was classified as rural. Urbanization is heavily concentrated in the southwestern coastal areas. The city of Colombo is unrivaled as the metropolitan hub of the nation. A 1963 population of 511,644 was enumerated in the Colombo municipal council area. Within the greater Colombo metropolitan area are four of the island's five most populous cities with a total population of about 775,000, almost 40 per cent of the entire urban population of the island. Jaffna, the largest city outside of the greater Colombo area, has less than one-fifth the population of the city of Colombo and about one-eighth the population of greater Colombo.[3]

Agriculture accounts for about 40 per cent of the gross domestic product, with tea contributing the largest share, followed by rice, the staple food of the population. Services and trade are the largest components of the nonagricultural sector (Table 3). The economic system is geared to the production of tea, rubber, and coconuts for export and the importation of manufactured goods and food requirements beyond local production. Although the volume of agricultural production and exports has been rising, steadily declining world market prices for Ceylon's principal export crops have contributed to chronic balance-of-payments difficulties. Stringent import restrictions since 1960 have led to the development of light manufacturing industries producing substitutes for consumer goods which were formerly imported. Nonetheless, economic performance generally has been poor, and efforts at economic expansion have met with slight success. The rapid rise in population combined with sluggish economic growth has led to a critical problem of unemployment and underemploy-

[3] *Ibid.,* Tables 22–24, pp. 39–42.

Table 3.   Gross domestic product, 1967

Industry	Million rupees	Per cent
Agriculture		
Tea	818.1	10.1
Rice	663.0	8.2
Other food crops	459.5	5.7
Coconut products	401.4	5.0
Rubber	254.0	3.1
Livestock	228.1	2.8
Fisheries	187.4	2.3
Other	265.1	3.3
	3,276.6	
Less: banking, insurance, etc.	23.9	
Value added by agriculture	3,252.7	40.1
Services	1,102.6	13.6
Wholesale and retail trade	919.9	11.3
Transport and communications	796.3	9.8
Manufacturing	620.2	7.7
Construction	555.4	6.9
Public administration and defense	426.6	5.3
Banking, insurance, etc.	106.2	1.3
Other	321.9	4.0
Total gross domestic product	8,101.8	100.0

Source: Ceylon, Department of Census and Statistics, *Statistical Abstract of Ceylon, 1967–1968* (Colombo: Department of Government Printing, 1970), Table 179, p. 254.

ment, which is particularly severe among educated youths. Nearly 15 per cent of the labor force was estimated to be unemployed in 1969–1970. Among youths aged fifteen to twenty-four with a secondary education, unemployment reached 70 per cent.[4] In ad-

[4] *Matching Employment Opportunities and Expectations: A Programme of Action for Ceylon,* Vol. I: *The Report of an Inter-Agency Team Or-*

dition to the overt unemployment, underemployment in the form of part-time or seasonal jobs or the sharing of work is believed to be widespread.

More than half of all gainfully employed persons are engaged in agriculture and related pursuits (Table 4). About two-thirds of the gainfully employed are paid workers.[5] The high proportion

Table 4. Gainfully employed population by industry, 1963

Industry	Number	Per cent
Agriculture, forestry, hunting, and fishing	1,681,937	52.5
Services	494,082	15.5
Manufacturing	313,425	9.8
Commerce	289,485	9.1
Transport, storage, and communication	137,598	4.3
Construction	85,131	2.7
Other and activities not adequately described	193,467	6.1
Total gainfully employed	3,195,125	100.0

Source: Ceylon, Department of Census and Statistics, *Statistical Pocket Book of Ceylon, 1970* (Colombo: Department of Government Printing, 1970), Table 18, p. 37.

of paid workers, relative to other developing countries with a labor force concentrated in agriculture, results from the important position occupied by tea, rubber, and coconut production, which is largely carried out on estates employing wage labor. Ceylon possesses a vigorous and rapidly growing labor movement.

---

ganised by the International Labour Office (Geneva: International Labour Office, 1971), pp. 3–4, 25–28.

[5] Ceylon, Department of Census and Statistics, *Census of Population, Ceylon, 1963*, Vol. I, Part II: "The Gainfully Employed Population, Tables Based on a 10% Sample" (Colombo: Government Press, 1967), Table 2, p. 4.

In 1967, nearly 1,454,000 employees belonged to trade unions, compared to about 360,000 in 1955 and 144,000 in 1945.[6]

Per capita gross national product in 1970 was Rs. 928 (about $155),[7] which although low in comparison with the industrialized nations of the West was moderately high relative to other countries in the region.[8] A 1963 survey found average urban incomes to be about double rural nonestate incomes and four times the size of incomes on the estates. Inequality of income distribution had declined since a survey in 1953, but remained marked, with a large proportion of the sample clustered at the lower income levels. Nearly two-thirds of the persons included in the sample, with incomes of Rs. 300 a month or less, received only 7.6 per cent of the total income received by all persons in the sample, while at the higher income levels a mere 0.4 per cent of the persons in the sample received an almost equal proportion of the income, 7.1 per cent.[9]

[6] Robert N. Kearney, *Trade Unions and Politics in Ceylon* (Berkeley: University of California Press, 1971), p. 16.

[7] Central Bank of Ceylon, *Annual Report of the Monetary Board to the Minister of Finance for the Year 1970* (Colombo: Central Bank of Ceylon, 1971), Appendix II, Table 1. In 1967, the official exchange rate of the Ceylon rupee was devalued from $0.20 to $0.17, and the following year a second rate of about $0.11 was applied for certain purposes to encourage the earning of hard currency. The world market rate was generally even lower. For the conversion of rupees into dollars, the official exchange rate of $0.17 has been used, but the resulting dollar figure should be considered as only a very rough indication of the rupee value.

[8] Ceylon's 1968 per capita gross domestic product of $140 was significantly higher than that of India ($78), Burma ($70), and Indonesia ($93). It was only slightly higher than that of Pakistan ($130), and lower than that of Malaysia ($280) and the Philippines ($294). United Nations, Statistical Office, *Statistical Yearbook, 1970* (New York: United Nations Publication, 1971), Table 184, pp. 597–601.

[9] *Ceylon Investment Guide: The General Economic Environment* (Colombo: Industrial Development Board, Ministry of Industries and

Ceylon has attained a remarkably high level of education and literacy. At the 1963 census, the literacy rate for all persons five years of age and over was nearly 72 per cent.[10] Almost eight of every ten males and two of every three females were literate. Steady advances in literacy have been recorded since the first census in 1881 (see Table 5). A significant feature of the growth in literacy, which distinguishes Ceylon from many other developing societies, is the rapid progress made in female literacy during

Table 5. Growth in literacy of population five years of age and over, 1881–1963

Year	Per cent literate		
	All persons	Males	Females
1881	17.4	29.8	3.1
1891	21.7	36.1	5.3
1901	26.4	42.0	8.5
1911	31.0	47.2	12.5
1921	39.9	56.3	21.2
1946	57.8	70.1	43.8
1953	65.4	75.9	53.6
1963	71.9	79.4	63.8

Source: Ceylon, Department of Census and Statistics, *Statistical Abstract of Ceylon, 1967–1968* (Colombo: Department of Government Printing, 1970), Table 20, p. 35; Ceylon, Department of Census and Statistics, *Statistical Pocket Book of Ceylon, 1970* (Colombo: Department of Government Printing, 1970), Table 11, p. 27.

Fisheries, 1968), pp. 79–80. It has been noted, however, that income inequality appears to be less marked in Ceylon than in most developing countries. *Matching Employment Opportunities and Expectations,* p. 55n.

[10] The 6,452,800 literates in 1963 constituted 61 per cent of the total population. This compares with the 24 per cent of the total population of India which was literate in 1961. *India: A Reference Annual, 1965* (Delhi: Publications Division, Ministry of Information and Broadcasting, 1965), p. 68.

the present century. Among the major ethnic communities, literacy of persons five years of age and over in 1963 varied from 79 per cent for the low-country Sinhalese and 77 per cent for the Ceylon Tamils to 51 per cent for the Indian Tamils. On a regional basis, literacy rates ranged from 85 per cent in the Colombo district to 52 per cent in the thinly populated jungle district of Monaragala. The five administrative districts with the highest literacy rates, all above 75 per cent, were Jaffna in the north and Puttalam, Colombo, Kalutara, and Galle, which form a belt along the west coast (see Map 1, p. 9). The five districts with the lowest rates of literacy—Batticaloa, Nuwara Eliya, Badulla, Amparai, and Monaragala—are clustered in the southeast corner of the island.[11]

The growth in literacy reflects a swift expansion of education commencing in the late nineteenth century and accelerating in the last three decades. By 1969, school enrollments had reached almost 2,670,000.[12] Education in government schools has been free from the primary through the university level since 1945. The educational level attained by persons fifteen years of age and older at the time of the 1963 census is presented in Table 6. About one-fifth had completed at least eight years of education and 45 per cent had completed the fifth year or more. Nearly 20,000 persons had university degrees or the equivalent. While educational levels are higher among the urban than among the rural population, the extent of education in the rural areas is striking. Although one-fourth had no schooling, more than 40

[11] Ceylon, Department of Census and Statistics, *Census of Population, Ceylon, 1963*, Vol. I, Part I: "General Characteristics, Tables Based on a 10% Sample" (Colombo: Government Press, 1967), Tables 14–15, pp. 52–54.

[12] Ceylon, Department of Census and Statistics, *Statistical Pocket Book of Ceylon, 1970* (Colombo: Department of Government Printing, 1970), Table 31, p. 48.

Table 6. Educational attainment of persons fifteen years of age and over, 1963

Highest level attained	Per cent		
	Ceylon	Urban	Rural
No schooling	23	11	26
Below standard 3	9	6	10
Standard 3	19	16	19
Standard 5	26	28	25
Standard 8	11	17	10
General Certificate of Education[a]	8	15	7
University degree[b]	—	1	—
Unspecified	4	6	4
Total	100	100	100[c]

[a] Including education beyond the General Certificate of Education (Ordinary Level) and technical training not equivalent to a university degree. Examination for the GCE (Ordinary Level) is taken after the fifth year of secondary education (the tenth year of schooling) at sixteen-plus years of age. A further two years of "higher school" intended as preparation for university study leads to examination for the GCE (Advanced Level), which also serves as a university entrance examination.

[b] Including technical training equivalent to a university degree and graduate degrees.

[c] Does not add to 100 per cent due to rounding.

Source: Ceylon, Department of Census and Statistics, *Census of Population, Ceylon, 1963*, Vol. I, Part I: "General Characteristics, Tables Based on a 10% Sample" (Colombo: Government Press, 1967), Table 16, pp. 55–57.

per cent of the rural population aged fifteen and over had reached a fifth standard or higher education. The proportion climbed to 55 per cent among rural youths between fifteen and twenty-four years of age. By 1969–1970, 19 per cent of the urban and 13 per cent of the rural nonstate labor force, but only 1 per cent of the estate labor force, had completed studies through the

General Certificate of Education (Ordinary Level), representing ten years of schooling.[13]

With the spectacularly rising literacy and expanding school enrollments, a socially mobilized mass public has apparently emerged. A 1964 survey of newspaper readership, radio listening, and movie attendance discovered a very high level of contact with mass communications media (Table 7). For the island, the survey found that 53 per cent of the men and 23 per cent of the women read some periodical publication, 58 per cent of the men and 33 per cent of the women listened to the radio, and 57 per cent of the men and 36 per cent of the women attended movies. Slightly more than 80 per cent of the men and more than half the women throughout the island were reached by one or more of the media. Media contact was consistently smaller for the rural than for the urban population and for women than for men in all strata and for all types of media (with the single exception of movie attendance by urban upper-middle-class women). Although lower than in urban areas, remarkably high exposure to the media was discovered in the rural villages, particularly in the "wet zone" of the southern and western coastal plains, where nearly two-thirds of the island's rural population lives. Among rural women of the north-central and eastern "dry zone," the Jaffna Peninsula, and the estates, media contact was virtually limited to radio-listening and movie attendance. For men, while the estates and rural Jaffna lagged behind the island average in all but movie attendance, no segment of the sample was without significant contact with mass communications media.

The survey also confirmed the compartmentalization of the population by language. It was found that 42 per cent of the men and 16 per cent of the women read only Sinhalese publications, 3 per cent of the men and 1 per cent of the women read only

[13] *Matching Employment Opportunities and Expectations,* p. 23.

Table 7. Contact with mass communications media, 1964 (in per cent)

Media contact	Total Ceylon	Urban				Rural				
		Total urban	Upper middle class[a]	Lower middle class[b]	Working class	Total rural	Wet zone	Dry zone	Rural Jaffna	Estate Tamils
Reading some publication[c]										
Men	53	80	100	94	67	45	54	38	24	18
Women	23	65	98	83	47	13	17	5	7	3
Reading daily newspaper										
Men	42	71	100	89	51	34	42	29	18	9
Women	15	49	96	73	26	6	8	3	3	1
Reading weekly newspaper										
Men	41	71	98	85	51	33	41	27	17	13
Women	19	54	95	77	36	10	15	5	5	2

Listening to the radio									
Men	58	73	93	81	60	55	57	59	48	37
Women	33	62	89	79	45	26	25	32	25	15
Attending movies									
Men	57	77	83	73	72	52	53	54	45	57
Women	36	62	85	71	61	29	30	35	37	13
Contacted by one or more of the media studied									
Men	82	95	100	100	91	79	82	81	72	66
Women	57	87	100	97	78	49	50	56	53	27

[a] Called "upper and middle class" in the survey, and including persons with a family income of over Rs. 500 per month.

[b] Including persons with a family income of Rs. 200–500 per month.

[c] Defined as having read a daily newspaper on the preceding day, a weekly newspaper during the preceding seven days, a fortnightly publication during the preceding two weeks, or a monthly publication during the preceding four weeks.

Source: "Readership Survey, Ceylon, April–June 1964, Conducted for the Audit Bureau of Circulations Limited by the Market Research Department of Lever Brothers (Ceylon) Limited" (mimeographed; Colombo, Sept. 1964), Tables 4 and 5.

Tamil publications, and 3 per cent of the men and 4 per cent of the women read only English publications. Almost the only bilingual readership involved English publications. Only 4 per cent of the men and 3 per cent of the women read both English and Sinhalese publications, while less than 0.5 per cent of the men and none of the women read both English and Tamil publications. The reading of Sinhalese, Tamil, and English publications was confined to a minute section of the urban upper-middle class.[14]

Four daily newspapers with average circulations exceeding 50,000 and eleven with average circulations between 10,000 and 50,000 were published on the island in 1966. The average circulation of three weekly newspapers exceeded 100,000, that of four ranged between 50,000 and 100,000, and that of fourteen was between 10,000 and 50,000. Sinhalese-language newspapers accounted for slightly more than half the daily and three-fourths of the weekly circulation. About one-fourth of the daily and one-sixth of the weekly circulation consisted of newspapers published in English, and one-fifth of the daily and one-tenth of the weekly circulation consisted of newspapers published in Tamil.[15] Nearly 10 million copies of books representing 1,200 titles, three-quarters in the Sinhalese language, were published in Ceylon during the same year.[16]

Historical Background

The history of Ceylon and the Sinhalese people conventionally commences with the arrival, 25 centuries ago, of a north Indian

[14] "Readership Survey, Ceylon, April–June 1964, Conducted for the Audit Bureau of Circulations Limited by the Market Research Department of Lever Brothers (Ceylon) Limited" (mimeographed; Colombo, Sept. 1964), Table 17.

[15] Ceylon, Department of Census and Statistics, *Ceylon Year Book, 1968* (Colombo: Government Press, 1968), pp. 317–318.

[16] *Statistical Abstract of Ceylon, 1967–1968*, Table 282, p. 365.

prince, Vijaya, and a band of 700 followers. According to Sinhalese tradition, the landing of Vijaya coincided with the Buddha's death and attainment of Nirvana. As recorded in Ceylon's ancient chronicle, the *Mahāvaṃsa,* the Buddha informed the god Sakka (Indra) of Vijaya's arrival in Ceylon and declared: "In Laṅkā, O lord of gods, will my religion be established, therefore carefully protect him with his followers and Laṅkā."[17] In about the fifth century, B.C., Aryan-speaking peoples from northern India settled on the island, probably intermingling with earlier inhabitants and assimilating migrations of Dravidian-speaking peoples from South India, to form the Sinhalese people. In the third century, B.C., the Sinhalese were converted to Buddhism, according to Sinhalese tradition by Mahinda, son of the Indian emperor Asoka. Over the next few centuries, a flourishing civilization began to develop around the city of Anuradhapura in the north-central dry zone, ushering in the "golden age" of Sinhalese history. The Anuradhapura civilization was based on a technologically advanced system of irrigation reservoirs and canals, constructed and maintained by a succession of monarchs over a period of more than 1,000 years. The extent and complexity of the irrigation system indicated not only a high technological level but a considerable degree of organizational and administrative capacity. In addition to the irrigation system, temples and shrines were built and literary and artistic works produced. Early contacts existed with Rome, Egypt, and China, and commercial and political connections with South India appear to have been common. From the seventh century, the Sinhalese were increasingly drawn into the wars of South India resulting from the rise of the Pandya and Chola empires. In the eleventh century, the capital was shifted westward from Anuradhapura to Polonnaruva.

[17] *The Mahāvaṃsa or the Great Chronicle of Ceylon,* trans. by Wilhelm Geiger (Colombo: Ceylon Government Information Department, 1960), p. 55.

Political organization was decentralized, with the outlying provinces under officials called *dissavas,* who obtained greater or lesser autonomy depending on the strength of the monarch and the extent of his distraction by foreign invasions or other problems. Three areas of Ceylon came to be identified, sometimes administered as provinces of a united kingdom and occasionally constituting independent or virtually independent kingdoms. Rajarata or the Royal Country, the center of the Sinhalese civilization surrounding Anuradhapura and Polonnaruva, lay in the dry zone to the north of the central highlands. In the far southeast was Ruhuna. The southwest coastal plains were known as Dakunudesa, the South Land. In addition, the central highlands, called Malaya, were usually under weak control from the Rajarata. The notion of a politically unified Ceylon, consolidated by a single monarch "under one umbrella," was strong, although the authority of the Rajarata king was often weak or absent in the distant provinces. Although South Indians occasionally occupied the thrones of Sinhalese kingdoms, in almost 2,000 years prior to the sixteenth century a major portion of Ceylon was ruled as a part of a foreign kingdom only once, for a period of seventy-five years in the eleventh century, when the Rajarata was annexed by the South Indian Chola empire.

Religion and government were closely intertwined. Kings were the patrons of Buddhism and the guardians of the sangha (Buddhist clergy). Many temples and monasteries were built, and large tracts of land were given by kings for the support of monasteries. The sangha seems to have been influential in affairs of state, including mediation of the frequent dynastic disputes. Although monarchs were absolute and began to claim divine status, the notion persisted that they were bound to govern in accordance with the Buddhist doctrine, an early suggestion of constitutionalism or the rule of law. The society was rigidly stratified, and occupations were hereditary. Social and economic relationships were ordered on a feudal pattern of land tenure linked to service obligations. Rank was almost entirely ascriptive, and royal officials were drawn exclusively from the most privileged stratum. A large section of the society was composed of cultivators, who assumed a status of authority and respectability in the locality. Ranked hierarchically under them were persons in craft and service occupations.

The classic Sinhalese dry-zone civilization began to decline by the thirteenth century, torn by dynastic conflicts and under pressure from South Indian invasions. Gradual decay overtook the irrigation system which was essential for the support of a large agricultural population in the dry zone. The Sinhalese began shifting to the southern and western wet zone. Jungle reclaimed vast tracts of the central dry zone and enveloped the temples and pavilions of the once-flourishing civilization.

From early times, Tamil-speaking people had drifted to the island from South India. Many were presumably assimilated into the Sinhalese population. After the tenth century, their numbers increased and they began to form a distinct and sizable separate group, by the thirteenth century establishing an independent kingdom in the North around the Jaffna Peninsula. By the fifteenth century, the island contained three kingdoms, one in the southwest with its capital at Kotte near the present city of Colombo, one in the highlands with its capital at Kandy, and the northern Tamil kingdom.

Until the sixteenth century, contacts with India largely shaped the society and influenced the course of history of the Ceylonese. Thereafter, European nations were to provide the principal external influence on the island. Ceylon lies on the maritime highway linking Europe and the Middle East with the Far East and Southeast Asia. Foreign traders had called at its shores for centuries, but the expansion of European exploration and trade in the sixteenth century brought a new contact which was to have

profound implications for the island. As the Sinhalese shifted to
the wet zone, production of spices, particularly cinnamon, began
to increase, attracting Arab, Indian, and later European traders.
In 1505, the Portuguese arrived on the island seeking spices and
conversions to Christianity and remaining to obtain political control of the coastal areas. The Portuguese had reduced the Kingdom of Kotte to a virtual protectorate by mid-century, and in
1597 they assumed sovereignty over its territory. A few decades
later Jaffna was annexed by Portugal. Only the Kandyan Kingdom remained independent, ruling the central highlands and the
east coast. After protracted warfare, the king of Kandy sought
Dutch assistance against the Portuguese, who were expelled in
1658. However, the Dutch, attracted by the cinnamon trade,
retained for themselves the coastal territories they seized from
Portugal and remained on the island for 140 years. In the eighteenth century, they obtained control of the east coast, leaving
the Kandyan Kingdom landlocked.

Ceylon's strategic location for the defense of Britain's expanding Indian empire stimulated British interest in the island at the
end of the eighteenth century. Overtures by the Kandyan king,
who sought military support against the Dutch, brought British
forces to the island, leading to the expulsion of the Dutch in
1796. Repeating the experience of the preceding century, the
British proceeded to install themselves in control of the former
Dutch territories. After a brief period of administration by the
East India Company, the British possessions in Ceylon were
placed under the Colonial Office in 1801, separating Ceylon
from India and allowing the island to follow an independent path
of development over the century and a half of British rule. In
1815, after nearly three centuries of pressure from European
powers, the Kandyan Kingdom was extinguished and all of Ceylon was brought under British rule. Despite rebellions in the
Kandyan areas in 1818 and 1848, the nineteenth century wit-

nessed the consolidation of British administration and growth of British economic and cultural penetration.

The nearly three centuries of Portuguese and Dutch involvement on the island had only a marginal and localized impact, producing few fundamental changes in the social and economic patterns of the great majority of the Ceylonese people. The Portuguese had encouraged cinnamon production and introduced the Roman Catholic church. A large number of Portuguese words entered the Sinhalese language and many Ceylonese adopted Portuguese personal names. Under the Dutch, canals and roads were built, primary education was expanded, Roman-Dutch law was introduced, and a shift from subsistence agriculture to production for the market was encouraged. Portuguese and Dutch rule did not extend beyond the coastal areas, however, and both powers governed their territories much as they had been governed before the arrival of the Europeans. The nineteenth century, in contrast, brought the beginnings of major social, economic, and political changes which eventually were to touch the life of virtually every person on the island.

Far-reaching reforms in 1833 undermined the feudal system of service obligations and land tenure, ended caste and communal inequality in law, and promoted education in the English language. Indirect rule of the Kandyan areas was terminated and the island was brought under a uniform and centralized system of administration. The beginnings of urbanization and the creation of a modern bureaucracy led to the appearance of urban clerical, professional, and managerial occupations. Fundamental changes in the economy of the island followed the introduction of estate agriculture at mid-century. Huge tracts of uncultivated hill land were claimed by the colonial government and sold to European planters. Great estates spread through the Kandyan highlands, initially cultivating coffee and then switching to tea in the latter part of the century. Labor on the estates was provided by Tamils recruited in South India, introducing a new ethnic community into the population. An accelerating pace of economic activity and the construction of roads and railroads followed the growth of planting. Improvements in transportation and communication tended to break down the isolation of the villages and to allow the penetration of new economic and cultural influences. Education began to spread outward from Colombo and Jaffna. The erosion of the feudal basis of society, the gradually increasing availability of education, and the opening of new avenues of social mobility contributed to a weakening of the traditional rigid, ascriptive, and hierarchical features of the social order. By the end of the century, a Ceylonese middle class of significant size, created by the new economic and educational opportunities and concentrated in the expanding professions and public service, commerce, and planting, had appeared. The nascent middle class was largely educated in the English language and tended to adopt Western values, attitudes, and styles of living.

The growth of modern political consciousness and activity can be traced to a cluster of religious and social reform movements which appeared in the late nineteenth and early twentieth centuries. The earliest and strongest of the new forces was a Buddhist revival which had generated considerable momentum by the latter part of the nineteenth century, particularly in the coastal areas and among the social groups most affected by the recent social and economic changes. Many revivalist spokesmen were members of the middle class who had been educated in Christian missionary schools and had reacted to Christian proselytizing by developing enthusiasm for the regeneration of Buddhism, often combined with hostility toward Christianity and other Western intrusions. Buddhist counterattacks against Christian missionary activity produced a series of public debates and led to an outpouring of polemical pamphlets and newspapers.

The Buddhist Theosophical Society, a lay organization founded in 1880, championed the Buddhist cause and began to establish Buddhist schools. A militant Buddhist revivalist, Anagarika Dharmapala, energetically spread a message of Buddhist and Sinhalese resurgence, which he linked with strident criticism of Western cultural penetration and political domination.

The Buddhist revival was closely followed by a growth of social welfare and reform movements spearheaded by members of the new middle class. In the first two decades of the twentieth century a temperance movement gained considerable force, becoming a vehicle for nationalist and anticolonial sentiments. Sinhalese-language newspapers, novels, and plays appeared in increasing numbers, frequently denouncing the cultural impact of the West and glorifying Sinhalese culture and history. At about the same time, the beginnings of an organized labor movement appeared among the workers of Colombo. The island's first major strike was called by Colombo printers in 1893, to be followed by a railway strike in 1912, railway and harbor strikes in 1920, and a general strike in 1923. The first durable labor organization, the Ceylon Labour Union, was formed in 1922.

Demands for constitutional reform had largely been limited to the resident British merchants and planters until the closing decades of the nineteenth century. By the end of the century, however, agitation for greater self-government had begun to grow within the ranks of the new Ceylonese middle class. No major change in the colony's system of government had been made since 1833. The colonial governor, responsible to the Colonial Office in London, had complete authority over the governmental machinery. A Legislative Council had been established in 1833, but it was dominated by official members who were senior public servants and the minority of unofficial members were nominated by the governor to represent ethnic communities. The unofficial members were three Europeans, a Sinhalese, a Tamil, and a Burgher until 1889, when a Kandyan Sinhalese and a Muslim were added. An Executive Council, also created in 1833 to advise the governor, was composed entirely of senior government officials until 1920.

In a famous memorandum to the Colonial Office, drafted in 1908, James Peiris, a Sinhalese nationalist leader, cited major social and economic changes which the island had experienced since 1833 and called for two "urgently needed" Legislative Council reforms, "the abolition of the present system of racial representation, and the introduction of the elective principle in place of nomination."[18] In 1912, the first non-European elected members entered the Legislative Council.[19] One Burgher and two European representatives were elected by communal constituencies. An additional member, representing the "educated Ceylonese," was elected on a very narrow franchise consisting of persons of all communities except Europeans and Burghers who had passed the Cambridge junior certificate examination or owned property worth Rs. 30,000. However, six other unofficial members were nominated by the governor, and a majority of official members was maintained in the council. The constitutional reforms were generally disappointing to the Ceylonese desiring a greater voice in governing the colony.

Sentiment for self-rule was sharpened by the colonial government's reaction to an outbreak of riots between Sinhalese Buddhists and Muslims in 1915. Apparently fearing a rebellion, the government resorted to measures judged by Ceylonese opinion to have been inappropriately severe and largely directed against in-

[18] James Peiris, "Memorandum," in S. W. R. D. Bandaranaike (ed.), *The Hand-Book of the Ceylon National Congress, 1919–1928* (Colombo: H. W. Cave & Co., 1928), p. 9.

[19] After 1855, three unofficial European members had been selected by the Chamber of Commerce, the Planters' Association, and the general European community.

nocent persons. Martial law was imposed, a number of persons were summarily executed, and many prominent Sinhalese, particularly leaders of the temperance movement, were imprisoned. The episode seemed to be a stark and tragic demonstration of the need for representative and responsible government. Soon thereafter an organized movement emerged to seek increasing Ceylonese control of the government; eventually it's objective was extended into a demand for independence. The Ceylon Reform League, founded in 1917, combined in 1919 with the Ceylon National Association to form the Ceylon National Congress, dedicated "to secure for the people of Ceylon responsible Government and the status of a self-governing member of the British Empire."[20] The Congress was composed almost entirely of middle-class lawyers, planters, landowners, businessmen, and retired public servants, and for many decades political activity scarcely extended beyond the ranks of the small, Westernized, predominantly urban middle class.

In the years following the founding of the Congress, constitutional revisions came rapidly. In 1921, for the first time, the Legislative Council contained an unofficial majority and included members elected from territorial constituencies (see Table 8). In addition to fourteen official members, the council consisted of twenty-three unofficial members, eleven elected from territorial constituencies, five elected by communal constituencies or associations, and seven nominated by the governor. A further shift toward election and noncommunal representation occurred four years later. Of thirty-seven unofficial members in the restructured Legislative Council of 1924, twenty-three were elected from territorial and eleven from communal constituencies. Educational and property qualifications sharply restricted the franchise, however, and the powers of the governor were largely undiminished.

[20] "Constitution of the Ceylon National Congress," in Bandaranaike, *The Hand-Book of the Ceylon National Congress,* Appendix H, p. 162.

Table 8. Composition of legislative chambers, 1833–1946

Type of member	Legislative Council, 1833–1889	Legislative Council, 1889–1911	Legislative Council, 1912–1920	Legislative Council, 1921–1924	Legislative Council, 1924–1930	State Council, 1931–1946
Official members	9	9	11	14	12	3
Unofficial members						
Nominated	6ᵃ	5	6	7	3	8
Elected, communal constituencies		3ᵃ	3	5	11	
Elected, other basis			1ᵇ			
Elected, territorial constituencies				11	23	50
Total members	15	17	21	37	49	61

ᵃ Between 1855 and 1911, three Europeans were elected by the Chamber of Commerce, the Planters' Association, and the general European community.

ᵇ Elected by the "educated Ceylonese" excluding Europeans and Burghers.

Source: S. G. Perera, A History of Ceylon, Vol.II: The British Period and After, 1796–1956, rev. by V. Perniola (7th ed.; Colombo: Associated Newspapers of Ceylon, Ltd., 1959), Chapters VII and XII; G. C. Mendis, Ceylon Under the British (2nd ed.; Colombo: Colombo Apothecaries Co., Ltd., 1948), Chapter X; and Great Britain, Colonial Office, Ceylon: Report of the Commission on Constitutional Reform, Cmd. 6677 (London: His Majesty's Stationery Office, 1945), pp. 7–18.

A major transition in the political evolution of Ceylon came with the adoption in 1931 of the Donoughmore constitution (named for the head of the Colonial Office commission recommending the constitutional revision). The Donoughmore proposals were described as intended "to transfer to the elected representatives of the people complete control over the internal affairs of the Island, subject only to provisions which will ensure that they are helped by the advice of experienced officials and to the exercise by the Governor of certain safeguarding powers."[21] With the Donoughmore constitution, election triumphed over nomination and communal representation disappeared, except for a few appointed legislators named to represent minority communities. A State Council was created consisting of sixty-one members, fifty of whom were elected from territorial constituencies. Eight additional members were appointed by the governor and three were senior colonial officials. Even more dramatic was the constitution's introduction of universal adult suffrage. As a result of the drastic extension of the franchise, the number of eligible voters jumped from 205,000 in 1924 to more than 1,500,-000 in 1931.[22] The experimental executive-committee system by which the State Council sought to exercise executive functions, modeled on the London County Council, was generally viewed as unsatisfactory and was abandoned in favor of a cabinet system at the next constitutional revision in 1946. The Donoughmore constitution nonetheless provided the framework for a modern political process based on broad popular participation and competitive elections.

[21] Great Britain, Colonial Office, *Ceylon: Report of the Special Commission on the Constitution,* Cmd. 3131 (London: His Majesty's Stationery Office, 1928), p. 149.

[22] Great Britain, Colonial Office, *Ceylon: Report of the Commission on Constitutional Reform,* Cmd. 6677 (London: His Majesty's Stationery Office, 1945), p. 54.

From an early date the independence movement was divided between radicals and moderate constitutional reformers. The moderates, who maintained a cautious and gradualist approach to political reform, dominated the Ceylon National Congress, which was pledged to act "by constitutional methods by a reform of the existing system of Government and Administration."[23] In 1927, the moderate leadership of the Congress argued for retention of a limited franchise based on educational and property qualifications in opposition to proposals for universal suffrage. The radicals differed not only in their impatience for independence but also in their concern with domestic social and economic problems. While generally of middle-class backgrounds, they expressed sympathy for the plight of the lower classes and sought to stimulate mass political consciousness through agitational techniques. The Young Lanka League, founded in 1915, early reflected the radical viewpoint. Although affiliated with the Ceylon National Congress after 1919, the league was frequently in conflict with the cautious Congress leadership. In 1928, A. E. Goonesinha, a Young Lanka League radical, withdrew from the Congress to found the Labour Party. A Marxist party, the Lanka Sama Samaja Party, was formed in 1935 and won two seats in the 1936 State Council election.

A second political cleavage developed between the Sinhalese and the Ceylon Tamils. At the commencement of the movement for self-government, hope for communal harmony was strong. A Tamil, Sir Ponnambalam Arunachalam, became the first president of the Ceylon National Congress in 1919. Within two years, however, most Tamil leaders had left the Congress in a dispute over communal representation, leaving the organization largely composed of low-country Sinhalese. Communal rivalry intensified with the constitutional changes shifting political power into the

[23] "Constitution of the Ceylon National Congress," p. 162.

hands of popularly elected representatives. Universal suffrage and territorial constituencies assured political dominance for the large Sinhalese majority. A Ceylon Tamil boycott of the 1931 election, protesting the rigorously majoritarian Donoughmore constitution, left four Northern Province seats unfilled in the first State Council. In 1936, an entirely Sinhalese slate of executive-committee chairmen was selected by the State Council, demonstrating the implicit power of the Sinhalese majority. During constitutional debates in anticipation of independence, a scheme to limit Sinhalese to half the membership of the legislature and half the cabinet appointments was championed by Tamil spokesmen. The Colonial Office commission charged with recommending the future constitution rejected the scheme in favor of a constitutional order which, although including provisions enhancing the representation of the minorities and prohibiting communally discriminatory legislation, was basically majoritarian and noncommunal. The constitution, as amended in 1947 to provide for complete independence and with minor subsequent amendments, served Ceylon until 1972.

By the end of the Second World War, independence was recognized as imminent. Negotiations between Ceylonese political leaders and British officials proceded in an orderly and generally amicable fashion with little emotion or conflict. Ceylon is often said to have gained independence as a by-product of the Indian independence struggle. General strikes in 1946 and 1947 are thought to have hastened the process, but generally the last decades of the passage to independence were marked by little coercive pressure and an absence of violence. Because independence came without arduous struggle and with little drama, the independence movement directly contributed little to creating mass political consciousness or to disturbing existing social and political relationships. Nonetheless, the cumulative effect of the perennial debates on constitutional revision, the agitation of the small but vocal bands of radicals, and particularly the introduction of universal suffrage and election campaigns had already stimulated political awareness in the towns and cities and had laid the groundwork for the seepage of political consciousness down to the village masses. Within a decade of independence, the population was highly politicized, voter participation in elections was soaring, and a process of popularization of politics had commenced. Increasingly, ordinary people became aware that their own problems and needs could be ameliorated through political action.

The effective entry of new and broader social groups into the political system is often identified with an election in 1956, which not only produced the first of a series of transfers of power between opposing political parties but marked the first explicit and concerted effort to win electoral support by direct appeal to the broad masses of the village population on issues of specific and immediate concern to them. Popular support was mobilized to defeat the party in power since independence by appealing to the religious, linguistic, and material grievances and aspirations of the rural Sinhalese Buddhist masses. The success of the mass popular appeals forced virtually all parties and politicians to alter their programs and perspectives to accomodate more adequately the wants and needs of the common people. The rising currents of populism and egalitarianism have been intertwined with a surge of majoritarianism among the Sinhalese-speaking Buddhists, who constitute a large majority of the island's people and who suffer from a sense of past discrimination and neglect. The "common people" often came to be identified with the majority community, and socialist and egalitarian policies intended to improve the circumstances of the underprivileged classes were combined with actions to enhance the status and opportunities of the Sinhalese and the Buddhists.

2. Structure and Process of Government

On May 22, 1972, at the astrologically determined auspicious moment of 12:43 P.M., a new constitution was proclaimed for the Republic of Sri Lanka, marking the first extensive constitutional revision since 1947, when the 1946 constitution was amended to provide for independence. The constitution of 1972, approved by a Constituent Assembly composed of the members of parliament, reflected the populist and socialist currents of the preceding decades, but the basic structure of government it created did not appear to differ radically from that set forth in the earlier constitution.

The strong influence of British constitutional forms and practices has been clearly evident in the government institutions of Ceylon. Under the constitution which had served Ceylon since independence, executive authority and control of administration was vested in a cabinet headed by a prime minister. The cabinet was responsible to and dependent for its continuation in office on the lower house of parliament, the House of Representatives. A feeble upper chamber, the Senate, which had only delaying powers in respect to legislation and no power to overturn the Government,[1] had been abolished in 1971. The judicial system

[1] Following a practice common in Ceylon and other countries with parliamentary systems, the word "Government"—capitalized—is used in this work to refer to the political executive or Ministry. Uncapitalized,

was capped by the Supreme Court of Ceylon. The basic formal institutions were completed by the governor-general, who served as ceremonial head of state and the constitutional equivalent of the British monarch. The new constitution declared Ceylon to be a republic, and a president replaced the governor-general as the ceremonial head of state. Legislative powers were vested in a single chamber, the National State Assembly, which is the successor to the House of Representatives. The cabinet, led by a prime minister, is responsible to the National State Assembly. The system of government has continued to be unitary in form and highly centralized. Power and responsibility are more fully concentrated in the hands of the assembly and cabinet than in the earlier constitution by the abolition of two independent agencies, the Public Service Commission and the Judical Service Commission, and by a prohibition on judicial review of legislation. The Ceylonese courts had assumed the function of interpreting the constitution and invalidating legislation on constitutional grounds. Under the 1972 constitution, bills questioned on grounds of constitutionality may be referred to a special Constitutional Court for an advisory opinion before enactment. If a bill is declared to be inconsistent with the constitution, it may nonetheless be enacted if it receives a two-thirds majority in the National State Assembly. The constitutionality of a legislative enactment may not be questioned in the regular courts. Although a greater concentration of power is evident, the newly designed legislative and executive institutions seem likely to function generally as did their predecessors under the 1946 constitution. The organization of government under the 1972 constitution is depicted in Figure 1.

The new constitution, although adopted overwhelmingly by the Constituent Assembly, stirred sharp controversy. Spokesmen

"government" is used to refer generally to the entire political and administrative apparatus of the state.

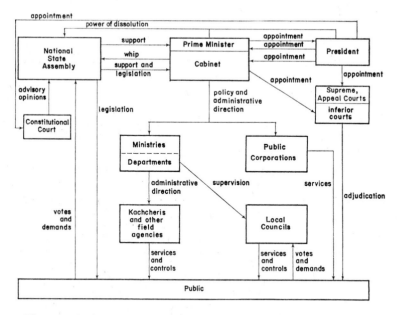

Figure 1. Simplified diagram of government organization

for the island's minorities denounced provisions designating Sinhalese as the official language and specifying a special status for Buddhism. Others charged that the constitution contained authoritarian features and would pave the way for a "constitutional dictatorship." The abolition of judicial review, the incorporation in the constitution of emergency powers formerly contained in ordinary legislation, and the absence of guarantees for property rights were frequent targets of criticism. The constitution's nonjusticiable "Principles of State Policy" reflected the egalitarian and collectivist ideology of the United Front Government which drafted the document. Among the principles enumerated as guides to lawmaking and governance were "the development of collective forms of property such as State property or co-operative property, in the means of production, distribution and exchange as a means of ending exploitation of man by man," and the endeavor "to eliminate economic and social privilege, disparity and exploitation and ensure equality of opportunity to all citizens."[2]

The Legislature

Constitutionally, the National State Assembly is "the supreme instrument of State power of the Republic."[3] In practice, however, as in other parliamentary systems, effective control over legislation has been obtained by the cabinet through tight control of the business of the chamber and the unrelenting exercise of the whip on parliamentary votes. Legislation, control of the budget, and oversight of administrative actions have not vanished but in ordinary circumstances have atrophied as effective functions of the legislature. The principal power of the assembly resides in its ability to dismiss a Government. Twice under the earlier constitution Governments lost votes of confidence in parliament and resigned and called new elections. A Government formed by the United National Party in March 1960 fell on its first test of confidence, producing the second general election of 1960. In December 1964, a coalition Government consisting of the Sri Lanka Freedom Party and the Lanka Sama Samaja Party lost a confidence motion by a single vote after fourteen SLFP M.P.'s crossed the aisle to the opposition. Parliament was dissolved and the 1965 election followed.

The maximum term of parliament, formerly five years, was

[2] *The Constitution of Sri Lanka (Ceylon)* (Colombo: Department of Government Printing, 1972), p. 9.

[3] *Ibid.*, p. 3. Although the new constitution does not refer specifically to the legislative assembly as the parliament, the assembly members are designated as "Members of Parliament." *Ibid.*, p. 16. The term "parliament" will be used in this work to refer to the legislatures existing under both the 1946 and the 1972 constitutions.

extended to six years by the new constitution.[4] Whether the change will lengthen the actual duration of parliaments is uncertain, as political circumstances usually have forced elections before the expiration of the constitutionally designated maximum period. Only the 1965–1970 parliament completed its full five-year term. Except for the parliament chosen in March 1960, which was almost immediately dissolved, parliaments have survived an average of four years and three months from first meeting to dissolution.

ORGANIZATION AND FUNCTIONING OF THE LEGISLATURE

The legislative chamber's formal organization and procedures closely follow British parliamentary practice. A speaker presides over the assembly, aided by a deputy speaker, who also serves as chairman of committees, and by a deputy chairman of committees. All three are members of parliament. A clerk of the house and a sergeant-at-arms and their assistants constitute the professional staff of parliament. Much of the work of the chamber is done in a committee of the whole house. There are also two nonspecialized standing committees and select committees, including a public accounts committee, the chairman of which was a member of the opposition until 1970.[5] The speaker is ostensibly nonpartisan. The convention of not contesting the speaker's seat

[4] The first term of the National State Assembly is to extend for a maximum of five years from the date of adoption of the constitution, which could mean that the M.P.'s elected in 1970 would remain in office for seven years. The expiration of the maximum term is to operate as an automatic dissolution, which is to be followed by a general election and the meeting of the new assembly within four months of the dissolution.

[5] LSSP member Bernard Soysa had served for many years as chairman of the public accounts committee and gained wide acclaim for his performance of the role. When the LSSP came to power with its United Front partners in 1970, Soysa was again chosen as chairman of the committee with the concurrence of the opposition.

has broken down, however, resulting in repeated election defeats of speakers. An incumbent speaker has not returned to parliament since 1952. As a result, except in the fourth parliament which was in session for less than a month in 1960, speakers have always been chosen by and politically associated with the party or coalition in power.

The Ceylonese legislative chamber maintains the physical separation between supporters and opponents of the Government of the British House of Commons. Individuals and small groups have crossed the aisle occasionally, and a few mavericks have changed sides several times over a period of years. The legislature has not, however, experienced the extreme instability and repeated switches from one side to the other which have plagued some parliamentary bodies. Until 1965, the parliamentary opposition was fragmented into mutually hostile groups and seldom resembled an alternative Government. Disagreements among opposition parties prevented the choosing of an official leader of the opposition until 1950. Subsequently, a leader of the opposition and a whip have represented the opposition in planning the business of the chamber, but the ideological and communal divisions within the opposition were frequently too great to permit agreement on anything except dissatisfaction with the Government. Following the 1956 and July 1960 elections, the LSSP and the Ceylon Communist Party elected to sit with the opposition but extended qualified pledges of support to the Government. While the UNP was in opposition between 1956 and 1965, other opposition parties often expended more time and energy in denouncing the UNP than in attacking the Government. With the 1965 election, the opposition for the first time constituted a coherent alternative Government and parliament was sharply divided into two unified blocs. A self-proclaimed National Government was formed by the UNP, the Federal Party, and several smaller parties. The three United Front parties in opposition—the SLFP, the LSSP, and the CP—formed a joint parliamentary group which met regularly throughout the term of parliament. Only three M.P.'s were not included in either the Government or the United Front parliamentary groups until the defection of the FP from the Government in 1968. The cohesion of the shattered opposition weakened, however, following the United Front's landslide election victory of 1970. The party situation in the House of Representatives immediately following the last three elections is shown in Table 9.

Rigorous party discipline is usually imposed on voting in the chamber. The standing orders of the UNP parliamentary party specify that each member "shall always vote in Parliament according to the Mandate of the Chairman conveyed through the

Table 9. Government and opposition alignments after recent elections

Government		Opposition	
Party	Seats	Party	Seats
		July 1960	
Sri Lanka Freedom Party	75	United National Party	30
Appointed members	6	Federal Party	16
		Lanka Sama Samaja Party[a]	12
		Ceylon Communist Party[a]	4
		Mahajana Eksath Peramuna	3
		Jathika Vimukthi Peramuna	2
		Lanka Prajathantravadi	
		Pakshaya	2
		Tamil Congress	1
		Independents	6
Total	81		76

Table 9. (cont.)

March 1965

United National Party	66	Sri Lanka Freedom Party	41
Federal Party	14	Lanka Sama Samaja Party	10
Sri Lanka Freedom		Ceylon Communist Party	4
Socialist Party	5	Independents	3
Tamil Congress	3		
Mahajana Eksath Peramuna	1		
Jathika Vimukthi Peramuna	1		
Independents	3		
Appointed members	6		
Total	99		58

May 1970

Sri Lanka Freedom Party	91	United National Party	17
Lanka Sama Samaja Party	19	Federal Party	13
Ceylon Communist Party	6	Tamil Congress	3
Independent	1	Independent	1
Appointed members	6		
Total	123		34

ª Extending qualified support to the Government.

Whip to the Party," although the party leader may permit an M.P. to abstain if a question of personal conscience is involved in a vote.[6] Individual M.P.'s occasionally defy the whip and vote against their party's position, but they are invariably expelled from the party or otherwise disciplined. Cabinet control of legislation is virtually total in ordinary circumstances. Government business takes most of the time of the assembly, including often the single day each fortnight supposedly reserved for private

[6] *United National Party Constitution* (Colombo: United National Party, 1962), p. 13.

members' bills. Bills not sponsored by the cabinet enjoy little consideration and less prospect of passage. A Prevention of Social Disabilities Act directed against caste discrimination, introduced by two FP M.P.'s in 1957, was a rare example of a significant legislative enactment resulting from a private member's bill.

Despite the virtual certainty of the eventual vote, parliament remains a lively forum for debate and an important medium of political communication. The chamber is used extensively as a platform to address the country, and there are few important public issues or events that do not receive attention in parliamentary debates. The debates are reported at length in the press and there seems to be relatively wide public awareness of the major happenings in parliament. The principal debates follow a "statement of Government policy" (formerly the "speech from the throne") which opens the annual legislative session and an annual budget speech. Another important parliamentary device is the adjournment debate, which is frequently employed to allow discussion of some immediate question of grave public concern such as a major strike, disorder, or other dramatic event. The half-hour daily question period has been used to capacity by M.P.'s, particularly those in the opposition, primarily to air individual constituents' grievances or complaints against specific administrative actions.

The former second chamber of parliament, the Senate, which was abolished in 1971, played a minor role in the legislative process and attracted much criticism. Half the thirty senators were elected by the lower house by proportional representation, and half were appointed on the recommendation of the cabinet. Consequently, the governing party was ordinarily able to obtain a majority of seats in the Senate after being in office through one biennial election of senators. Only after the 1970 election, on the eve of its abolition, did the Senate serve as a significant obstacle to the Government's legislative proposals. Such utility as the

Senate possessed was not in policy making or in acting as an effective brake on the lower chamber, but in supplying a means for parties to reward supporters or give symbolic recognition to certain groups and in providing some flexibility to the parliamentary system. Many senators were party loyalists who failed to win seats in the popularly elected house. Some were members of ethnic, religious, or caste groups chosen to attract the political support of the groups to which they belonged. The Senate performed an additional, perhaps more important, political function. Every minister was required to be or to become within four months a member of one house of the legislature. On the infrequent occasions when it was thought desirable to name some individual to the cabinet who was not a member of parliament, the Government was able to recommend his appointment to the Senate. The most unusual use of the Senate resulted from the unique situation of the SLFP in July 1960. Although Sirimavo Bandaranaike campaigned for the party and was its recognized leader, she did not contest a parliamentary seat. When the SLFP emerged victorious in the election, she was named prime minister by the governor-general, then recommended her own appointment to the Senate. For nearly five years she served as prime minister while sitting in the second chamber.

THE GOVERNMENT PARLIAMENTARY GROUP

An important role in legislation and government policy making has been assumed by the Government Parliamentary Group, composed of the members of parliament who support the Government. The group has met regularly since the first session of parliament in 1947, but its strength and recalcitrance emerged only after 1956. Although the group's enhanced influence and independence was most apparent under the two Bandaranaike Governments in office between 1956 and 1965, it continued to play an active role under the 1965–1970 Government headed by

Dudley Senanayake and seems to have become a permanent feature of the legislative process in Ceylon. The group has regularly included a few independents or members of minor parties and the appointed M.P.'s, as well as the M.P.'s belonging to the governing party. When a coalition is in power, the M.P.'s of all parties backing the Government meet together in the group, which thus functions as one of the principal structural links and devices for coordination among the allied parties in the coalition.

The group regularly meets at the beginning of the week when parliament is in session to discuss business before the assembly and examine cabinet legislative proposals. Meetings of the group have been used by backbench M.P.'s as opportunities to discuss and criticize cabinet policies, to urge alternative courses of action on the ministers and party leaders, and even to denounce individual ministers. In a number of instances, cabinet-approved proposals of major legislation have been rejected by the group. The recalcitrance of the Government Parliamentary Group was felt soon after the 1956 election, when the cabinet's draft official-language bill was rejected and had to be rewritten to satisfy demands voiced by the group. After 1961, the cabinet prepared and submitted to the group several drafts of a bill to regulate the island's press, each of which was rejected in turn. A publicly announced cabinet decision to requisition a building under construction by a trade union was reversed in 1962 after the Government Parliamentary Group voted against the action.

Probably the most dramatic exercise of the group's power came in a turbulent fight over the 1962 budget. The budget speech of the minister of finance contained proposals for a sales tax and a reduction in the weekly ration of rice made available to consumers at a subsidized price. Sharp criticism of both proposals was voiced in an emergency meeting of the Government Parliamentary Group following the speech. The sales tax was withdrawn and the cut in the rice ration was twice postponed, but the minister of finance repeatedly insisted that the rice reduction would not be canceled and that the action had the unanimous support of the cabinet. After much public controversy, the minister of finance eventually announced to parliament the withdrawal of the rice ration cut and his resignation from the cabinet.

Informal subgroups have occasionally appeared within the Government Parliamentary Group. During the premiership of S. W. R. D. Bandaranaike, a "forward bloc" existed within the group with the objective of spurring the cabinet toward socialist measures. Under Sirimavo Bandaranaike's first Government, at a time when Kandyan grievances and demands were prominent, an advisory group consisting of M.P.'s representing Kandyan constituencies was formed within the Government Parliamentary Group. Following the 1965 election, seventeen advisory committees paralleling the seventeen ministries were created by the group. None of the subgroups, however, proved to be of lasting legislative importance.

MEMBERS OF PARLIAMENT

During its first term, the National State Assembly is to consist of the M.P.'s serving in the Constituent Assembly (and, hence, the House of Representatives) immediately before adoption of the new constitution. After 1960, the House of Representatives contained 151 M.P.'s elected by popular vote and six M.P.'s appointed on ministerial advice to represent interests deemed inadequately represented by the electoral process. Prior to 1960, the house was composed of ninety-five elected and six appointed members. After the first dissolution of the National State Assembly and a new election, the appointed M.P.'s will cease to exist and, if a fresh delimitation of constituencies has occurred, the number of elected M.P.'s could rise, as the size of the chamber is linked to population. Most elected M.P.'s have been returned as candidates of coherent and reasonably stable political parties. Although the number of parties represented in parliament has been large—nine obtained seats in July 1960 and in 1965—more than 90 per cent of all M.P.'s returned in the last three elections were candidates of parties formed before 1952, and 70 per cent belonged to either the UNP or the SLFP.

The ethnic composition of the chamber follows roughly the ethnic distribution of the population except for the largely non-citizen Indian Tamils (see Table 10). In 1970, Sinhalese held 81 per cent, Ceylon Tamils 13 per cent, and Ceylon Moors 5 per cent of the elective seats in the house, compared to the 79

Table 10.   Ethnic distribution of elected M.P.'s, 1947–1970

Ethnic group	1947	1952	1956	March 1960	July 1960	1965	1970
Sinhalese	68	75	74	122	121	122	123
Ceylon Tamils	13	12	12	18	18	17	19
Ceylon Moors	6	6	7	10	11	11	8
Burghers	1	1	1	1	1	1	1
Indian Tamils	7	1	0	0	0	0	0
Total	95	95	94[a]	151	151	151	151

[a] One person, a Sinhalese, was elected by two constituencies.
Source: For 1947–1956, S. Namasivayam, *Parliamentary Government in Ceylon, 1948–1958* (Colombo: K. V. G. de Silva & Sons, n.d.), p. 54. For 1960–1970, author's tabulation.

per cent, 12 per cent, and 7 per cent, respectively, of the citizens of Ceylon and the 71 per cent, 11 per cent, and 6 per cent, respectively, of the island's total population these communities constitute. In 1970, the appointed M.P.'s consisted of two Sinhalese, two persons of Indian extraction, a Ceylon Tamil, and a Ceylon Moor; in 1965, they included two Indian Tamils and a single Sinhalese, Ceylon Moor, Burgher, and European.

The educational background of elected M.P.'s is indicated in Table 11. A considerable number of the M.P.'s have consistently been graduates of universities or professional schools, and remarkably few have not attained at least a secondary education.

Table 11.   Educational backgrounds of M.P.'s[a]

Highest level completed	Per cent of M.P.'s elected in				
			July		
	1947	1956	1960	1965	1970
Primary or less	—	2	4	2	2
Secondary	31	41	43	47	46
Vocational beyond secondary	6	6	8	9	7
University or professional	47	43	40	37	41
Undetermined	16	7	5	5	3
Total[b]	100	100	100	100	100
Total number of M.P.'s elected	95	94[c]	151	151	151

[a] M.P.'s returned in 1952 and March 1960 are not included because of insufficient data.

[b] Some columns do not add to 100 per cent due to rounding.

[c] One individual was elected by two constituencies.

Source: Ceylon Daily News, *Parliament of Ceylon, 1947* (Colombo: Associated Newspapers of Ceylon, Ltd., n.d.), and the comparable Ceylon Daily News publications for 1956, 1960, 1965, and 1970, supplemented by information from the Colombo newspapers and the author's interviews with M.P.'s.

Despite the popularization of politics over the last two decades, the proportion of M.P.'s with higher educations has fallen only slightly since independence (although the number attending foreign universities or the prestige preparatory schools on the island has declined). While the M.P. is increasingly required to be accessible to his constituents, informed about local circumstances and problems, and articulate in Sinhalese or Tamil, he must also, in order to fulfill the expectations of his constituents, be able to deal effectively with party leaders, ministers, and public servants. This generally requires a relatively high level of education and sophistication.

The principal occupations of elected M.P.'s appear in Table 12. While the dominance of lawyers had declined by 1956, law-

Table 12. Principal occupations of M.P.'s[a]

Principal occupation	Per cent of M.P.'s elected in				
	1947	1956	July 1960	1965	1970
Lawyer	35	23	20	24	26
Planter, landowner	17	16	21	18	10
Public servant[b]	13	10	15	15	13
Businessman, trader	11	12	11	13	15
Teacher, educator	7	15	13	11	18
Political party or trade union official[e]	6	7	5	2	4
Writer, journalist	5	5	3	3	3
Cultivator	—	—	2	1	2
Other	1	7	7	9	6
Undetermined	5	4	3	5	4
Total[d]	100	100	100	100	100
Total number of M.P.'s elected	95	94[e]	151	151	151

[a] M.P.'s returned in 1952 and March 1960 are not included because of insufficient data.

[b] Includes employees of public corporations.

[e] This category has been used only for those M.P.'s who were substantially engaged in party or trade union tasks and apparently had no other occupation of significance either prior to entering or while serving in parliament. Many other M.P.'s are also party or trade union officials.

[d] Some columns do not add to 100 per cent due to rounding.

[e] One individual was elected by two constituencies.

Source: See Table 11.

yers have continued to form the principal occupational group in parliament. Schoolteachers have increased in number since 1947. An M.P. elected in 1956, a postal peon prior to the election, was often called the first working-class member of parliament. In 1960, a small handful of craftsmen and cultivators first appeared in parliament. An ex-laborer and a former pavement hawker, both later successful in business, had by 1970 served in parliament for at least a decade. Nonetheless, M.P.'s have continued to be drawn primarily from the prestigious and relatively well-paying occupations. The previous experience of M.P.'s in elective office is presented in Table 13. Since the political shift of 1956, a large majority of successful parliamentary candidates have previously served in parliament. Nearly half the M.P.'s have

Table 13.   Political experience of M.P.'s

| | Per cent of M.P.'s elected in | | | |
| | | July | | |
Type of experience	1956	1960	1965	1970
Service on local government bodies[a]				
Municipal councils	11	10	11	11
Urban councils	10	9	11	7
Town councils	4	2	4	3
Village councils	15	25	25	24
Total	40	46	51	45
Prior service in the House of Representatives	40	77[b]	72	63

[a] M.P.'s who had served on more than one type of local government body were classified according to the type on which they had served for the longest period. In 1968, there were 12 municipal councils, 34 urban councils, 79 town councils, and 516 village councils.

[b] Of M.P.'s elected in July 1960, 38 per cent had served only in the brief fourth parliament elected in March 1960, while 39 per cent had served in parliament prior to 1960.

Source: See Table 11.

served on elective local government bodies, which have become important training grounds for national politics.

Although Ceylon was the first modern nation to install a woman prime minister, parliament has remained an overwhelmingly male institution. Along with 145 men, six women entered the House of Representatives in 1970, the largest number of women ever elected to the chamber. Four women were returned as M.P.'s in 1965, and earlier the number of women ranged between one and three. All have been elected from Sinhalese areas.

The appointed M.P.'s have generally served to represent planting and commercial interests and the smaller minorities such as the Burghers and Muslims. Since 1958, they have also included Sinhalese members of low-status and disadvantaged castes which are fairly large but have enjoyed little representation in parliament, and after 1960 the largely voteless Indian Tamils have been represented by appointed M.P.'s. The appointed M.P.'s have with rare exceptions voted with the Government of the day in all parliamentary divisions. On some occasions, they have provided the margin by which a Government has survived a test in parliament. However, in the critical vote of December 1964, which overturned the SLFP-LSSP coalition Government by a single vote, one appointed M.P. voted against the Government and a second abstained. An appointed M.P. was for the first time named a minister in 1960, allowing a Muslim to be included in the cabinet when presumably no elected Muslim M.P. with suitable partisan and other qualifications was found. In 1970, two appointed M.P.'s, a Muslim and a member of a large but disadvantaged Sinhalese caste, were included in the cabinet.

M.P.'S AND CONSTITUENTS

The relationship between the M.P. and his constituents has undergone a marked change in recent years, reflecting changes both in the techniques of mobilizing votes and in popular attitudes toward the government. The changing role of the M.P. has followed a rapid decline in deference voting and a steep rise in popular expectations of services they may receive from the government. Prior to independence, a candidate frequently was able to win election by obtaining support from traditionally eminent landowning families, village headmen, and similar persons of local influence within his constituency. The rural voters were said to be impressed by the candidate who traveled in an automobile, wore Western clothing, and was educated in the English language. By about 1956, however, interest—which was often parochial and particularistic—had begun to replace deference in determining voting behavior. Many M.P.'s concluded that the performance of personal services for their constituents had become one of the essential keys to electoral success.

M.P.'s have been performing a growing number of tasks for individual constituents for more than a decade. The small size of Ceylon and the existence of cheap public transportation has meant that a villager with a problem is likely to board a bus for Colombo in order to seek the assistance of his M.P., frequently accompanied by a small band of relatives and neighbors to support his claim and lend him encouragement. A reduction in the size of parliamentary constituencies in 1959 probably increased popular reliance on the M.P. by bringing the M.P. closer to his constituents. The lobby of the parliament building is commonly filled with constituents waiting to see their representatives. M.P.'s returning to their residences often find the compound and verandah crowded with waiting constituents. As an example of the contacts between M.P.'s and constituents, one M.P. reportedly has devoted a day each week to visiting his constituency, and he has regularly seen between two and three hundred persons seeking his assistance. On other days of the week an average of about fifty constituents have come to Colombo by bus to present their requests at his home.[7] Veteran Communist M.P. Pieter Keuneman was described as spending each morning

attending to the many people who call daily to see him—constituents, Party members and others with problems big and small, about which they want Keuneman's advice and help. These problems cover a wide field—housing, rent, employment, exploitation by slum landlords, harassment by the police or other Government authorities, schools, sanitation, shortages of essential articles at co-operative stores and experiences of delays and other vexations at the hands of Government and local government bureaucrats.[8]

Since the emergence of a participatory, competitive political process more than four decades ago, parochialism and "parish-pump" politics have always been evident and, as in other newly independent developing countries, representatives have often displayed less concern with the content of general policies than with the specific application of the existing policy regarding an individual pension, application, job or other claim. In part, this tendency is a legacy of colonial rule, when the absence of effective popular control of government hampered the growth of concern with or knowledge of the policy-making process, but when rapidly growing social services and government activities did stimulate awareness of administrative actions as they impinged upon individuals. The unsophisticated villagers with narrow horizons also were presumably more inclined to think in terms of the immediate and specific rather than of the abstract and distant. The incomplete emergence of a popular sense of functional or class interests may also have encouraged political office-seekers to emphasize specific individual services over generalized policy positions.

[7] Author's interview, July 23, 1971.

[8] Basil Perera, *Pieter Keuneman—A Profile* (Colombo: Ceylon Communist Party, 1967), p. 131.

While these considerations have been receding with increased experience in representative democracy and with advances in education and mobility, the pervasive scarcity of resources—insufficient jobs, schools, hospitals, and other amenities and opportunities—has worsened relative to rapidly growing aspirations, intensifying the rivalry for the resources that are available. Furthermore, a lack of administrative capacity has often imperiled the implementation of existing policies. There is little value in obtaining policy decisions in favor of grand welfare and development schemes when as a result of bureaucratic inertia, confusion, or indifference the individual is unable to obtain the pension, medical care, or other benefits to which he is entitled under long-established policies.

The changing role of the M.P. reflects a fundamental process of political development. The citizen has become increasingly aware not only of the benefits he may derive from the government, but of the interconnections among voting and election campaigns, the services of the M.P., and the extensive operations of the administrative machinery of government. The M.P. has come to occupy a central position in a shift from "subject" to "participant" political culture.[9] The M.P. has assumed a major burden in the trend for the government to move closer to the people and become increasingly responsive to their demands. Some of the changes which have occurred in the political system were captured in a message by Prime Minister Sirimavo Bandaranaike:

Democratic Government implies that the elected representatives

[9] "Subject" orientations to the political system, in which awareness is essentially limited to administrative "outputs," and "participant" orientations, in which awareness and actual or potential involvement extends to the political "inputs" of demands and preferences, are described in Gabriel A. Almond and Sidney Verba, *The Civic Culture* (Boston: Little, Brown and Co., 1965), pp. 24–26.

must not only be in close sympathy with the aspirations of the people but be continuously responsive to their aims. We have moved far in this direction. In the old days there was a big gulf between the Government as rulers and the people as the ruled. This was a reflection of the colonialist habit of mind. Today, the people are more and more conscious that they are the real rulers and that the Government is their servant. Today, too, the average Member of Parliament is closer to the people's aspirations and accessible to them. He is not, as in the past, an outsider, when Members of Parliament were generally drawn from the ranks of the western-oriented monied classes.[10]

In response to constituents' pleas, M.P.'s regularly go from one government office to another seeking to expedite pensions, obtain rice ration books, locate employment, arrange admissions to schools and hospitals, and secure or prevent the transfer of teachers and other public employees. As the employment situation worsened, appeals for jobs began to swamp all other forms of requests for assistance. A marked rise in political interference in the public service is partly a product of this trend in the function of the M.P. The M.P.'s role as intermediary between the government and the public is becoming institutionalized with a growing tendency to channel public requests, particularly for employment, through the M.P. In 1971, a person wishing employment in the government service was required to obtain a certificate from the M.P. representing his constituency to be considered for appointment. The mounting volume of individual appeals from constituents has made heavy demands on the time and energy of M.P.'s, seriously distracting them from their legislative functions. It has also been a significant source of tensions between ministers and backbenchers, as the backbenchers have

[10] "Prime Minister's Independence Day Message," *Ceylon Today*, XIV (Feb. 1965), 7,

deluged ministers with requests for patronage and parochial benefits.

The Cabinet and Executive Authority

Government policy making and control of the administration are concentrated in the hands of the cabinet. The 1972 constitution provides for "a Cabinet of Ministers charged with the direction and control of the government of the Republic which shall be collectively responsible to the National State Assembly and answerable to the National State Assembly on all matters for which they are responsible."[11] All ministers are included within the cabinet, which until 1965 usually contained between thirteen and fifteen members. The smallest were the caretaker cabinets formed in 1959–1960 by W. Dahanayake and Dudley Senanayake, with ten and eight ministers, respectively. The cabinet headed by Dudley Senanayake in 1965 contained seventeen ministers and was later expanded to nineteen, while that formed by Sirimavo Bandaranaike in 1970 contained twenty-one, the largest cabinet to date. The progressive enlargement of cabinets since 1964 reflects the existence of coalition Governments, composed of several parties with claims to ministerial appointments. Nearly all ministers have had executive responsibility for one or more administrative departments grouped in a ministry, although occasionally a minister without portfolio or with very light departmental responsibilities has been appointed.

Also included in the Government, but not in the cabinet, are deputy ministers, called parliamentary secretaries until 1972, who serve as legislative aides to the ministers and occasionally as acting ministers in the absence of the ministers. Prior to 1970, the number of parliamentary secretaries varied from nine to sixteen, ex-

[11] *The Constitution of Sri Lanka (Ceylon)*, p. 38.

cept for the brief UNP Government of 1960, which had none. In 1970, twenty parliamentary secretaries were appointed.

With the exception of the traumatic years 1959–1960, Ceylon has not experienced the serious executive instability often associated with multiparty systems, despite a proliferation of political parties and frequent coalition Governments. In the fifteen months preceding the July 1960 election, Ceylon had four cabinets and three prime ministers. SLFP leader S. W. R. D. Bandaranaike reconstructed his cabinet at the breakup of his coalition Government in May 1959. The following September he was assassinated. W. Dahanayake became prime minister and continued with essentially the same cabinet until December, when he abruptly broke with the SLFP and dismissed the ministers who remained with that party. Dahanayake's new cabinet was swept away by the March 1960 election. The cabinet formed by UNP leader Dudley Senanayake in March survived only until July. A few cabinet changes or reshuffles have been made between elections due to the death or retirement of ministers or occasionally as a result of political developments. An unusually rapid turnover of finance ministers occurred in 1962–1964, when five persons held the post within two years. Ordinarily, however, changes in the personnel of cabinets have been relatively small and continuity of policy and leading ministers has generally been maintained between elections. The only election which failed to produce a viable Government supported by a parliamentary majority was that of March 1960. Even that apparent deadlock may not have been unresolvable. When the UNP Government was defeated in parliament, leaders of parties holding a majority of seats asked the governor-general to allow the SLFP to form an alternative Government, which they pledged to support. Nonetheless, on the advice of his UNP ministers, the governor-general dissolved parliament and called for a new election.

FUNCTIONING OF THE CABINET

The Ceylonese executive functions according to the typical pattern of parliamentary systems. The cabinet is collectively responsible for broad policy decisions and the general conduct of government. In addition, each minister has particular responsibility for the policies and operations of his ministry. Cabinet meetings usually are held for about half a day each week, with many informal contacts among individual ministers or senior public servants in the ministries. Cabinet deliberations are conducted in secret, but leaks of cabinet discussions and decisions are notorious. In the collective duties of the cabinet, strong leadership is ordinarily exercised by the prime minister, who profits from his political position as leader of the party (or the principal party) in power and as the public symbol of the party and the Government. While virtually all major policy questions confronting the Government are considered by the cabinet, and decisions are registered in the name of the cabinet, the degree of collegial deliberation and decision appears to be minimal. In each cabinet, a few of the more powerful ministers seem to have enjoyed considerable autonomy in running their ministeries and in determining policy on matters related to ministry functions, with only formal deference paid to collective responsibility. The formal cabinet meeting probably has functioned chiefly as a device for ratifying decisions taken by the prime minister or by individual ministers in their own spheres of activity, or for confirming the results of bargaining and compromises between rival ministers. Between 1965 and 1970, extensive and reportedly effective use was made of cabinet subcommittees as policy-making and coordinating devices, but the regular use of subcommittees seemed to decline with the installation of the United Front Government in 1970, although a few ad hoc subcommittees were constituted.

While the principle of cabinet solidarity and collective responsibility is given verbal deference, it operates uncertainly and with many violations in practice. Policy and personal differences between ministers have regularly been reported in the press, discussed in political circles, and only thinly veiled by the participants in public. A singularly high level of cabinet discord and an unusual lack of control by the prime minister existed from 1956 to 1959 in the coalition Government headed by S. W. R. D. Bandaranaike. The turbulence culminated in a collision between a group of SLFP ministers and two ministers belonging to the SLFP's small coalition partner, the Viplavakari Lanka Sama Samaja Party.[12] In May 1959, ten SLFP ministers refused to attend cabinet meetings for ten days in an effort to force Bandaranaike to dismiss the two VLSSP ministers. After attempting to compromise and placate both factions, Bandaranaike eventually succumbed to the pressure and, without notifying the VLSSP ministers, reshuffled their ministries, removing several activities from their control. The two promptly resigned and crossed the floor, bringing the coalition to an end and making it possible for the now entirely SLFP cabinet to resume meeting. Discord within a cabinet did not at any other time reach this level of public conflict. Nonetheless, in virtually every cabinet some clashes and rivalries have been known. The tendency seems to be for a large volume of ministerial disputes and disagreements to be taken to the prime minister for his personal mediation or decision, as he is the only person with the authority and prestige to gain acceptance for his disposition of an issue by all ministers. Prominent among the matters which divide cabinets and produce rivalries between ministers are programs which would lend prestige and

[12] After 1959, the VLSSP called itself the Mahajana Eksath Peramuna (People's United Front), the name of the coalition that had been formed in 1956 by Bandaranaike, consisting of the SLFP, the VLSSP, a small group which was later absorbed into the SLFP, and a few independents.

power to one of the ministers, particularly those which would create large numbers of jobs or other sources of patronage under the control of one minister. Not only matters of prestige and political strength, but caste and communal considerations have frequently figured in the rivalries.

Most of the attention and energy of ministers is absorbed by responsibilities for their individual ministries. Marked differences exist among ministers in their performance of their role. Some reportedly are content to serve as spokesman for the ministry in parliament and to convey major policy questions to the cabinet or prime minister for decision, with little apparent interest in the internal functioning or performance of the ministry, except occasionally to obtain patronage or favors for political supporters. Others immerse themselves in the administrative operations of the ministry and give personal attention not only to the larger questions of policy but also to routine bureaucratic procedures and practices. Infrequently, a minister has established a reputation as an effective and vigorous administrator. More often, a minister is evaluated in terms of his strength in the party, support among the public, and debating skill in parliament.

COMPOSITION AND CHARACTERISTICS OF CABINETS

Political and communal considerations are of major importance in determining the size and composition of cabinets and the distribution of portfolios. The prime minister is constitutionally authorized to determine the number of ministers and the allocation of responsibilities among them. But while the prime minister ordinarily enjoys some discretion in ministerial appointments, a number of factors tend to limit his freedom. If more than one party is supporting the Government, portfolios must be distributed on the basis of negotiations among the coalition parties. In the 1964 SLFP-LSSP coalition, the LSSP received three portfolios, including the powerful Ministry of Finance, while the

SLFP retained twelve. Prior to the 1970 election, agreement had been reached among the United Front parties on the ministries to be received by the SLFP's two allies, the LSSP and the CP. Named to the cabinet were seventeen SLFP ministers, three LSSP ministers, and a single CP minister. The cabinet formed in 1965 by the self-styled National Government, which was supported by six political parties,[13] included twelve UNP members, three members of the Sri Lanka Freedom Socialist Party (composed primarily of SLFP dissidents who had broken with the SLFP in 1964), and one member each from the Federal Party and the Mahajana Eksath Peramuna. FP representation in the cabinet was politically important and the Ministry of Local Government was of particular concern to the Federalists. Consequently, the prime minister presumably had little choice but to assign the ministry to the FP's selection. The small SLFSP and MEP parliamentary contingents contained three prominent ex-ministers (one a former prime minister) who had to be accomodated in the cabinet. Within his own party, a prime minister is required to satisfy leading party figures and to provide for the representation of various communities and castes. Former ministers and persons with political strength within the party are difficult to exclude.

Every cabinet has been overwhelmingly Sinhalese and Buddhist in composition, but each has included one Muslim, except momentarily in 1959–1960 when two were included, and at least one Christian, except for a few years after 1965. The cabinet constituted in 1965 consisted of fifteen Buddhists, one Muslim, and one Hindu. A Christian was given a ministry in 1968, molifying complaints by Christians of exclusion from the cabinet. The cabinet formed in 1970 included fourteen Buddhists, three

[13] Also backing the National Government was a seventh organization, the Ceylon Workers' Congress, a trade union which serves as a spokesman in politics for the Indian Tamil minority.

Christians, one Muslim, and two Marxists of Christian background who are difficult to classify according to religion (two other Marxists in the cabinet are classified as Buddhists). Until 1956, each cabinet had contained two Tamils, but with the eruption of the official-language controversy and the growing cleavage between communities no Tamil served in the cabinet between 1956 and 1965. A Tamil Hindu member of the FP held a cabinet post from 1965 until his party left the Government in 1968, when he was replaced by a Sinhalese. The ethnic composition of recent cabinets is indicated in Table 14.

Table 14.   Ethnic composition of cabinets, 1960–1970

Ethnic group	Number of ministers appointed in					
	March 1960	July 1960	June 1964	March 1965	Sept. 1968	May 1970
Sinhalese	7	10	14	15	18	18
Ceylon Tamils	0	0	0	1	0	1
Moors	1	1	1	1	1	1
Burghers	0	0	0	0	0	1
Total	8	11	15	17	19	21

Source: Author's tabulation.

Sinhalese ministers have been predominately from the Goyigama caste, but cabinets have regularly included members of the Karāva and Salāgama castes, and occasionally a member of one of the "lower" castes. The 1960 SLFP cabinet contained seven Goyigama and single Salāgama, Karāva, and Durāva ministers, in addition to one Muslim. The cabinet formed in 1965 included twelve Goyigama ministers and single members from the Karāva, Salāgama, and Batgam castes, as well as a Muslim and a Vellala Tamil. Later changes brought into the cabinet a second

Karāva and a member of the small Hinnā caste. The eighteen Sinhalese ministers named to the cabinet in 1970 included thirteen Goyigamas, two Karāvas, two Salāgamas, and one Vahumpura.

Most ministers have had extensive political experience and many have previously served in cabinets. Of the twenty-one ministers appointed in 1970, eleven were former ministers. Four, including two senators and an appointed M.P., had not served previously in parliament. The seventeen with previous parliamentary experience averaged nearly fourteen years' service in the House of Representatives. Three had been members of parliament continuously since 1947 and one had been a member of the pre-independence State Council. The seventeen-member cabinet named in 1965 included nine ex-ministers, two of whom had previously been prime minister. Only two, one of whom was the mayor of Colombo and the other a former solicitor-general of Ceylon, were without previous parliamentary experience. The remaining fifteen averaged ten years of parliamentary service.

By occupational background, the ministers appointed in 1970 included seven lawyers, three former public servants, three businessmen, two educators, and a housewife, a judge, an engineer, a planter, a journalist, and a diplomat-politician. Several, however, had in fact devoted their adult lives to politics. Thirteen were university or law school graduates, seven had completed secondary educations, and one had less than a secondary education. The cabinet formed in 1965 included five lawyers, three former public servants, two schoolteachers, two businessmen, two planters, one journalist, one medical doctor, and one who could only be classified as a politician. The ministers in 1970 averaged about fifty-five years of age, a few years younger than the ministers appointed in 1965. Only two women have ever served in the cabinet, including Sirimavo Bandaranaike, who in 1970 commenced her second term as prime minister.

THE PRIME MINISTER

Except during the confused days of 1959–1960, the prime minister has been the undisputed and effective head of his party, the party with the largest representation in parliament. The authority and prestige of the prime minister extends beyond the cabinet and the party to the country, and he must often personally assume responsibility for delicate or controversial matters. When the official-language issue was critical after 1956, Prime Minister S. W. R. D. Bandaranaike assumed personal responsibility for official-language affairs. When Dudley Senanayake became prime minister in 1965, he also held the portfolio of the newly created Ministry of Planning and Economic Affairs, as expeditious economic development was considered crucial and the prime minister was presumed to be the only person certain to secure compliance and cooperation from all ministers. When Sirimavo Bandaranaike assumed the premiership in 1970, she retained the ministry, renamed the Ministry of Planning and Employment in recognition of the mounting unemployment problem, under her personal control. The stature and popular esteem of the prime minister is generally far above that of his colleagues and, on controversial matters, assurances of direct control by the prime minister are calculated to generate trust and confidence.

The prime minister has not only been required to deal personally with disagreements among his ministers, but also has been almost constantly called upon to intervene in innumerable matters outside the cabinet such as labor disputes, grievances of particular categories of public servants, and complaints of private associations and groups. The tendency—which seems endemic in Ceylon and is observable at all levels of government—to send petitions and delegations to the highest authority possible reaches its pinnacle with the prime minister. An unsatisfactory resolution of an appeal seemingly is not accepted until it has been passed up to the personal attention of the highest executive authority.

Six persons have served as prime minister of Ceylon. All have been Sinhalese and Buddhists and of the Goyigama caste. All but one were members of wealthy and prominent families. Only W. Dahanayake, a one-time schoolteacher, was of modest means and not related to either the Senanayake or the Bandaranaike families. All except Sirimavo Bandaranaike were veteran politicians and legislators who had begun their legislative careers in the State Council before independence. Dudley Senanayake, who has been prime minister three times, had compiled a total of nearly seven years in the premiership when his party was defeated in the 1970 election. His father, D. S. Senanayake, held the premiership for four and one-half years. Mrs. Bandaranaike's first term as prime minister lasted four years and eight months, and in 1970 she commenced her second term. S. W. R. D. Bandaranaike held the premiership for nearly three and one-half years and Sir John Kotelawala for about two and one-half years. Dahanayake held the post for six months.

Succession to the premiership has posed difficult problems at times. Following an election, the leader of the largest party in parliament is by convention summoned to form a Government. Only in March 1960 was the Government so formed unable to command the confidence of the parliament. However, when a prime minister dies in office or retires, considerable confusion and intraparty conflict may ensue. The first prime minister, D. S. Senanayake, died in office in 1952 and, after an acrimonious intraparty struggle, was succeeded by his son, Dudley Senanayake, by-passing the latter's cousin, Sir John Kotelawala, who expected the post. Within two years, the younger Senanayake voluntarily relinquished the premiership to Kotelawala with the intention of abandoning politics. Following the UNP debacle in 1956, Kotelawala was persuaded to retire and return party leadership to Senanayake. When Prime Minister S. W. R. D. Bandaranaike was assassinated in 1959, his chief lieutenant, C. P. de Silva, was abroad undergoing medical treatment and W. Dahanayake was named prime minister as the ranking cabinet minister. Dahanayake, although the titular head of the SLFP, almost immediately broke with the party. When C. P. de Silva succeeded to leadership of the SLFP, the governor-general was asked to dismiss Dahanayake and appoint de Silva prime minister as the leader of the largest party in parliament. Dahanayake, however, ordered the dissolution of parliament and a new election, held in March 1960. Prior to the July 1960 election, de Silva relinquished SLFP leadership to Bandaranaike's widow, Sirimavo Bandaranaike, who had emerged from the March election as the party's most effective campaigner. When her party was victorious, Mrs. Bandaranaike was named prime minister and appointed to the Senate.

THE PRESIDENT

The ceremonial head of state and commander-in-chief of the armed forces under the 1972 constitution is the president of the republic, who is nominated by the prime minister for a four-year term of office. Presumably, the presidency created by the new constitution will closely resemble the earlier office of governor-general. The president is constitutionally required to act on ministerial advice in the performance of his duties, except in the appointment of a prime minister and in certain cases of dissolution of parliament. Even in appointing a prime minister, he will ordinarily have little latitude, as his selection must command the confidence of a majority in the National State Assembly. In unusual circumstances when the results of an election are particularly ambiguous or when a prime minister dies in office it is possible that the president may exercise some discretion. For the most part, however, his role, like that of the earlier governor-general, apparently will be formal and ceremonial, not effective and political.

Sir Oliver Goonetilleke, the first Ceylonese governor-general, who held the post from 1954 to 1962, played a personal role of some significance at several critical junctures, not because of the formal requirements of his office but because of his personal relationships with the prime ministers and the uses which prime ministers wished to make of his talents. Goonetilleke had been a close political adviser to the first two prime ministers, and after becoming governor-general he continued in this relationship with Prime Minister Sir John Kotelawala. Despite his intimate associations with the leaders of the UNP, Goonetilleke's effective role expanded to remarkable dimensions after the UNP's fall from power in 1956. Prime Minister S. W. R. D. Bandaranaike, faced with an extremely turbulent political environment and by circumstances or temperment unable himself to control events, depended repeatedly on Goonetilleke for executive leadership or mediation in emergency situations. With the explosion of communal riots in 1958, Bandaranaike virtually abdicated to the governor-general the authority to deal with the island's most serious emergency in many decades. Goonetilleke assumed direct control over the police, military, and civil administration in suppressing the violence and restoring law and order. Bandaranaike further obtained the assistance of the governor-general in a series of critical strikes in 1958–1959, and sought to use the governor-general to conciliate conflicting factions within his own cabinet in May 1959.

Goonetilleke did not appear to enjoy the confidence of Mrs. Bandaranaike, and his scope for action was considerably reduced with the commencement of her premiership. Early in 1962, a plot to seize control of the government by a small group of military and police officers was uncovered. The conspirators reportedly planned to obtain, either by persuasion or coercion, the governor-general's authorization for an emergency military regime.[14] Although cabinet spokesmen were careful not to accuse him of complicity, a month after the plot was discovered Goonetilleke was replaced as governor-general. His successor, William Gopallawa, performed his duties unobtrusively and did not appear to extend the role of the office beyond the formal and ceremonial. Despite his appointment by and personal connections with the SLFP leadership, he continued to hold office after the 1965 change in Government and appeared to maintain correctly nonpartisan behavior throughout the five-year duration of the UNP-dominated Government. His son, however, successfully sought election to parliament in 1970 as an SLFP candidate. On the promulgation of the new constitution in 1972, Gopallawa became the first president of the Republic of Sri Lanka.

The Public Service and Administration

The public service is one of the few modern structures in Ceylon possessing the skills and organization required to realize the goals sought by contemporary society. A trained, experienced, and capable bureaucracy and a coherent administrative system seemingly were among the nation's most valuable assets at independence. In the intervening years, the public service has been assigned a wide range of new functions and responsibilities. At the same time that it has been confronted with the challenge of new and vastly expanded responsibilities, the public service has been subjected to a series of social and economic stresses and increasing political penetration. Many features of bureaucracy and administration have attracted sharp public criticism. Although widely denounced as lethargic, backward-looking, and insensitive to public desires or convenience, the public service nonetheless

[14] *Coup d'Etat: Statement Read on Behalf of the Government by Felix R. Dias Bandaranaike, Parliamentary Secretary for Defence and External Affairs, in the House of Representatives on 13.2.62* (Colombo: Government Press, 1962), p. 7.

contains much of the island's talent, inspiration, and expertise, which is vital to the nation's hopes for progress and order.

STRUCTURE OF THE PUBLIC SERVICE

The public service is stratified into three major levels, sharply differentiated by status and pay. The highest level is composed of the administrative, professional, and technical officers, termed staff officers, who account for only about 4 per cent of all public servants (see Table 15). Below the staff officers are the employees of the intermediate grades, called "subordinate employees," including clerks, stenographers, policemen, field inspectors, and a number of other categories of public servants. At the bottom of

Table 15.   Employees of government departments, 1970[a]

Type of employee	Number	Per cent
Administrative, professional, and technical officers of staff rank	9,289	4.1
Subordinate employees	82,851	36.9
Minor employees	120,358	53.5
Other employees	12,319	5.5
Total	224,817	100.0

[a] Excludes approximately 90,000 teachers in government schools.
Source: Central Bank of Ceylon, Annual Report of the Monetary Board to the Minister of Finance for the Year 1970 (Colombo: Central Bank of Ceylon, 1971), p. 214.

the hierarchy are more than half of all public servants, termed "minor employees," among whom are the lower grades of office workers such as peons, messengers, and watchers, as well as considerable numbers of skilled and unskilled laborers. Promotions between levels have been extremely rare, despite some recent attempts to expand opportunities for movement to higher levels.

Staff officers are primarily university graduates. Generally, the clerical and other intermediate-level employees have completed secondary schools or technical training schools, but with the vastly worsening employment situation university graduates have been seeking posts in the clerical grades with increasing frequency. About 19,000 government clerks are included in the interdepartmental General Clerical Service. Other subordinate and most minor employees belong to departmental services.

A Ceylon Administrative Service (CAS) was formed in 1963, absorbing 209 members of the Ceylon Civil Service (CCS) and 642 departmental staff officers. The venerable CCS, Ceylon's minature counterpart of the famous Indian Civil Service, had come under heavy attack after independence as a relic of colonialism and a bastion of privilege. The formation of a unified administrative service was a reform widely advocated for years. After 1963, however, sharp controversy raged over the advantageous terms under which the former CCS officers were absorbed into the new CAS. As constituted in 1963, the CAS was stratified into five classes, the lowest of which was divided into two grades. After a number of re-examinations and proposals for reorganization, in 1971 the CAS was restructured into three classes, containing 100, 300, and 936 posts, respectively. Direct recruitment to the CAS is open to university graduates between twenty-two and twenty-six years of age. In the first examination, 421 applicants sought 40 vacancies, and in 1968, 6,404 applications were received for 151 openings.[15] In response to previous criticism of the lack of mobility in the public service, direct recruitment by open competitive examination is limited to 55 per cent of the vacancies available, while a competitive examination restricted

[15] *Annual Report of the Public Service Commission, 1963,* Sessional Paper V—1964 (Colombo: Government Press, 1964), p. 3; *Annual Report of the Public Service Commission, 1968,* Sessional Paper VI—1969 (Colombo: Government Press, 1969), p. 2.

to public servants with at least ten years' service in subordinate grades is to supply 25 per cent of the CAS recruits and another 20 per cent may enter by promotion from the clerical service without competitive examination.[16]

The demand for public employment has long been strong; with mounting unemployment in recent years it has reached tidal proportions. A bureaucratic career has been made attractive by the prestige and high social status traditionally enjoyed by public servants and by the value placed on security of tenure and pension rights in the society, reinforced by severely limited alternative sources of employment. The value system and the wage structure provide particularly strong incentives for seeking white-collar posts, a tendency strengthened by the proclivity of the educational system to grind out clerks and schoolteachers. With a rapid growth in the number of university and secondary-school graduates during the past decade, the scramble for white-collar government jobs has become an acute social problem. Pressures for employment presumably have combined with the expansion of government functions to produce a steady increase in the size of the public service. Excluding government schoolteachers and public corporation employees, the number of central government employees climbed from about 82,000 in 1948/1949 to nearly 225,000 in 1970.[17]

CHARACTERISTICS OF ADMINISTRATION

Government administration in Ceylon is characterized by marked departmentalization and weak integration of ministries. The nearly one hundred departments are the second-level ad-

[16] "Minute on the Ceylon Administrative Service," *Ceylon Government Gazette Extraordinary*, No. 14,996/12 (Feb. 9, 1972).

[17] The 1948/1949 figure is from *Report of the Salaries and Cadre Commission, 1953,* Part II, Sessional Paper XVII—1953 (Colombo: Government Press, 1953), Appendix I, p. 554. The 1970 figure is from Table 15.

ministrative units, comparable to the bureaus of many other administrative systems. A half-dozen or more departments are usually grouped together to form a ministry, under the direction of a cabinet minister. The number of ministries seems dependent principally on political considerations which dictate the size of the cabinet. The post of permanent secretary (retitled secretary in 1972) was created at independence as the administrative head of the ministry and the minister's principal policy adviser. For nearly two decades, however, little effort was made to integrate the departments within ministries. Staff functions were performed and files were maintained by each department, which remained as a self-contained and sometimes virtually autonomous unit, subject to frequent shifts from one ministry to another. Departments, particularly in the absence of clearly defined ministry goals, are claimed not infrequently to have worked at cross-purposes or to have duplicated efforts, inhibiting effective planning, implementation of programs, and ministerial control.

In 1966, after repeated recommendations, the Ministry of Local Government became the first fully integrated ministry. The departments within it were transformed into divisions of the ministry, department heads formerly titled commissioners became senior assistant secretaries of the ministry, and responsibility for personnel and budgetary matters was shifted from the departments to the ministry. The Ministries of Health and Education subsequently were partially integrated, but little progress toward the integration of other ministries has been registered. The common absence of ministry integration, while complicating coordination and direction, may provide some administrative flexibility by facilitating the regrouping of departments and functions to accomodate changing objectives and priorities.

Until 1965, permanent secretaries, although considered outside the career public service, were invariably selected from the top ranks of the bureaucracy. In 1965 and again in 1970, a number of permanent secretaries were appointed from outside the public service. Some were experts in specialized fields such as economics or education, and others were political appointees who held the confidence of the minister. Political loyalty appeared to be an additional qualification for the experts from outside and for the administrators promoted from within the public service. Only five of eighteen permanent secretaries were retained after the 1970 change in Government. Three of the new appointees in 1970 were drawn from university faculties. Also in 1970, the post of additional permanent secretary was created for the first time in a few ministries. The implications of the changing position and character of the permanent secretary for ministry operations remain to be determined, but it is often claimed that Ceylon is moving away from the British and toward the American practice regarding political appointments at high administrative levels.

The district is the basic unit of field administration. There are currently twenty-two districts, with an average population of about half a million. The population of the Colombo district exceeds two million and that of the Kandy district is slightly more than one million. The smallest district contains about 60,-000 inhabitants. District administration is headed by an officer with the title of government agent, the Ceylonese counterpart of the collector or deputy commissioner of India. Government agents report to the Home Ministry, although their responsibilties range over the activities of a large number of departments and ministries. The office of the government agent, known as a kach-cheri, was once the focus of all government field activities. Despite the growth of specialized departments with their own field staffs, the government agent has retained a wide variety of responsibilities, including coordination of field activities not under his direct control, and he continues to be regarded as the center and symbol of government authority in his district. A report on district administration in 1967 noted: "Traditions reaching back almost one hundred and fifty years find embodiment in the institution of the Government Agent. They flow from his earlier role in his area as the representative of the Raj, and the variety of commitments that were associated with that role."[18] As growing emphasis has been placed on social and economic development in recent years, the government agent has been assigned increasingly heavy developmental responsibilities.

Each district is subdivided into divisions headed by divisional revenue officers. The twenty-two districts contain 118 divisions and the number of divisions per district ranges from twelve to two. A grama sevaka (village servant) is responsible for a large village or a cluster of smaller villages within the division. In 1963, grama sevakas, who are selected through competitive examination and are transferable, replaced village headmen, who were local residents commonly selected on the basis of ascriptive criteria and were often viewed as the last vestige of a semifeudal pattern of administration. In addition to the grama sevakas, public servants engaged in agricutural extension work and similar functions operate at the village level. In 1969, public employees working at the village level totaled about 6,700.[19]

PUBLIC CORPORATIONS

In recent years, public corporations entirely owned and controlled by the government have grown rapidly in number and have assumed increasing importance in government economic endeavors. Public corporations are engaged in a wide range of

[18] "Report of the Committee of Permanent Secretaries on District Organization for Agricultural Development Work" (mimeographed; Colombo, Feb. 10, 1967), p. 7.

[19] "Task Force on Administrative Reforms: Interim Report on the Machinery of Government" (mimeographed; Colombo, Nov. 15, 1969), p. 32.

activities including transportation, banking, insurance, petroleum distribution, radio broadcasting, wholesale and retail trade, and river valley development. Enterprises called state industrial corporations, of which twenty were functioning in 1970, are involved in small-scale manufacturing. Employees of public corporations are not considered to be members of the public service and are not subject to public service regulations and pay scales. In 1970, public corporations and a few other semiautonomous government institutions employed nearly 167,000 persons. The number of employees of the state industrial corporations grew from about 5,000 in 1962 to more than 22,000 in 1970, while between 1964 and 1970 the staff of the Ceylon Transport Board, which operates the island's bus services, almost doubled, climbing from about 26,000 to nearly 50,000.[20]

The corporate device was adopted in an effort to obtain flexibility in financial, administrative, and personnel practices. However, the corporations have tended to adopt regulations and practices from the conventional departments, often resulting in reproduction of the rigidities which the corporations were created to escape. Except for financial institutions, public corporations are subject to close ministerial supervision and appear to enjoy little autonomy. Responsibility for their day-to-day operations is vested in a chairman and board of directors, but ministerial intervention in routine activities, particularly matters of recruitment and discipline, seems to be common. The corporations have filled many of their administrative posts with staff officers obtained

[20] The 1970 figures are from Central Bank of Ceylon, *Annual Report of the Monetary Board to the Minister of Finance for the Year 1970* (Colombo: Central Bank of Ceylon, 1971), pp. 65–80. The 1962 figure for state industrial corporations is from "Prospects for Industrialisation," *Ceylon Today,* XI (Sept. 1962), 1. The figure for the CTB in 1964 is from *Nationalised Bus Service,* Information Brochure no. 4 (Colombo: Department of Broadcasting and Information, 1964), p. 4.

temporarily from the public service. Chairmen and directors of the larger corporations frequently have been persons from outside the public service and the corporation staff who are identified politically with the party in power at the time. The smaller corporations are often headed by public servants, some of whom serve as chairmen or directors in addition to their regular public service duties. After 1970, elective employees' councils were created in all public corporations to allow employee participation in corporation management.

The corporations seem to have been particularly susceptible to political favoritism and patronage in recruitment, assignment, promotion, and discipline. Patronage is thought to have played a major role in the staffing of many public corporations and intervention by political officeholders in promotions and disciplinary actions reportedly has been common. The tremendous growth in the corporations' staffs has been attributed in part to the desire of ministers and M.P.'s to secure opportunities for patronage.

BUREAUCRATIC PERFORMANCE

The public service appears to have been relatively successful in performing the conventional regulatory and service functions of government, although its capacity as an instrument of economic development is less certain. In the crisis and confusion of the 1958 communal riots and the 1971 insurrection, field officers of the public service often responded with courage and decisiveness and played a major role in stemming the disorders. Nonetheless, much dissatisfaction with the bureaucracy's performance is evident both within and outside the public service. Organization, training, and personnel practices have all been subjected to criticism, but probably the most severe condemnations have been directed toward the attitudes and behavior of public servants. In the performance of their functions, bureaucrats tend toward a meticulous adherence to the details of rules, regulations, and established procedures, with little evident ability or inclination to exercise discretion or initiative. Often routine procedures and practices have become ritualized to the point that the routine appears to be accorded greater value than attainment of the objective for which the routine was established. An immense amount of time and effort is expended in the passage of papers from clerk to clerk for initialing and forwarding to the next clerk. Each letter or form must be handled by an astounding number of persons within an office and often by an amazing number of offices before final disposition. At any point, action may be held up for days, weeks, or even months. Furthermore, it is frequently alleged that public servants are apathetic, indolent, and indifferent toward organizational goals and public desires. Absenteeism, lack of discipline, and inattention to duties are often cited as characteristics of public servants' behavior.

The frequent absence of motivation toward achievement or diligence in the performance of duties is commonly linked with the promotion policies and security of tenure of the public service. Bureaucratic recruitment is based on merit, determined more or less competitively. However, after a recruit has entered the public service, normally immediately after leaving school, status and advancement are little related to achievement. Promotions and salary increases are based almost entirely on seniority and age, at least until the highest administrative grades are reached. In appealing for promotions based on performance and merit, a committee on administrative reform concluded: "There is no special incentive to one in the Public Service to make a special effort under the present conditions. It is hardly surprising that the Public Service is neither enterprising nor dynamic in this context."[21] At the top rungs of the bureaucratic hierarchy, demonstrated ability appears again to operate as a major con-

[21] *Report of the Committee on Administrative Reforms,* Sessional Paper IX—1966 (Colombo: Government Press, 1966), p. 17.

sideration in promotion and assignment, diluted perhaps only by political considerations. The top administrators are probably as capable and conscientious as their counterparts in any public bureaucracy and are frequently saddled with overwhelming responsibilities and duties. Accomplishment may be impressive. Below a few score senior positions, however, little incentive is provided for conscientious performance or maximum effort.

The alienation, lack of discipline, and indifference to organizational objectives often attributed to the bureaucracy appear to be related to the social and economic stresses and the bureaucratic and political circumstances confronting public servants. During the past two decades, the bureaucracy has felt reverberations of major political transformations, intense partisan contests, and communal tensions and conflict. Such traumatic events as the communal riots of 1958 and the insurrection of 1971 heightened the turbulence of the bureaucracy's social environment. In the same period, the public service has undergone a considerable expansion, assumed wide new functions and responsibilities, and been subjected to repeated demands for reform. The changeover from English to Sinhalese as the language of administration after 1956 created some administrative confusion and considerable demoralization among public servants educated in the English language. Progressive politicization of the public service has tended to undermine conventional notions of discipline, duty, and authority. Frustrations have been generated by conditions of economic scarcity, sharp class and status differentials, and the disruptive experiences of social and economic change. Economic insecurity has been heightened by a constantly rising cost of living. Allowances granted in 1967 temporarily stemmed a decade-long decline in the real wages of public servants.[22] Until 1970, public

[22] Central Bank of Ceylon, *Annual Report of the Monetary Board to the Minister of Finance for the Year 1967* (Colombo: Central Bank of Ceylon, 1968), pp. 139–140.

service salaries had not undergone a major revision since 1951.

Indicative of spreading grievances and discontents within the public service is a steep rise in the size and militancy of trade unionism among public servants. Trade union rights with some restrictions were extended to government employees in 1948. Membership in public service trade unions climbed from 52,000 in 1954 to 115,000 five years later, and by 1968 had passed 257,000 (including government schoolteachers).[23] The growth in size has been matched by increasing militancy. Public servants have repeatedly resorted to strikes and demonstrations over a variety of grievances. A public servants' strike in 1968, which lasted twenty-five days, was claimed to have involved more than 200,000 public employees and to be the largest strike ever to hit the public service. Public servants also participated in politically motivated protest strikes in 1953, 1959, 1962, 1964, and 1966. In addition to strikes, public servants have resorted to "work-to-rule" campaigns, by which they have adhered with such elaborate attention to the details of procedures and regulations that the work of the office was thrown into confusion or brought to a standstill. Aggressive trade unionism appears to have become an important channel for articulating grievances and protest within the middle and lower levels of the public service.

POLITICIZATION OF THE PUBLIC SERVICE

The Ceylonese public service has become increasingly politicized over a period of more than a decade. A tendency for ministers and other politicians to intervene in routine administrative activities has long been evident, but the extent of penetration throughout the bureaucracy of political pressures and influences has increased tremendously in recent years. The trend has been reinforced by the willingness of public servants to accede to poli-

---

[23] *Administration Report of the Commissioner of Labour* for the years 1954–1967/1968 (Colombo: Government Press, 1955–1969).

ticians' requests and, with increasing frequency, to seek political favor for themselves. The 1946 constitution created an autonomous Public Service Commission intended to insulate the bureaucracy from political interference. The commission, however, complicated lines of authority and responsibility without demonstrably inhibiting the growth of political intervention in public service matters and was eliminated by the 1972 constitution.

Some suspicions and tensions between elected officials and career public servants are almost inevitable in any system of government containing both. Ceylonese public servants have occasionally displayed attitudes of superiority and disdain toward politicians. One M.P. reportedly was told when he asked a public servant the reason for a shortage of water buffaloes that "the buffaloes are now in Parliament."[24] Political officeholders have, however, generally obtained supremacy over bureaucrats by being able to affect transfers, promotions, assignments, and retirements. A senior public servant once explained: "Power lies where there is the right to [determine] promotion and preference. In our system of administration, it is not the Permanent Secretary who determines promotions and other preferences. . . . [These decisions] tend to lie in the political sector and naturally power lies there."[25] Public servants who have refused to cooperate with politicians have found themselves subjected to a variety of difficulties and pressures. Ministers frequently support their political followers in disputes with public servants. M.P.'s often denounce individual public servants by name on the floor of parliament, an unnerving experience for public servants because of the possibility of being called to account by the minister or being quietly transferred to an undesirable post. Senior administrators with sturdy

[24] Ceylon, House of Representatives, *Parliamentary Debates (Hansard)*, vol. 48, col. 2738 (Sept. 10, 1962).

[25] "Seminar on the Role of the Public Service," *Training Digest* (Journal of the Academy of Administrative Studies), I (Jan. 1969), 49.

reputations for competence and integrity have often been able to resist politicians' requests, but the junior staff officers and middle-level supervisors have seldom been in a position to dismiss lightly the threats or requests of politicians.

Two types of developments have contributed to the progressive politicization of the bureaucracy. The first is a growing tendency for political influences to be exerted over administrative actions. Political intervention in a multitude of bureaucratic operations has resulted from the political officeholders' desire for patronage and benefits for supporters or constituents. Steeply rising popular demands and expectations have added to the pressures for political intervention. The M.P. has responded to constituents' pleas by attempting to influence public servants to obtain desired actions. Politicians have tended to intervene at the point at which action may be taken, often at a fairly low level of the administrative hierarchy, and to go to higher levels of the bureaucracy or to the minister only if satisfaction cannot be obtained at the lower level. This type of intervention has been practiced by members of all political parties under every recent Government. Bureaucratic incapacity, inertia, and indolence have commonly been cited by politicians as necessitating their intervention. As one M.P. complained: "It is only when the administrative machinery functions properly that the effects of government policy are felt tangibly by the people. If the [public service] officers do not take any interest whatsoever to see that the policies of the Government are put into effect what is the use of our being M.P.s? We cannot get anything done at the kachcheri."[26] The politicians have been attempting to develop important new linkages within the political system and to heighten government responsiveness to public wants and needs. Their paramount concern, however, frequently has been for their individual political fortunes, and

[26] Ceylon, House of Representatives, *Parliamentary Debates* (*Hansard*), vol. 87, col. 1447 (Sept. 5, 1969).

their intervention in administration has often been directed toward obtaining immediate advantages exclusively for their own supporters. Public servants, although not always adjusting gracefully to the postindependence changes, may in some cases have possessed a longer-run and more universalistic outlook on government activities and services than the politicians.

Political intervention has extended beyond administrative services to the public to envelop such internal public service matters as recruitment, transfers, promotions, retirements, and discipline. Often the public servant concerned has sought intervention on his behalf by an M.P. or minister. Political influences reportedly have become so pervasive as to disrupt seriously the formally established procedures governing transfers, promotions, and disciplinary actions. Public employees in the lower grades often have taken grievances with a superior to the minister, from whom they frequently have received a sympathetic hearing, sometimes followed by orders countermanding the superior. Serious problems of authority reportedly have arisen because supervisors hesitate to discipline their subordinates for fear a complaint will be made through a trade union or other nonbureaucratic channel to a minister or another politician. While inadequate bureaucratic performance is often cited in justification of political intervention in administration, the pervasiveness of political involvement may further reduce administrative capabilities and undermine the basis of a professionalized public service by disrupting regular procedures, eroding discipline, and substituting political influence for more relevant administrative criteria in determining assignments and promotions.

A second and separate development in the politicization of the bureaucracy is a tendency for tests of political loyalty to be applied for certain assignments within the career public service. Ministers and M.P.'s have long sought to transfer or otherwise rid themselves of public servants assigned to their ministry or constituency who were suspected of sympathy with the political opposition. This appears to stem largely from fear that the public servant will reveal confidential information or otherwise act to discredit the political officeholder or subvert his popular support. While most evident at the higher levels, the tendency is said to extend down to divisional revenue officers and sometimes even to schoolteachers in an M.P.'s constituency. In recent years, particularly with the formation of the United Front Government in 1970, politicians in power have tended to demand a positive commitment to the objectives of the Government of the day from permanent secretaries, department heads, and other ranking administrators involved in priority programs. Political parties coming to power dedicated to major, extensive, and innovative actions are more likely to value and seek positive commitment to their goals by public servants than parties with more limited and conventional objectives, as procrastination and inertia appear to be among the principal obstacles to the attainment of their goals. The bureaucracy has exhibited a marked tendency to continue to implement the same policy in the same manner indefinitely, and considerable effort is required to secure a shift in policy objectives or methods of implementation. Hence, for the crucial posts in executing their priority programs, political leaders have tended to seek public servants who are not merely neutral, with its suggestion of indifference, but are positively committed to the objectives of the program and the Government.

Parallel to the growing political penetration of bureaucratic activities, a trend toward increasing partisanship by public servants and their organizations has emerged. Until 1970, public service regulations prohibited public servants from engaging in political activities or belonging to political organizations, and statutory restrictions prohibited political involvement or connections by public servants' trade unions. While the restrictions ordinarily inhibited overt and conspicuous partisan activities, many violations were claimed to have occurred. During the 1970 election campaign, an SLFP leader and ex-minister called on public servants to work openly for the United Front, promising that after it came to power it would reinstate public servants who had been penalized for political activities.[27] Many trade unions of public servants had long maintained informal links with political parties. After the 1966 United Front–sponsored political strike, disciplinary action was taken against large numbers of participating government employees, probably helping to propel their unions into a more overtly partisan role. The prominent Government Clerical Service Union in 1970 publicly called for the defeat of the incumbent UNP-dominated Government. The organization's journal declared on the eve of the election: "We are now thrown [in]to the position of finding a political solution. Let us therefore take our opportunity in this General Election. . . . Let us ensure the defeat of the UNP Combine."[28]

The granting of political rights to public servants had been discussed for a number of years and was promised in the 1970 United Front election manifesto. After the United Front victory, prohibitions on political activity and membership in political organizations were removed for civilian government employees below the staff grades. Restrictions on public servants' trade unions were also eliminated. While the granting of political rights could intensify partisanship within the public service, the action may have represented little beyond the formalization of the situation which had developed in practice.

Local Government

Local representative institutions have existed for more than a century in the major cities. Elected municipal councils were

[27] *Ceylon Daily News,* April 1, 1970, p. 1.
[28] *Red Tape* (Journal of the Government Clerical Service Union), May 1970, p. 4.

formed in Colombo and Kandy in 1866 and in Galle the following year. Subsequently, elective local bodies were created in the smaller cities and towns and eventually in the villages. In 1968, 12 municipal councils, 34 urban councils, 79 town councils, and 516 village councils existed. All of Ceylon except for a small area under the River Valleys Development Board was within the jurisdiction of one of the local government bodies. About one-tenth of the island's population lived in municipal council areas and nearly 80 per cent in village council areas.

Outside of the major cities, local councils have sharply limited powers and resources and enjoy little autonomy. Their functions chiefly deal with sanitation, health, utilities, and roads. Services provided are much greater in the urban areas, but even the village councils provide a significant range of services (see Table 16). All municipal councils and most urban councils provide dispensaries, piped water, and electricity. About one-third of the village councils maintain dispensaries, but only about one-eighth provide piped water or electricity. Conservancy services (principally sanitation and refuse collection) are supplied by all municipal, urban, and town councils, but by less than half of the village councils. In 1968, local councils employed more than 27,000 persons, nearly 15,000 of whom worked for the twelve municipal councils.[29] Council employees belong to a centrally organized Local Government Service.

All local councils function under the supervision of the central Ministry of Local Government, which exercises close scrutiny over their activities. Chairmen of local councils have frequently been removed, or the entire council has been suspended or dissolved, on ministry findings of malfeasance or incompetence. Even in Colombo, the municipal council was dissolved in 1957

[29] Ceylon, Department of Census and Statistics, *Statistical Pocket Book of Ceylon, 1970* (Colombo: Department of Government Printing, 1970), Table 84, p. 115.

Table 16. Facilities provided by local councils, 1968

| Type of council | Number | Number providing | | | | | | | | Miles of road per 10,000 inhabitants |
		Dispensaries	Cemeteries	Piped Water	Electricity	Conservancy	Parks, playgrounds	Libraries	
Municipal	12	12	12	12	12	12	12	12	6.3
Urban	34	32	32	22	31	34	30	32	9.5
Town	79	26	52	16	53	79	33	55	12.0
Village	516	182	375	65	70	214	139	252	25.3

Source: Ceylon, Department of Census and Statistics, *Statistical Pocket Book of Ceylon, 1970* (Colombo: Department of Government Printing, 1970), Tables 84 and 86, pp. 115, 117.

and municipal affairs were administered for two years by a special commissioner appointed by the Ministry of Local Government. The council dissolution was precipitated by a strike of municipal employees which disrupted health, sanitation, and other municipal functions. Suspension or dissolution of village and town councils has been much more common. Partisan motives have occasionally been ascribed to the ministry's intervention. In the year following the 1970 election, it was claimed that at least twenty councils were dissolved, all of which were controlled by parties in opposition in the national parliament.[30]

The term of office of local councils was lengthened from three to four years in 1969. Municipal elections have been fought essentially on party lines in the cities and towns since parties first appeared at the national level more than a quarter of a century ago. Within the first decade of independence, party competition spread rapidly to the village council elections as well. In the last dozen years local elections have been dominated by clashes between candidates of the major national parties. Alliances and fronts created for parliamentary elections have often continued to function for local elections. Municipal politics, particularly in Colombo, are closely linked with national politics and many persons are simultaneously active in both. Six of seven M.P.'s elected from Colombo constituencies in the 1970 parliamentary election had served on the Colombo municipal council. Three ministers in the national cabinet named in 1965 were sitting members of the Colombo municipal council. The UNP has dominated Colombo municipal politics almost continuously since independence. In 1961, the municipal council was enlarged and constituencies were reapportioned by the SLFP-controlled Ministry of Local Government in a presumed effort to reduce UNP strength in the council. An election the following year, however,

[30] Ceylon, Senate, *Parliamentary Debates* (*Hansard*), vol. 32, cols. 1367–1368 (June 17, 1971).

resulted in the UNP capturing forty of the forty-seven seats in the enlarged council.

In view of the limited functions and powers of local councils, particularly those in rural areas, political competition in local elections has been surprisingly vigorous. Political cleavages in village council politics, although often masked by party labels and ideological rhetoric, seem frequently to reflect long-standing local factional rivalries, and the council elections appear to serve as an arena for the clashes between rival clans, castes, or locally prominent personages. Furthermore, while council members have few benefits to dispense directly, they are commonly linked to the national network of patronage and favors and may influence the dissemination of central government jobs and services. Local councils have also become channels for movement to higher levels of politics and may attract the ambitious by the prospect of serving as a springboard for election to parliament.

Relations between locally elected bodies and the field agencies of the central government have seldom been harmonious. The kachcheri system of field administration has come to symbolize highly centralized paternalistic rule from Colombo, often accompanied by disinterest in the opinions or preferences of the people of the locality. In an effort to decentralize and democratize field administration, several proposals have been advanced since the 1950's to create representative bodies on a regional or district level. Among the more fully developed was a 1968 scheme for the creation of district councils which would "not be local authorities but would be an extension of the Central Government activities taking over some functions now performed by the Kachcheries" and operating under the control of the central ministers.[31] The proposals, however, regularly became entangled

[31] *Proposals for the Establishment of District Councils Under the Direction and Control of the Central Government* (Colombo: Government Press, 1968), p. 9.

in controversy surrounding Federal Party demands for regional autonomy for the Tamil minority and were abandoned.

After the 1970 election, several types of bodies were established to represent local opinion in the implementation of central government programs. The most widely publicized were "people's committees" created to oversee administration and expose corruption at the local level and to serve as chanels of communication between the central government and the public. About 9,000 people's committees, each containing eleven members, were formed. The committees were, however, given only investigative and advisory powers, and their members were appointed by a central minister. In addition, advisory development councils and committees were established at the local and district levels. The new institutions seem to have few resources and to be essentially limited to advisory functions. Their relationship with the existing elective local councils is somewhat ambiguous. Whether they will have a major impact on government activities at the local level remains to be determined. Government in Ceylon seems likely to remain highly centralized, with power, resources, and popular interest concentrated at the national level.

3. Political
Parties

There are few more striking or significant features of the Ceylonese political system than the vigorous and effective competition that occurs between political parties. By 1970, control of the government had passed between opposing parties as a result of free and orderly elections no less than five times. In each parliamentary election after 1952 the governing party or coalition was expelled from office. The clash of parties has not only determined the personnel making up the political executive but has demonstrably altered the content and direction of government policies and actions. Although the party system has been in existence in Ceylon for no more than a quarter of a century, political parties displaying a considerable degree of coherence and resilience have established themselves at the center of the political process, and partisan loyalties and party voting have apparently become entrenched among the population.

The 1947 election, held shortly before independence, was the first to be fought essentially on party lines, although as early as 1928 a small, now defunct Labour Party was formed, and in 1935 a group of young radicals inspired by anti-colonialism and socialism founded the first Marxist party, the Lanka Sama Samaja Party, the oldest party still in existence. Earlier political organizations, denied any prospect of winning and exercising power by colonial rule, operated as agitational groups or discussion societies, rather than as political parties. Except for the ideo-

Party	Year founded	Principal original leader(s)	Catalyst for founding
Lanka Sama Samaja Party	1935	N. M. Perera, Philip Gunawardena, Colvin R. de Silva, and others	Nationalism and social protest, largely among young graduates of Western universities
Ceylon Communist Party	1943	S. A. Wickremasinghe, Pieter Keuneman	United Socialist Party transformed into the Ceylon Communist Party; followed a 1940 split in the LSSP over the LSSP's condemnation of the Third International
Tamil Congress	1944	G. G. Ponnambalam	Constitutional debate in anticipation of independence
United National Party	1946	D. S. Senanayake	Approach of independence and imminent pre-independence election
Federal Party	1949	S. J. V. Chelvanayakam	Split in the TC following denial of citizenship to Indian Tamils and TC cooperation with the UNP Government
Mahajana Eksath Peramuna [originally Viplavakari Lanka Sama Samaja Party]	1950	Philip Gunawardena	Split in the LSSP over ideological and tactical questions, largely related to "proletarian internationalism" and identification with the Sinhalese working class
Sri Lanka Freedom Party	1951	S. W. R. D. Bandaranaike	Break away from the UNP, stemming from conflict over succession to UNP leadership, reinforced by policy differences
Ceylon Communist Party ["left"]	1963	N. Sanmugathasan	Split in the CP, largely on the issues of the ideological conflict between Moscow and Peking
Lanka Sama Samaja Party (Revolutionary)	1964	Bala Tampoe, Edmund Samarakkody	Split in the LSSP following LSSP agreement to enter a coalition Government with a "bourgeois" party

Table 18. Party performance in parliamentary elections, 1947–1970

Party	1947 Per cent popular vote	1947 Number seats won	1952 Per cent popular vote	1952 Number seats won	1956 Per cent popular vote	1956 Number seats won	March 1960 Per cent popular vote	March 1960 Number seats won
United National Party	39.9	42[a]	44.1	54	27.3	8	29.4	50
Sri Lanka Freedom Party	—	—	15.5	9	40.7[b]	51[b]	20.9	46
Lanka Sama Samaja Party	16.9[c]	15[c]	13.1	9	10.2	14	10.5	10
Communist Party	3.7	3	5.7[d]	4[d]	4.5	3	4.8	3
Federal Party	—	—	1.9	2	5.4	10	5.7	15
Tamil Congress	4.3	7	2.8	4	0.3	1	1.2	1
Other parties	6.2	7	2.9	2	0.6	—	18.3[e]	19[e]
Independents	28.9	21	14.0	11	11.0	8	9.1	7
Total[f]	100.0	95	100.0	95	100.0	95	100.0	151

[a] One UNP candidate was returned unopposed.
[b] Results for the Mahajana Eksath Peramuna coalition, the principal component of which was the SLFP.
[c] Includes two factions contesting the election separately.
[d] Results for a united front of the CP and the VLSSP. Three Communists and one VLSSP member were elected.
[e] Includes the MEP (the former VLSSP), which secured 10.5 per cent of the popular vote and 10 seats.
[f] Some columns do not add to 100.0 per cent due to rounding.
[g] One candidate of the UNP and one of the LSSP were returned unopposed.
[h] One SLFP candidate was returned unopposed.
[i] Includes the LSSP(R), "left" CP, Eela Thamil Ottumai Munnani, and United Left Front, the candidates of which were treated as independents in the official results.
[j] Includes the Sinhala Mahajana Pakshaya, the candidates of which were treated as independents in the official results.

Party	July 1960		1965		1970	
	Per cent popular vote	Number seats won	Per cent popular vote	Number seats won	Per cent popular vote	Number seats won
United National Party	37.6	30	39.3	66[g]	37.9	17
Sri Lanka Freedom Party	33.6	75	30.2	41	36.9	91[h]
Lanka Sama Samaja Party	7.4	12	7.5	10[g]	8.7	19
Communist Party	3.0	4	2.7	4	3.4	6
Federal Party	7.0	16	5.4	14	4.9	13
Tamil Congress	1.5	1	2.4	3	2.3	3
Other parties	5.3	7	6.7[i]	7	1.3[j]	—
Independents	4.6	6	5.8	6	4.6	2
Total[z]	100.0	151	100.0	151	100.0	151

Source: For 1947: Ceylon Daily News, *Parliament of Ceylon, 1947* (Colombo: Associated Newspapers of Ceylon, Ltd., n.d.). For 1952: I. D. S. Weerawardana, "The General Elections in Ceylon, 1952," *Ceylon Historical Journal,* II (July–Oct. 1952), 111–178. For 1956: I. D. S. Weerawardana, *Ceylon General Election, 1956* (Colombo: M. D. Gunasena & Co., Ltd., 1960); and Ceylon Daily News, *Parliament of Ceylon, 1956* (Colombo: Associated Newspapers of Ceylon, Ltd., n.d.). For March and July 1960: *Report on the Parliamentary General Elections, 19th March and 20th July, 1960,* Sessional Paper II—1962 (Colombo: Government Press, 1962); and Ceylon Daily News, *Parliaments of Ceylon, 1960* (Colombo: Associated Newspapers of Ceylon, Ltd., n.d.). For 1965: *Report on the Sixth Parliamentary General Election of Ceylon, 22nd March, 1965,* Sessional Paper XX—1966 (Colombo: Government Press, 1966). For 1970: *Report on the Seventh Parliamentary General Election in Ceylon, 27th May, 1970,* Sessional Paper VII—1971 (Colombo: Department of Government Printing, 1971). Also, for all elections: Ceylon, Department of Elections, *Results of Parliamentary General Elections in Ceylon, 1947–1970* (Colombo: Department of Government Printing, 1971).

logically motivated parties, all significant political parties still in existence were formed between 1944 and 1951 (see Table 17). Party formation in that period was prompted by intense constitutional debate in anticipation of independence and the emergence of new political patterns and issues in the first years after independence. Subsequently, considerable institutionalization of the party system has occurred, and voting according to party labels seems to have become a firmly established practice for the overwhelming majority of the Ceylonese electorate.

Competitive Pluralism

The party system is not only competitive, but highly pluralistic. The election performance of parties (Table 18) reveals a wide scattering of popular votes and parliamentary representation among half a dozen durable parties, along with a number of less stable parties and independents.

ALTERNATIONS IN POWER

No party enjoys a perpetual dominance, nor is one party so situated that it is virtually assured of inclusion in a governing coalition. The alternations in power within a pluralistic party system result from the existence of two relatively large opposing parties, the United National Party and the Sri Lanka Freedom Party, one of which has formed the core of each Government since independence. The UNP, founded in 1946, formed the Government with a few minor allies from 1947 until its defeat in 1956, held power briefly in 1960, and returned in 1965 as the principal component of a governing coalition. The SLFP, founded in 1951 after a split in the UNP, either formed the Government or was the dominant coalition partner in the Government from 1956 to 1965, except for a few months in 1960. In 1970, the SLFP and its United Front allies administered a resounding defeat to the UNP and returned to power with an overwhelming majority in parliament. The capacity of each of the two major parties to survive election defeats and remain in existence as a viable alternative has been significantly enhanced by the prospect that the party may return to power at the next election.

Both the UNP and the SLFP are sufficiently large to be within plausible reach of power, which encourages the hope of victory and hence tends to intensify the competition. Also, the two are closely enough balanced in many constituencies to allow small shifts in votes or the benefits of electoral alliances with smaller parties to tip the balance from one to the other. Throughout the Sinhalese areas of the island, political competition tended to develop into a UNP-SLFP contest with the 1956 election. Although the UNP outpolled the SLFP by a small margin in each of the four subsequent elections, the popular vote of the two parties has remained fairly close. However, the number of seats won in parliament has fluctuated widely from one election to the next. Figures 2 and 3 depict the swings in proportions of the popular vote and parliamentary seats won by the UNP and the SLFP. In view of the relative stability of the smaller parties' electoral strength (Figures 4 and 5), it is evident that the major shifts occur between the UNP and the SLFP, and a gain by one is largely at the expense of the other, as suggested by Figure 3.

Since the confused election of March 1960, the proportion of votes won by each of the two major contenders has remained remarkably stable. The UNP proportion has held between 37 and 40 per cent, while the SLFP proportion has varied by only a slightly wider margin, from 30 to 37 per cent. The wide swings in seats won, despite a relatively consistent showing in popular votes, is largely explained by the use of a plurality, predominately single-member-district electoral system, where a small shift in votes within an electoral district can cause the seat to change from one party to another. If a similar shift occurs in a number

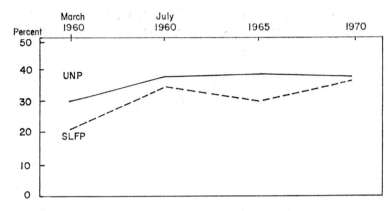

Figure 2. UNP and SLFP per cent of popular vote in last four elections

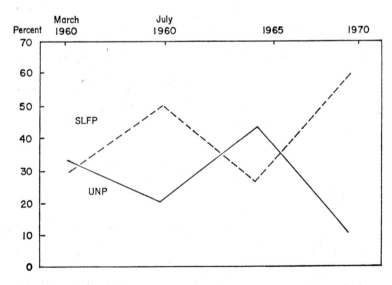

Figure 3. UNP and SLFP per cent of parliamentary seats won in last four elections

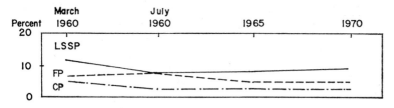

Figure 4. LSSP, FP, and CP per cent of popular vote in last four elections

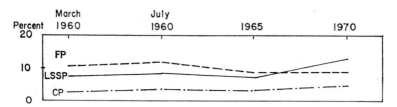

Figure 5. LSSP, FP, and CP per cent of parliamentary seats won in last four elections

of constituencies, a party may lose or gain a considerable number of seats on a modest change in votes.[1]

Ceylon provides a striking example of the "turnover" pattern of party competition, with the party or parties in power being defeated in five consecutive elections, in marked contrast with the "hegemonic" or "Congress-dominant" party system of neighboring India.[2] The emergence of a turnover pattern was possible in

[1] On the effects of the electoral system, see Chapter 4.

[2] The distinction between the "turnover" and the "hegemonic" patterns of party competition is made in Joseph LaPalombara and Myron Weiner, "The Origin and Development of Political Parties," in LaPalombara and Weiner (eds.), *Political Parties and Political Development* (Princeton, N.J.: Princeton University Press, 1966), pp. 35–36. On the Indian party

Ceylon because of the absence of any party with a dominant position and strong nationwide organization such as the Indian National Congress enjoyed at independence. The Ceylon National Congress never possessed the organizational strength or popular base of its Indian counterpart. The Ceylonese organization suffered a loss of authority by the departure of most Ceylon Tamil leaders within two years of its founding, leaving it as a largely Sinhalese organization. With the appearance of a popularly elected national legislature, the State Council, in 1931, the legislative chamber tended to become the focus of politics, and independence came essentially through negotiations between the legislative leaders and the British authorities. The Congress did not function as a political party in State Council elections or as a unified and disciplined group within the legislature. D. S. Senanayake, the leader of the State Council and later the first prime minister of Ceylon, resigned from the Congress in 1943 in protest against the admission of Communists to membership. Probably because of its organizational limitations and its lack of communal inclusiveness, the Congress was not converted into a national political party at independence, but rather was incorporated into the newly formed UNP and soon vanished. The UNP initially sought to be a broad national "umbrella" party, but never fully succeeded either in bringing in the ethnic minorities or in establishing a mass popular base. With growing mass political awareness and activism in the first decade after independence, the UNP found itself out of touch with popular aspirations and ineptly led. The rout of the UNP in 1956, after nine years in office, undoubtedly had a tremendous psychological impact by demonstrating conclusively that the governing party was

---

system, see Rajni Kothari, *Politics in India* (New Delhi: Orient Longmans, Ltd., 1970), pp. 153–205.

not invincible and that substantial changes in the composition and policies of Governments were possible through election contests.

The swing of popular support away from the governing party or parties which regularly has appeared since 1956 suggests the presence of an "opposition mentality" within the Ceylonese electorate. Growing mass political awareness and social mobilization, particularly since the mid-1950's, have produced high expectations and insistent demands among the public, further stimulated by the vigorous competition between parties. The financial and administrative resources available to any Government, however, are severely limited. The result is that performance falls below party promises and presumed public expectations. Opposition parties vigorously exploit the failures and weaknesses of the Government's performance and argue that with power they would fulfill promises and register major achievements. Dissatisfaction with past performance leads a section of the electorate to shift their votes to the opposition, and with the near balance obtaining between the UNP and the SLFP, the result is the defeat of the incumbent Government. The new Government, however, facing constraints and lack of resources much like those confronting its predecessor, also performs unsatisfactorily, leading to a repeat of the cycle. Through 1970, the pattern resulted in orderly alternations in power. The eventual effects on popular opinion of repeated disappointments and failures of achievement, however, is difficult to predict. At some point frustration could mount against the system itself, leading to apathy or turmoil and attacks on the basic character of the system. The bitter alienation of a portion of the island's youth apparent in the 1971 insurrection evidently stemmed in part from conviction that few substantial differences distinguished the two groups of politicians who alternated in office.

STABILIZED PLURALISM

The lines of competition between the two major contenders are complicated by the existence of a number of smaller parties which are able to mobilize only limited electoral support but remain as active participants in the system. In addition to independents, candidates of thirteen parties contested the 1965 election and eight parties offered candidates in 1970. Independents and ephemeral parties, however, have declined to negligible proportions, and the striking feature of the system's pluralism is the resilience and durability of the smaller parties. In 1970, all but two of 151 parliamentary seats and 94 per cent of the popular votes were captured by parties that had been in existence for at least nineteen years. In addition to the SLFP and the UNP, four parties—the Lanka Sama Samaja Party, the Ceylon Communist Party, the Federal Party, and the Tamil Congress—have contested every parliamentary election since 1952 and have returned at least one member to parliament in each. These four small but durable parties have consistently accounted for about one-fifth of the popular vote. They have survived and retained a stable base of support by narrowly focusing their efforts and appeal. The FP and the TC have exclusively championed the interests of the Tamil minority. The LSSP and the CP have relied on ideological commitment backed by sustained organizational and agitational activities in restricted areas. The party system therefore exhibits not only a marked pluralism but also a considerable degree of stability.

Both communal and ideological cleavages have contributed to the multiplicity of parties functioning in Ceylon. The Ceylon Tamils have tended to support parties exclusively dedicated to serving the interests of the Tamil community, particularly since 1956, when the eruption of the official-language issue deepened the political gulf between the Sinhalese and the Tamils. In 1956, the Tamil Congress was displaced by the Federal Party as the leading party of the Ceylon Tamils, although the former party has remained in existence, captured a few parliamentary seats, and provided competition for the Federal Party in the Tamil areas. Except for scattered FP support from east-coast Muslims, both parties depend entirely on the votes of the Ceylon Tamil community. The two parties consistently divide between them about one-tenth of the seats in parliament and one-twelfth of the popular vote in each election, reflecting their strength within and limitation to the Ceylon Tamil community.

Fissures and schisms have produced several Marxist parties which trace a common origin to the Lanka Sama Samaja Party. A clash between the Trotskyists and Communists within the LSSP in 1940 led to the expulsion of the Communists, who formed the Ceylon Communist Party in 1943. A 1950 split in the LSSP produced the Viplavakari Lanka Sama Samaja Party, which since 1959 has called itself the Mahajana Eksath Peramuna. In 1963, the CP split into two separate parties, each claiming to be the Ceylon Communist Party.[3] When the Samasamajists entered a coalition with the SLFP the following year, a group of orthodox Trotskyist dissidents broke with the LSSP to form the Lanka Sama Samaja Party (Revolutionary). The 1965 election found six self-proclaimed Marxist parties in contention. None of the dissident Marxist parties formed since 1963 has been able to attract even modest electoral support, although the "left" Communists and the LSSP(R) have enjoyed some influence in the trade union movement.

The electoral performance of the LSSP and the CP suggests that each has possessed a stable core of dependable support, which has neither expanded nor contracted appreciably in a quarter of a century. In each election prior to 1970, Samasama-

[3] References to the CP after the 1963 split will be to the pro-Moscow party. The considerably weaker pro-Peking party will be cited as the "left" CP.

jist candidates consistently amassed about 300,000 votes. The number of votes captured by Communist candidates, although fluctuating somewhat more widely, generally ranged around 100,000. The United Front landslide in 1970 boosted the Samasamajist vote to nearly 435,000, and that of the CP to nearly 170,000. While the number of votes the two parties have obtained has remained relatively static, the Ceylonese electorate has steadily expanded, with the result that the proportion of the popular vote won by the two parties has gradually declined since 1947. The evident electoral strength of the LSSP and CP, however, has been restricted by their electoral agreements with the SLFP in four of the last five elections, as a result of which the two Marxist parties combined have contested less than one-fourth of all constituencies. In the 1970 United Front sweep, every LSSP and CP candidate except a few sacrificial candidates in the Northern Province was elected. The consolidation of the United Front with the SLFP has probably tended to freeze the position of the LSSP and the CP. The two Marxist parties are unable to extend their electoral efforts appreciably, as the SLFP has appropriated for its own candidates virtually all constituencies not in the areas of long-standing Marxist strength, but the LSSP and the CP also are not crowded out of existence by the clash of the major contenders. In the constituencies assigned to them, they constitute the practical alternative to the UNP and, hence, one of the two major competitors.

While the UNP and the SLFP usually divide more than two-thirds of the seats in parliament between them, the persistent strength of other parties generally denies clear control of parliament to either of the two largest parties. The frequent necessity for coalitions has considerably broadened the opportunities for sharing in the exercise of government power, even for quite small parties. All four of the durable smaller parties have participated in governing coalitions, as have the Mahajana Eksath Peramuna, the Jathika Vimukthi Peramuna,[4] and several short-lived parties. The possibility of sharing in the exercise of power has probably contributed to the survival of the smaller parties. Ideological considerations, however, tend to limit their bargaining flexibility. The LSSP and the CP are implacably opposed to the UNP and face the practical choice of either cooperating with the SLFP or remaining in opposition. On several occasions since 1960, the SLFP and the UNP have vied for Federal Party support, but the FP's parliamentary strength is not sufficiently great to assure for it a pivotal role in the formation of coalitions. It participated in a coalition Government only once, from 1965 to 1968. The small MEP is the only party to have served in coalition cabinets with both the SLFP and the UNP.

Although party loyalties may not be as firmly established in Ceylon as in some countries with much older party systems, desertion of one's party is a hazardous venture. Some individuals have been able to ignore party labels and move from party to party. Many others, however, have experienced electoral setbacks on leaving their party. One of the more striking illustrations was provided by the LSSP dissidents who formed the LSSP(R) in 1964. Two LSSP(R) M.P.'s contested the same constituencies in 1965 which they had won in the preceding election as LSSP candidates. Each not only finished far behind the candidate of his former party but lost his deposit. Edmund Samarakkody, who collected more than 10,000 votes five years earlier, won only 278 votes in the same constituency, while the regular LSSP candidate received more than 13,000. Of eleven M.P.'s who deserted the

[4] The Jathika Vimukthi Peramuna (National Liberation Front) was founded by K. M. P. Rajaratna in the late 1950's. It backed the National Government formed in 1965 but was defunct by 1970. Rajaratna's party was unrelated to the Janatha Vimukthi Peramuna (People's Liberation Front) which was credited with launching the 1971 insurrection. The latter organization is discussed in Chapter 6.

SLFP in 1964 and sought re-election the following year from the same constituencies which they had represented, most of them under the label of the Sri Lanka Freedom Socialist Party, seven were defeated, although they enjoyed the support of the victorious UNP and their former party generally suffered reverses in the election.

REGIONAL PATTERNS OF COMPETITION

A pronounced regional pattern is evident in the competition among parties. The most prominent regional variation, constituting a subsystem of the Ceylonese party system, is found in the Northern Province and a major portion of the Eastern Province, the home of the Ceylon Tamil minority. Electoral competition in the Tamil areas is primarily between the Federal Party and the Tamil Congress. Independent candidates also are more prevalent in the North and East than in the remainder of the country. Neither the FP nor the TC attempts to mobilize support through the rest of the island. In the Northern Province, the Marxists regularly offer a few candidates to symbolize their concern with the Tamil minority, and in 1970 the UNP contested one seat and the SLFP two seats, but their efforts have been little more than gestures. In the Eastern Province, with a communally mixed population (44 per cent Ceylon Tamil, 34 per cent Ceylon Moor, and 20 per cent Sinhalese), the FP, the UNP, and the SLFP all have had some following, and independent candidates have shown considerably more strength than in any other province. The FP appears to have received support primarily from the Tamils; the SLFP has depended primarily on the Sinhalese, although it may have made some inroads into the Muslim vote; and UNP strength seems to have been largely based on Muslim voters, with some Sinhalese and Tamil support.

The UNP and the SLFP display relatively strong support

throughout the island except in the Northern and Eastern Provinces. UNP strength relative to the SLFP is located in the coastal Western, North-Western, and Southern Provinces, and in the southwestern inland province of Sabaragamuwa. UNP performance in the cities is striking. Of ten parliamentary seats in Colombo, Kandy, and Galle, the UNP won seven in 1970, while capturing only seventeen seats throughout the island. Six months prior to its crushing defeat in the parliamentary election, the UNP won thirty-five of forty-seven seats in the Colombo municipal council. UNP strength in the cities probably reflects its appeal to middle-class voters and support by the ethnic and religious minorities which are numerous in the cities. SLFP strength is apparent in the more traditional and less developed Uva and North-Central Provinces in the interior.

LSSP and CP votes are heavily concentrated in the southwestern corner of Ceylon, from Colombo on the southwest coast to the island's southern tip. Both parties have met with some electoral successes in the city of Colombo. The LSSP has been consistently strong along a narrow coastal belt extending south from Colombo and in a cluster of constituencies a short distance inland in the Western Province and Sabaragamuwa. Communist voting strength is found primarily on the south coast. The Marxist strongholds are in the area of highest population density, in which urbanization, the development of education and transportation, and dependence on wage employment or production for the market are greatest. The Marxists have engaged in intensive organizational, agitational, and social service activities in these areas for nearly four decades. The LSSP and the CP also are thought to have profited from caste-protest votes along the southwestern and southern coastal belts, where Marxist strength tends to coincide with concentrations of the Karāva, Salāgama, and Durāva castes.

MINOR PARTIES AND INDEPENDENTS

Contests by minor parties and independents sometimes do not reflect serious expectations of victory, but are intended to divide the vote of one of the major parties. Occasionally, when candidates of opposing major parties are of differing castes or religions, supporters of one will encourage a frivolous candidacy by an individual of the same caste or religion as the opposing candidate, hoping to deprive him of some votes which he would otherwise be likely to receive on caste or religious grounds. The occasional attempts of small or new parties to contest a large number of seats regularly end in disaster. The Sinhala Mahajana Pakshaya (Sinhalese People's Party), formed on the eve of the 1970 election, fielded forty-nine candidates, of whom none was successful and forty-eight lost their deposits. The party averaged a mere 404 votes per candidate. Only slightly less humiliating was the 1965 debacle of the MEP. The party nominated sixty-one candidates, of whom only one was elected and fifty-five lost their deposits. The MEP entered the election informally allied with the UNP and a large number of the MEP candidates were thought to be frivolous candidates intended to split the vote to the advantage of the UNP.

Ephemeral parties often appear after splits in the major parties and within a short time either disintegrate or are absorbed into one of the major parties. Upon breaking with the SLFP in 1959, Prime Minister W. Dahanayake formed the Lanka Prajathantravadi Pakshaya (Ceylon Democratic Party) which contested the two elections of 1960 with little success and thereafter crumbled rapidly. In 1965, what remained of the party (essentially, Dahanayake and the party's name and election symbol) merged with another ephemeral party, the Sri Lanka Freedom Socialist Party, formed by former SLFP M.P.'s who split with their party in 1964. The new party fought the 1965 election allied to the UNP and won five seats. By 1970, it had been absorbed into the UNP. Hence it served as a temporary bridge over which a group of dissidents shifted from one major party to another. Other small parties have been similarly absorbed by the larger ones. Thus, the tiny Labour Party was swallowed by the UNP in the early years of independence, and the Bhasha Peramuna was absorbed by the SLFP shortly after the 1956 election.

At the edge of the Ceylonese party system is an important "quasi-party," the Ceylon Workers' Congress. The CWC is, in fact, a trade union and does not function as a political party in that it does not nominate candidates for office or formulate a program covering broad issues of public policy. It is nonetheless recognized as possessing a separate political identity as spokesman for an otherwise largely unrepresented segment of the population, engages in political bargaining and electioneering, and, indeed, has secured representation in parliament. The CWC was established as an estate workers' trade union by the Ceylon Indian Congress, a political organization formed in 1939 to champion the interests of the Indian Tamil community, and swiftly grew into the largest labor organization on the island. The Ceylon Indian Congress won seven parliamentary seats in 1947, but after most Indian Tamils were excluded from Ceylonese citizenship and the franchise a few years later, the party, renamed the Ceylon Democratic Congress, atrophied and eventually was disbanded. The CWC assumed the role of political spokesman for the Indian Tamil community, prominently involving itself in the issues of the Indian Tamils' citizenship and repatriation to India.

Although a large proportion of its clientele lacks the franchise, the CWC has been able to play a significant political role by bargaining among competing parties for its endorsement and support. The Indian Tamils possessing citizenship and the vote, numbering about 134,000 in 1964, are considered marginally important in a number of parliamentary constituencies in the estate areas. The CWC worked for the SLFP among Indian

Tamils during the July 1960 election, and after the SLFP's victory, CWC president S. Thondaman was named an appointed member of parliament. By the 1965 election, the CWC had shifted to the UNP camp, publicly endorsing the UNP and vigorously campaigning for UNP candidates in the estate areas. After the UNP victory, Thondaman and a second CWC officer were named appointed M.P.'s. The CWC's quasi-party role is suggested by the opposition's labeling of the National Government formed in 1965 by the UNP and several smaller groups as the *hath havula* or seven-part coalition, referring to the six political parties and the CWC which initially backed it. CWC support for the UNP continued through 1970, and when the UNP was swept from power the CWC lost its representation in parliament. The United Front Government formed in 1970 named as an appointed M.P. the head of the Democratic Workers' Congress, the CWC's principal rival as an estate workers' trade union.

Independents have declined to a negligible factor in election contests, although a number of independent candidates continue to clutter the ballot. The decline of independents is depicted in Table 19. Of the eighty-seven independent candidates in 1970, seventy-three lost their deposits and only two were elected. Many of the independents appear in the Northern and Eastern Prov-

Table 19. Independent candidates in parliamentary elections, 1947–1970

	1947	1952	1956	March 1960	July 1960	1965	1970
Number contesting	181	85	64	168	39	96	87
Number elected	21	11	8	7	6	6	2
Per cent of popular vote won	29	14	11	9	5	6	5

Source: See Table 18.

inces, probably due to the greater persistence of traditional social structure and attitudes and the less vigorous and pluralistic party competition there. Except in 1965, at least half the successful independent candidates have been from these two provinces. Much of the Eastern Province and the Northern Province outside the Jaffna Peninsula is relatively backward in terms of education, penetration by mass communications media, and the development of associational groups cutting across kin and caste loyalties. Politics has tended to be parochial, relative to the rest of the island, and to revolve around personalities, local concerns, and caste or community. Consequently, the importance of party organizations or programs is reduced. One Eastern Province politician who had received the nomination of the FP, then decided to seek election as an independent, explained, "I am sure of being elected if I stand for election under any banner as personal merits and sincerity counts [sic] more here than party politics."[5] Independent candidacy also sometimes is a temporary expedient, resulting either from disagreements with a party to which the candidate formerly belonged or from circumstances which prevent contesting the seat as a party candidate. Among the successful independents in 1965, for example, were R. G. Senanayake, who had earlier broken with the SLFP and soon after the election rejoined that party (only to be expelled again a few years later), and Percy Samaraweera, a former UNP candidate who entered the contest as an independent when an electoral agreement between the UNP and the Jathika Vimukthi Peramuna denied him the UNP nomination for the seat he had previously contested.

Party Positions and Perspectives

On the basis of their predominant perspectives and purposes,

[5] Ceylon, House of Representatives, *Parliamentary Debates (Hansard)*, vol. 25, col. 504 (July 8, 1959).

political parties in Ceylon can be roughly categorized as (1) pragmatic, "power-oriented," or (2) ideological, "mission-oriented," or (3) personality parties (Table 20). The largest parties are essentially pragmatic parties geared to the capture of power, in which personal ambitions and the distribution of jobs and favors play a large role. Policies and goals frequently shift with pre-

Table 20. Recently active parties classified by predominant perspective and purposes[a]

Predominantly ideological, "mission-oriented"	Predominantly pragmatic, "power-oriented"	Predominantly personality
FP	UNP	◀––– TC
LSSP –––▶	◀––SLFP	MEP
CP –––▶		SMP
LSSP(R) –––––––––––––––––––––––▶		
"Left" CP–––––––––––––––––––––––▶		

[a] Arrows indicate the direction of recent trends.

sumed changes in popular opinion and calculations of electoral advantage. The "mission-oriented" parties tend to be the durable smaller parties. Intent on achieving certain specific objectives, they manage to hold a core of devoted supporters but fail to attract more general support because of their unwillingness to abandon or dilute their doctrines and mission for wider popularity. Prominent among the "mission-oriented" parties are the Marxist parties, although the Federal Party, in its determination to achieve regional autonomy for the Tamils and exclusive concern with the Tamil community, displays similar characteristics.

The personality parties are the very small parties organized around an individual leader and generally reflecting his personal convictions or ambitions. Most of the small parties which have appeared briefly and then disintegrated are of this type. However, the TC, which at least until very recently was one of the more unambiguous examples of a personality party, is among the oldest existing parties in Ceylon, and the MEP was essentially the personal following of Philip Gunawardena from 1950 until his death in 1972. Parties seldom fit perfectly into one classification, and a single party may have characteristics of more than one type. The SLFP began as primarily a personality party formed around S. W. R. D. Bandaranaike, but over most of its history it has been predominantly a pragmatic, "power-oriented" party. Yet, in recent years, it has tended to become more ideological. The LSSP, long a classic "mission-oriented" party, seems gradually to have become more pragmatic over the past decade. The small LSSP(R) appears to be an archtype "mission-oriented" party, but in some respects it is a projection of the irrepressible personality of its leader, Bala Tampoe.

THE UNITED NATIONAL PARTY

The UNP is regularly characterized as the party of the Right in the Ceylonese political context. It is essentially a pragmatic party, with little sense of mission or dedication to specific social or economic goals. A 1963 statement of party policy noted that "the policy and programme of a political party must necessarily change with the changes that take place in a country."[6] Probably the strongest and most enduring conviction of the party is that it is a bulwark against revolutionary upheaval and a protector of individual liberty. At independence, voices within the UNP spoke

[6] United National Party, *What We Believe* (Colombo: United National Party, 1963), p. 11.

of progress, social welfare, and reform, but over the following years the accent shifted to stability and order. Originally attracting the backing of a substantial part of the commercial and propertied classes, the party has often found itself cast in the role of defender of the status quo. With the political and ideological changes which followed independence, the UNP was frequently accused of being the party of the wealthy and the privileged.

After the UNP's devastating 1956 defeat, a concerted effort was launched to revitalize the party and refurbish its image. A revised program intended to broaden the party's appeal was adopted in 1958. The program embraced democratic socialism and urged progress in education, social services, and economic development, but tempered its reformism by insistence on orderly change with a minimum of social disruption. The party's democratic socialism was described as "the middle road in opposition to total State ownership and management on the one hand and the ownership and management by a few capitalists on the other."[7] Major stress was placed on economic development after the UNP returned to power in 1965. In contrast with the policies of the preceding SLFP Government, however, the development efforts tended to be concentrated on agriculture, and considerable scope was permitted to private enterprise.

The UNP has tended, with some lapses, to hold a relatively secular and integrative social outlook. The party originally attracted some members of all communities except the Indian Tamils, and it has been fairly successful in retaining support among the Christian and Muslim minorities. Although the UNP mobilized scant electoral support in the Tamil areas, some Ceylon Tamils remained in the party until 1956, when an abrupt UNP acceptance of Sinhalese as the only official language cost it all

[7] *Progress Through Stability: United National Party Manifesto* (Colombo: United National Party, 1958), p. 7.

semblance of Tamil support for almost a decade. From 1956 to 1960, the UNP seemed intent on demonstrating greater opposition to Tamil demands than did the SLFP. Nonetheless, by 1965, the UNP was able to collaborate with the minorities in the National Government and to capture one parliamentary seat from a constituency with a Tamil majority. The UNP's 1970 election manifesto argued that "the divisive tendencies that were in evidence earlier have been largely eliminated and conscious and deliberate attempts have been made to strengthen unity and amity among communities."[8] Despite its generally integrative, secular approach to ethnic and religious communities, the UNP was often accused of caste exclusiveness, particularly in its early years, and its alleged Goyigama domination incurred the hostility of many other castes, notably the articulate Salāgama and Karāva castes.

Although frequently on the defensive because of its identification with conservatism and privilege in a period of growing populism, the UNP has enjoyed a number of advantages, including the support of most of the island's press and possession of a relatively strong and well-financed party organization. As it has frequently been in power, the possession or anticipation of the fruits of office have helped to bind the party together. The UNP's crushing election defeat in 1970 sparked searching debate on its future strategy and role. Deputy leader J. R. Jayewardene argued for cooperation with the United Front Government, while the party's leader, Dudley Senanayake, demanded a more conventional role of opposition to the Government.

THE SRI LANKA FREEDOM PARTY

The SLFP appeared within a few years of independence as a reformist but nonrevolutionary alternative to the generally con-

[8] United National Party, *For Stability and Progress: U.N.P. Manifesto, 1970* (Colombo: United National Party, 1970), unpaged.

servative UNP. Styling itself the "party of the common man," the SLFP focused its concern on the language, religion, and material well-being of the Sinhalese rural masses. The party benefited from identification with the sociopolitical changes of 1956, when the Sinhalese-speaking village schoolteachers, ayurvedic physicians, small traders, and petty landowners suddenly found a voice and significance in politics they had not previously enjoyed. The strength of the SLFP has always rested in the villages of the interior, away from the urban centers and the cosmopolitan seaboard. Propounding the party's outlook in 1961, an SLFP minister announced:

We have set a standard . . . which we have declared to the people of this country. . . . What is that standard? A very simple standard: we stand by the interests of the rural people of this country. . . . [The] common people of this country, the rural people of this country can rest assured that we shall never let them down.[9]

The party grew out of the Sinhala Maha Sabha, an organization formed by S. W. R. D. Bandaranaike in 1937 to speak for the Sinhalese community in politics, and the SLFP retained a predominantly Sinhalese perspective and character. A few Muslims and Christians have been active in the party, but its basic appeal has consistently been directed toward the Sinhalese Buddhists. SLFP leader Sirimavo Bandaranaike told a 1967 party conference, "We believe that the Sinhala Buddhists sincerely accept [the] Sri Lanka Freedom Party as the only party that will not betray the rights of the Sinhala Buddhists."[10]

Although professing democratic socialism and displaying a strong strand of populism, the SLFP has often seemed to lack a coherent outlook or clearly defined goals. After it first came to

[9] Ceylon, House of Representatives, *Parliamentary Debates* (*Hansard*), vol. 43, cols. 936–937 (July 27, 1961).

[10] *Ceylon Observer,* July 21, 1967, p. 10.

power, the lure of patronage added to the heterogeneity of the party and further blurred its outlook. The principal policy thrust of the SLFP was toward the destruction of privileges of colonial origin, which included the subordination of those educated in the Sinhalese language to those educated in English, the felt educational and employment disadvantages of the Sinhalese Buddhists relative to the Tamils and the Christians, and the inferior status and opportunities of the villagers relative to the urban dwellers. Prior to 1960, the party was more strongly identified with linguistic and religious sentiments than with class protest, but the communal and class appeals were always intertwined. After Sirimavo Bandaranaike assumed leadership in 1960, the party began to become more radical and more insistent on egalitarian social reform. In Mrs. Bandaranaike's words:

We are not a chauvinistic Party. We are nationalist no doubt. But ours is not a backward looking Nationalism. . . . [SLFP founder S. W. R. D. Bandaranaike] was only too well aware that the people while they were deeply attached to their religious beliefs and cultural traditions, were also against economic exploitation and social oppression. . . . He believed that a genuine democracy had to free itself from grinding poverty [and] social inequality for the majority. Hence his fight to establish in this country a Socialist Democracy.[11]

After 1959, a series of defections and schisms decimated the party's conservative wing and contributed to a steady drift to the Left. W. Dahanayake, S. W. R. D. Bandaranaike's successor as prime minister, detached a portion of the more conservative party members when he left the SLFP at the end of 1959, and individual defections continued to erode the party's right wing. In 1964, one-time SLFP president C. P. de Silva bolted with a group of M.P.'s identified with the remnants of the SLFP's right

[11] Sirimavo Bandaranaike, "Forward Towards a Socialist Society," *Nation* (Colombo), July 21, 1967, p. 7.

wing in protest against the coalition with the LSSP. The attrition of the more conservative elements in the SLFP was accompanied by the appearance of many ex-Marxists in party posts and its parliamentary contingent. SLFP leaders, who once described the SLFP as a center party poised between the Marxists on the Left and the UNP on the Right, increasingly spoke of a polarization of political groups between the "progressives" and the "reactionaries." With the gradual radicalization of the party and its close association with the Marxists since 1964, the SLFP seems to have become more ideological and purposive, although it remains a heterogeneous and predominantly "power-oriented" party.

THE FEDERAL PARTY

The FP, also known by its Tamil name of the Ilankai Tamil Arasu Kadchi, is the self-declared champion and defender of the Ceylon Tamil minority. In 1956, after rising communal tensions, the FP became the dominant party of the Ceylon Tamils, a position it has maintained through four subsequent parliamentary elections. The overriding objective of the FP is the preservation of the unique and separate identity of the Ceylon Tamil community. Federalist beliefs rest on the conviction that the Tamils will remain threatened with domination and assimilation by the Sinhalese majority as long as the two peoples exist together in a unitary state subject to control by the majority. The party's mission, proclaimed in 1951, is "to work for the attainment of freedom for the Tamil-speaking people of Ceylon by the establishment of an autonomous Tamil state on the linguistic basis within the framework of a Federal Union of Ceylon."[12]

The FP was created after a 1949 split in the Tamil Congress

[12] *The Case for a Federal Constitution for Ceylon: Resolutions Passed at the First National Convention of the Ilankai Tamil Arasu Kadchi* (Colombo: Ilankai Tamil Arasu Kadchi, 1951), p. 9.

and has always been more militant and uncompromising than the TC. The TC, organized before mass politics took firm root, was the creation of G. G. Ponnambalam, a prominent Colombo lawyer, and has been largely a party of professionals and public servants, particularly sensitive to Tamil opportunities for education and white-collar employment in the urban centers of the South. The FP, in contrast, established a relatively broad popular base among Tamil schoolteachers, small landowners, merchants, and town functionaries. Its concern has been less with Tamil opportunities in the South than with the circumstances of the Ceylon Tamil community in the North and East. Preoccupation with questions of communal relations has caused the Federalists to ignore most other issues and questions of public policy. The FP's 1960 election manifesto noted that the party "concentrates all its attention to achieve freedom for the people whom they [sic] represent," and dismissed all noncommunal issues with the declaration that the party would "support all progressive measures introduced by any government in office."[13] A decade later, the party's manifesto observed: "The forces of the Right and the Left, in the South, are locked in a bitter struggle. . . . But we the Tamil-speaking people of Ceylon are . . . merely passive spectators of the scene having no part to play in this struggle."[14]

In their efforts to resist Sinhalese domination, the Federalists have sought to reinforce the solidarity and unity of the island's Tamil-speaking peoples. Within the Ceylon Tamil community, the FP has denounced the barriers of caste which divide the "untouchable" castes from the rest of Tamil society and have attempted to reduce the regional differences separating the Tamils of Jaffna from those of the Eastern Province. Appealing beyond

[13] *Manifesto of the Ilankai Tamil Arasu Kadchi* (Colombo: Ilankai Tamil Arasu Kadchi, 1960), p. 1.

[14] *Tribune* (Colombo), May 17, 1970, p. 3.

the Ceylon Tamil community, the FP has also sought backing from the largely Tamil-speaking Muslims in the Eastern Province and has made overtures to the Indian Tamils of the estate areas. The party, however, has succeeded in winning only scattered support among the east-coast Muslims, and its efforts to reach the estate population have produced slight evidence of success.

As a party explicitly identified with an ethnic minority, the FP can scarcely hope to capture a majority in parliament. The Federalists have alternately followed strategies of applying extraparliamentary pressure through hartals and satyagraha campaigns and attempting to utilize a pivotal position in parliament to bargain between the SLFP and the UNP for concessions in exchange for parliamentary support. On several occasions, the FP appeared to have scored major gains, only to see them evaporate in the face of mounting Sinhalese intransigence fanned by competition among the predominantly Sinhalese parties. Convinced that the interests of the Tamil people had been betrayed by the TC leadership in exchange for office shortly after independence, the FP leaders and activists have harbored a mistrust of ministerial appointments. The FP's possession of one portfolio in the National Government from 1965 to 1968 was self-consciously justified as a necessary expedient to weld together the governing coalition and safeguard Tamil interests from within the cabinet. An agreement on the language of administration was obtained, but a proposal for government decentralization through semiautonomous district councils was dropped by the National Government in the face of vigorous opposition attacks. The FP, facing internal strains and defections, shortly thereafter withdrew from the Government.

With the passage of years, the FP's seeming inability to gain its major objectives produced signs of restiveness within the party. Growing stresses within Tamil society resulting from mounting caste protest among the "untouchables" and a worsening employment problem for educated Tamil youths contributed to the political stir in the North during the late 1960's. No major challenge to FP electoral predominance in the North materialized by 1970, however. Despite a slight erosion of its electoral position and the defeat of several prominent leaders in the 1970 election, the party retained its standing as the chief political spokesman of the Ceylon Tamil minority. When FP proposals for a federal constitution were overwhelmingly rejected in 1971 by the Constituent Assembly empowered to draft a new constitution, the FP leadership ordered a boycott of the assembly, an action which precipitated a rift in the party. The following year, the Federalists declared a day of mourning when the new constitution was promulgated.

THE LANKA SAMA SAMAJA PARTY

Formed by a small group of young intellectuals in 1935, the LSSP is Ceylon's oldest existing political party, from which four additional parties have sprung. In its early years, the LSSP encompassed a variety of socialist and nationalist sentiments, but following the 1940 expulsion of the Communists the party became committed to Trotskyism and affiliated with the Fourth International. Samasamajists long boasted that theirs was the only Trotskyist party in the world to be represented in a national legislature, and in 1964 they claimed to be the first Trotskyists to serve in a national cabinet,[15] although entrance into the cabinet resulted in their expulsion from the Fourth International. The LSSP has always been the dominant party of the Ceylonese Left. At independence, it was the largest single party in opposition to to governing UNP, and the Samasamajists harbored expectations of eventually replacing the UNP in power. The emergence of the

[15] MEP leader Philip Gunawardena, who became a cabinet minister in 1956, claimed the distinction for himself, but he was regarded as an apostate by the Samasamajists.

SLFP as the principal alternative to the UNP in the early 1950's, however, robbed the LSSP of its hopes and led to a stagnation of the party's strength and influence. In 1964, the LSSP adopted a strategy of alliance with the SLFP and obtained its first taste of power. Defeated in 1965, the Samasamajists with their United Front allies won a stunning popular mandate in the 1970 election.

The LSSP's outlook is essentially that of a "mission-oriented" party, intent on the eventual attainment of certain social goals, and disdaining attempts to gain popular favor at the cost of principle. A party history, in noting that the LSSP's adherence to unpopular positions had cost it public support, asserted that, "as distinct from opportunist politicians to whom power is an end in itself, to the LSSP power is only a means to an end. That end is socialism."[16] Virtually all important party decisions are considered and debated in terms of Marxist and Trotskyist doctrine. Doctrinal disagreements contributed to party schisms in 1940, 1945, 1950, 1953, and 1964. The heated intraparty debate on joining a coalition with the SLFP in 1964, for example, turned on the question of the class character of the SLFP, as avoidance of "class collaboration" was considered an important tenet of Trotskyism. The opponents of coalition argued that the SLFP was a "bourgeois" party and thus the coalition would be both unwise and unprincipled. Advocates of the coalition did not base their argument on practical advantage or challenge the Trotskyist injunction against "class collaboration." Instead, they argued that the SLFP was a "leftward-moving" party—presumably at some transitional stage between a "bourgeois" and a "workers' " party. The heavy majority in favor of the coalition underscored the dominance of the pragmatic wing within the LSSP. The departure of the more dogmatic Samasamajists who formed the

[16] Leslie Goonewardene, *A Short History of the Lanka Sama Samaja Party* (Colombo: Lanka Sama Samaja Party, 1960), p. 54.

LSSP(R) accelerated a trend toward growing LSSP pragmatism and flexibility.

Indicative of the LSSP's increasing pragmatism and domestication is the party's retreat from dreams of revolutionary upheaval and acceptance of the parliamentary path to its goals. The party declared in 1950 that its basic objectives "cannot be realized through bourgeois parliaments."[17] Fourteen years later, however, the LSSP had entered a coalition with the non-Marxist SLFP, and subsequently the Samasamajists accommodated themselves to close alliance and a sharing of power not only with the SLFP but with their old ideological antagonists in the Ceylon Communist Party. The 1956 election, which toppled from power the Marxists' arch enemy, the UNP, demonstrated to the Samasamajists the potential of elections for producing major political changes. As explained by an LSSP leader in 1970, the party's early belief that capitalism could be overthrown and a socialist society established only by "the seizure of power by a mass uprising" gave way after the 1956 election to a conviction that "a Parliament elected by Universal Franchise is not merely a platform for proclaiming our views to the country, but also an instrument that can be used for the movement towards Socialism."[18]

The party has played a major role as a political educator and innovator, and has contributed to a strong ideological and class dimension of Ceylonese political rhetoric, which is reflected in other parties' policies and pronouncements. The LSSP claims to have first brought political discussion to the common people in their own language during the 1930's, and many Sinhalese words first adopted by the Samasamajists for such political terms as

[17] Lanka Sama Samaja Party, *Programme of Action, Adopted at the Unity Conference, June 4th, 1950* (Colombo: Lanka Sama Samaja Party, 1950), p. 4.

[18] Leslie Goonewardene, "New Outlook of the LSSP," *Ceylon Daily News,* Dec. 21, 1970, p. 4.

"socialist," "class," and "party" have come into standard usage in Sinhalese.[19] With the LSSP's increasing absorption in the immediate action problems of electoral politics and governance, some decline seems evident in the attention given to conscious, explicit definition of party policies and purposes. Nonetheless, the party probably remains the most self-consciously articulate and intellectually vigorous of Ceylonese parties.

The decision for alliance with the SLFP was a major turning point for the LSSP. After years of stagnating electoral fortunes and receding prospects, the party was able to revitalize itself with a new hope and sense of direction. In committing itself to the United Front, however, the LSSP faced the risk of losing its unique identity in the shadow of its much larger United Front partner. LSSP(R) leader Bala Tampoe highlighted the danger in an open letter to his former comrades of the LSSP, arguing that as a result of the alliance, "the LSSP has lost its own distinctive Samasamajist character, and has assumed more and more a political character that is hardly distinguishable from that of the SLFP."[20] The price of sharing power could be the eventual suffocation or assimilation of the party by its larger ally.

The LSSP, and the other Marxist parties it had spawned, faced a further challenge. By 1970, a restless crop of radical youth, educated in Sinhalese and of rural indigenous backgrounds, emerged with insistent demands for immediate solutions to the island's employment and other problems. The abrupt explosion of insurrectionary violence in 1971, directed against a self-proclaimed "People's Government," suggests the degree of alienation separat-

[19] For example, the Sinhalese *"sama samāja"* (literally, "equal society"), from which the party derives its name, was adopted as the equivalent of "socialist." The use of *"pakshaya"* and *"panthiya"* to refer, respectively, to "party" and "class" was pioneered by the Samasamajists.

[20] Bala Tampoe, "Open Letter to the Members of the Lanka Sama Samaja Party from the Lanka Sama Samaja Party (Revolutionary)" (mimeographed; Colombo, Aug. 9, 1969), p. 7.

ing Ceylon's "Old Left" of sophisticated, Westernized intellectuals from a section of the newly emergent radical youth. The LSSP and the other established Marxist parties had apparently failed to kindle a deep response among many of the young, village-bred youths with secondary or higher educations in Sinhalese, whose numbers had grown tremendously over the preceding decade.

THE UNITED FRONT

The formation of the United Front, binding together the SLFP, LSSP, and CP, represented a significant change in the political situation of Ceylon, leading toward an ideological polarization and a growing bipolar confrontation between the UNP and the United Front. Collaboration by the three parties originated in a shared hostility toward the UNP. Increasingly, the alliance was reinforced by a convergence of objectives and outlooks, as the LSSP and CP became more pragmatic and the SLFP became more radical. In 1956, the three parties joined in a "no-contest" electoral agreement intended to avoid contesting the same constituencies and splitting the anti-UNP vote. The arrangement was repeated in the July 1960 election. In 1963, after a period of estrangement from the SLFP, a short-lived United Left Front was formed by the LSSP, the CP, and the MEP. Early in 1964, the SLFP, faced with eroding parliamentary strength, opened negotiations with the United Left Front parties on the formation of a coalition Government. When the talks stalled, the LSSP abruptly agreed to enter the coalition without its Marxist allies. The CP, although excluded from the coalition, offered its support to the SLFP-LSSP Government and was allied to the coalition parties by an electoral agreement during the 1965 election. Soon after the election the Communists were admitted to membership in a three-party United Front.[21] While in

[21] Although the term "United Front" replaced "coalition" in popular

opposition between 1965 and 1970, the United Front adopted a common program and appeared to gain appreciably in cohesion.

The alliance has not been free of obvious stress, possibly accentuated by the magnitude of its 1970 election victory, which freed the SLFP of dependence on its allies. The SLFP in 1970 contested 108 parliamentary seats, leaving only twenty-three for the LSSP and nine for the CP, among which were seven seats in the North that the United Front parties had slight prospect of winning. Despite strong Communist protests, the SLFP put forward a candidate for the three-member Colombo Central constituency, although two of the three seats were expected to be captured by the UNP and the third was being defended by the CP general secretary, who had represented the constituency since 1947. Almost immediately after the 1970 assumption of power signs of restiveness within the CP and tensions between the CP and the LSSP appeared. Despite the SLFP shift to the Left over the preceding decade, the party remained a heterogeneous organization containing a wide assortment of attitudes ranging from admiration for Communist China to obscurantist communal sentiments. Furthermore, a strong desire seemed to exist within certain sections of the SLFP to preserve the separate identity of the party and avoid a coalescence with the Marxist parties. SLFP deputy leader Maithripala Senanayake assured a 1971 party conference that despite the United Front collaboration, "the SLFP would remain intact with its own policies."[22]

Party Organization and Membership

Party organization in Ceylon tends to be loose and informal. Each party maintains a headquarters with a small staff, and has

---

and party usage only after 1965, for simplicity the three-party alliance will be referred to in this work as the United Front from the commencement of the 1965 election campaign.

[22] *Ceylon Daily News,* Feb. 18, 1971, p. 1.

branches or comparable local units scattered throughout the island. Excluding the principal Marxist parties, which differ substantially in structure, a party is headed by a president, who is usually the most prominent leader of the party and the head of its parliamentary delegation. Other party officers customarily consist of a number of vice presidents, a general secretary or several joint secretaries, and a treasurer. M.P.'s predominate among the party officers and appear to control the extraparliamentary organization. Periodic party conferences serve as instruments for generating enthusiasm among the party's activists and local stalwarts and provide the leadership with a platform from which to enunciate party policy. Conferences seem intended to present an appearance of party unity and enthusiasm, and seldom seriously ponder alternatives of policy, leadership, or strategy.

The local units of all parties other than the Tamil parties tend to cluster in the Southwest. There are indications that many branches are the creatures of individual party stalwarts, and others function only at election time. Until 1956, Ceylonese parties, except possibly the LSSP and the CP, were virtually without local organization. The few party branches which existed were generally concentrated around the urban centers and often in practice represented no more than an individual party supporter and a few personal retainers. With the growth of popular political awareness and increasing intensity of party competition after 1956, attempts were made by both the SLFP and the UNP to extend their branch organizations. The UNP constitution was amended in 1961 in an attempt to disperse the party's local units more broadly through the rural areas and reduce the dominance of the Colombo area. After the UNP return to power in 1965, branches multiplied rapidly. By 1969, 1,907 branches were claimed, nearly double the 1,041 branches existing four years earlier.[23] Between 1956 and 1962, the number of SLFP

[23] The 1969 figure is from *United National Party 18th Annual Sessions,*

branches climbed from 74 to 546. Soaring party membership following the 1970 election victory led to a rapid growth in the number of SLFP branches, which had rocketed to nearly 4,000 by late 1970.[24] The FP maintains about twenty-five branches, clustered in the Tamil areas of the North and East except for one branch in Colombo and one in the highland estate areas.

The major non-Marxist parties all have formally defined memberships requiring certain simple procedures of enlistment and the payment of a small subscription, usually one rupee a year. Membership is open to virtually anyone willing to declare general agreement with the party's aims and an intention to support the party's candidates for public office. Nonetheless, party membership tends to be amorphous and to fluctuate widely with the changing party fortunes. At least until very recently, most party members have come from the middle class of the cities and towns or from among the planters, landowners, traders, schoolteachers, and other local notables in the rural areas. Although precise information on membership is usually unobtainable or unreliable, there are indications that parties are gradually developing mass memberships. In 1967, the SLFP was reported to include about 30,000 members.[25] Subsequently, an astonishing growth has been claimed, accelerated by the party's 1970 election triumph.

The LSSP and the CP are organized on Leninist lines, with a hierarchy extending from the primary units, called locals in the LSSP and branches in the CP, through periodic party conferences or congresses, to a central committee and a political bureau at the apex of the hierarchy. The chief executive officer of each party is the general secretary. Unlike the other parties, the Marx-

---

23rd & 24th February, 1969 (Colombo: United National Party, 1969), p. 30. The figure for 1965 was supplied to the author by the UNP headquarters in 1965.

[24] Information supplied to the author by the SLFP headquarters.

[25] Author's interview with the SLFP general secretary, Aug. 8, 1967.

ist parties have memberships that are sharply defined and bound together by a relatively strong *élan* and ideological commitment. A striking feature of the LSSP is the vigor of intraparty democracy. The Trotskyist orientation of the LSSP has led to great stress on the dangers of dictatorial control by a party bureaucracy, and the Samasamajist leaders seem ideologically and intellectually committed to the free debate of alternative policies, regular competitive election of officers, and adherence to majority decisions. The central committee is regularly elected at the party conference, with the number of aspirants far exceeding the membership of the committee. While the dozen top leaders are repeatedy re-elected, the relative position of each in the voting is considered a significant barometer of prestige within the party and shifting rank-and-file moods. Party conferences have produced spirited debates and in a few cases have resulted in sharp divisions. During major intraparty battles such as occurred in 1953 and 1964, arguments for conflicting courses of action have been circulated to the membership in Samasamajist publications and meetings. In 1964, the question of joining the SLFP in a coalition Government, which had produced a three-way division in the politbureau and central committee, was decided by vote of a party conference.

The LSSP has retained a small and selective membership, limited to activists versed in Marxist theory and willing to devote regular service to party activities. The small, active, ideologically oriented membership has made possible the vigorous rank-and-file participation in party affairs. The small membership, however, has also forced the party into heavy dependence on the energies of a relatively few individuals for a multiplicity of party tasks and has restricted the manifold public contacts necessary to mobilize mass electoral support. At about the time the party entered the 1964 coalition, LSSP membership gradually began to expand. By 1970, the membership had climbed to about 4,000, more than double that of 1962.[26] A further increase seems likely, despite lingering concern among the veteran Samasamajists that a rapid growth of membership may "dilute" the party, with a possible weakening of cohesion and dedication to traditional party principles.

The top CP leaders appear to maintain a firm grip on the party organization and to determine party policies and tactics unencumbered by internal debate or dissent. Strict internal discipline is thought to rest primarily on the leaders' control of a relatively large number of salaried party offices and jobs. A revolt by pro-Peking dissidents against the stoutly pro-Moscow position of the veteran party leaders in 1963 led to the expulsion of a number of second-level party functionaries and officials of the Communist-sponsored trade unions, who formed the "left" Communist Party. Among the charges leveled against the veteran party leaders by the "left" dissidents was that they had subverted intraparty democracy by failing to convene party congresses regularly, in an effort to maintain their hold on the party organs and forestall opposition to their policies. In the twenty years prior to the split, only six congresses had been held. Despite its Leninist heritage, the CP has not been as highly selective in recruitment of members as has the LSSP. The Communists have espoused the objective of building a mass party for more than a decade. Although the "left" Communists were able to muster little support, the 1963 schism initially cost the CP many of its enthusiastic young militants.

The two types of ancillary organizations utilized by nearly all political parties are youth leagues and trade unions. Each of the major parties maintains a youth league as its principal mass organization, recruiting ground, and link with the general public. In view of the small and primarily middle-class character of party

[26] Author's interviews with LSSP officers between 1962 and 1970.

membership, the youth leagues have assumed an important role for their associated parties in assembling participants for rallies and demonstrations, in conducting the house-to-house canvassing of election campaigns, and in projecting the party's influence beyond the narrow circle of party members. The LSSP, which at least until the last few years rigorously restricted party membership to a tight cadre of dedicated activists, has considered its youth league as a mass organization for supporters and sympathizers, irrespective of age, who were unable to meet the exacting requirements of party membership. During the past decade, the UNP has made particularly vigorous efforts to develop its youth league, which has become an important source of party workers and participants for party rallies. In 1961, the UNP youth league began to bring groups of young village men to Colombo for week-long courses of lectures and discussions. By 1965, 18,000 youths were claimed to have completed the course. The UNP youth league reportedly was built up from about 160 branches in 1960 to 2,800 branches containing about 200,000 members in 1970.[27]

The sponsorship of labor organizations has become a party activity almost as common as the organization of youth leagues. The Marxists entered the nascent labor movement in the 1930's and by independence had established a powerful trade union position. The Ceylon Federation of Labour, representing more than 100,000 workers, is aligned with the LSSP, and the Government Workers' Trade Union Federation also functions under Samasamajist guidance. The longstanding Communist labor federation, the Ceylon Trade Union Federation, was captured by the "left" Communists during the 1963 party split. The regular CP immediately created a rival organization, the Ceylon Federation of Trade Unions, which succeeded in attracting a large proportion of the older federation's membership. The Cen-

[27] Author's interviews with officers of the UNP youth league between 1961 and 1970.

tral Council of Ceylon Trade Unions is the labor center of the MEP. Marxists also lead or strongly influence a number of other labor organizations less conspicuously linked with the parties. The militant and influential Government Clerical Service Union, for example, is informally aligned with the LSSP, while Communist influence predominates in the huge Public Service Trade Union Federation. In 1956, other parties began to follow the Marxists' lead and to establish their own labor organizations. The first SLFP-sponsored trade unions were formed soon after the party came to power in 1956, and were grouped in a federation, the Sri Lanka Nidahas Vurthiya Samithi Sammelanaya, a few years later. Two trade unions were formed by the UNP in 1961, and the next year the Federal Party established a union primarily for Indian Tamil estate workers.

In 1963, the labor organizations allied with the LSSP, the CP, and the MEP joined with several prominent unaligned unions to form a Joint Committee of Trade Union Organizations, which embraced an impressively large and powerful section of the labor movement. When the SLFP-LSSP coalition was established in the following year, the coalition Government called for restraint on a series of demands drafted by the Joint Committee. A battle, largely fought on partisan lines, erupted over the demands and demolished the labor grouping. The name of the Joint Committee was resurrected at the end of 1965 for a labor grouping clearly aligned with the SLFP-LSSP-CP United Front and including only the unions associated with those three parties.

The Samasamajists and the Communists rely heavily on their trade unions to provide participants for mass rallies and demonstrations, and occasionally to dramatize a party protest or demand by staging a brief political strike. The control of labor organizations, with the ability to order strikes in such sensitive and highly visible areas as the transport system or the Colombo port, has contributed to the Marxist parties an element of extraparlia-

mentary power and influence. Other parties attach less significance to their labor organizations. As mass organizations, they are
probably smaller and less effective than the parties' youth leagues,
but they provide the party with an additional link with the public
and serve as a symbol of the party's concern for the common
people. Increasingly, the party in power has tended to view the
labor organization under its control as a means of defense against
costly or embarrassing strikes.

Another type of organization has assumed some prominence as
an SLFP auxiliary. The Islamic Socialist Front was formed soon
after the 1965 election by Badi-ud-in Mahmud, an SLFP vice
president and the only Muslim to serve in the Sirimavo Bandaranaike cabinet, to mobilize Muslim support for the SLFP. The
votes of many Muslims in the Southwest were captured regularly
by the UNP, contributing an important bloc of support for that
party in the city of Colombo. The Islamic Socialist Front sponsored pro-SLFP and pro-United Front meetings and rallies of
Muslims and in 1970 spearheaded SLFP election campaigning
in Muslim areas. Twelve members of the front contested the 1970
election as SLFP candidates. The organization's activities presumably contributed to modest SLFP inroads into the Muslim
vote.

4. Elections, Voting, and Campaigns

It is through competitive elections that the masses of the Ceylonese people most directly enter the political process and the authoritative expression of the popular will is obtained. Parliamentary election contests fought on party lines and involving reasonably specific and comprehensible issues have become a real and effective arbiter of politics in Ceylon, producing five changes in the political control of the government within twenty-three years of independence. Elections on the basis of universal suffrage were held in 1931 and 1936 for the State Council, the pre-independence legislature. In 1947, the first parliamentary election was held, and subsequent parliamentary elections were conducted in 1952, 1956, March and July 1960, 1965, and 1970. Few countries outside of Northern Europe and North America can boast as long a record of uninterrupted experience with free, open, and competitive national elections on a broad franchise.

The Electoral System

Parliamentary elections in Ceylon employ a plurality, primarily single-member-district electoral system. A single poll is held and the candidate receiving the greatest number of votes, even if fewer than a majority of all votes cast, is elected. Local elections are conducted separately, and no national official other than the member of parliament is chosen by direct popular election, so the

132

voter is faced only with the choice of a representative in parliament for his constituency. Under the 1959 delimitation of parliamentary constituencies, the 151 elected M.P.'s are chosen from 140 single-member constituencies, four two-member constituencies, and one three-member constituency. In the multimember constituencies, each voter may cast as many votes as there are representatives to be elected, which may all be given to a single candidate or may be distributed among several candidates. The two candidates, or three in the three-member constituency, with the largest number of votes are elected. Constituencies are small, with an average population of under 65,000 at the time of the 1959 delimitation. In 1970, registered voters averaged 37,966 per constituency and 36,457 per elected member of parliament.[1]

Parliamentary seats are distributed among the island's nine provinces on the basis of population, but additional seats are allocated to provinces on the basis of area, which has the effect of giving sparsely populated interior provinces a high proportion of parliamentary seats relative to the densely populated, more urbanized southwest quarter of the island. Each province is assigned one seat for every 75,000 persons it contains and another seat for every 1,000 square miles in its area. At the 1959 delimitation, 126 seats were distributed among the provinces on the basis of population and 25 on the basis of area. The provision of seats for area in addition to population was originally justified as enhancing the representation of the island's principal minorities. It has also been claimed that the political leaders at independence expected their own support to be based on the villages of

[1] Data on the 1970 election in this chapter are from *Report on the Seventh Parliamentary General Election in Ceylon, 27th May, 1970,* Sessional Paper VII—1971 (Colombo: Department of Government Printing, 1971). The 1965 election data are from *Report on the Sixth Parliamentary General Election of Ceylon, 22nd March, 1965,* Sessional Paper XX—1966 (Colombo: Government Press, 1966).

the interior and wished to minimize the parliamentary strength of their Marxist opponents, whose support lay in the densely populated Southwest.

Within the provinces, constituency boundaries are determined by a three-member, nonpartisan Delimitation Commission, which is to divide the province into electoral districts containing as nearly equal numbers of citizens as is practical in view of the geography, transportation facilities, and social composition of the province. The commission is empowered to draw constituency boundaries where feasible to allow representation of groups possessing a "community of interest"—construed as a common ethnic, religious, or caste identification—differing from that of the majority of the area. The commission may also create multi-member constituencies where to do so would make possible the representation of ethnic minorities that are not sufficiently concentrated territorially to obtain representation from a single-member constituency.[2] Multimember constituencies have been created primarily to permit representation of scattered pockets of Muslim voters. A few single-member constituencies were formed in 1959 to coincide with Muslim concentrations and pockets of disadvantaged and low-status Sinhalese castes.

While ethnic, religious, and caste bonds have been recognized in constituency demarcation, the basis of representation remains territorial. There are no seats reserved for members of particular communal groups or separate polls for different communities.[3]

[2] The creation of multimember constituencies was restricted to situations involving ethnic minorities in 1959. In the first delimitation, multimember constituencies could be established to facilitate representation of any community of interest, and a two-member constituency was formed on the southern coast to accomodate Sinhalese caste differences.

[3] In 1954, provision was made for a special election roll for citizens of Indian and Pakistani origin, who were to constitute a communally restricted electorate returning four M.P.'s and were not to be included on

Although a constituency may have been created expressly to facilitate representation of a specific minority, all persons residing within the constituency who meet the general requirements for the franchise are entitled to vote in a single poll, and anyone qualified to serve in parliament is free to contest the constituency and be elected.

The voice voters enjoy in the selection of a parliament differs markedly between provinces. The assignment of seats to provinces on the basis of area was intended to give a somewhat stronger voice to voters in the sparsely populated provinces. The divergence from equal representation, however, was greatly magnified by the subsequent denial of Ceylonese citizenship and of the franchise to the Indian Tamils, who are heavily concentrated in the central hill-country provinces. Their disfranchisement in 1949 resulted in the creation of many "rotten boroughs" containing very few eligible voters. Consequently, a constitutional amendment in 1959, while continuing the distribution of parliamentary seats between provinces on the basis of total population (including Indian Tamils and other noncitizens), provided for the drawing of constituency boundaries within provinces on the basis of the distribution of citizens of Ceylon. The result is an extremely wide variation between provinces in the number of eligible voters per representative in parliament. At the time of the 1970 election, the average number of registered voters per elected representative in the Western Province was more than double that in Uva Province. In sixteen single-member constituencies there were more than 50,000 registered voters in 1970, while six constituencies contained fewer than 20,000. The largest single-member constituency, an urban area adjoining Colombo, contained 70,236 registered voters, while the smallest, in remote Uva, held only 16,461.

---

the general election register. The provision was, however, repealed without ever being implemented.

PARTIES AND ELECTIONS

In most constituencies, elections constitute an effective two-party clash, despite the frequent presence of frivolous candidates. In 1970, the two leading candidates received 90 per cent or more of all votes cast in 114 of 119 single-member constituencies outside the Northern and Eastern Provinces (one was not contested). Although eight candidates crowded the ballot in the two-member Colombo South constituency, the two winning candidates divided 98 per cent of the votes. In the seven provinces outside the North and East, the prevailing pattern was a direct collision between the UNP and one of the United Front partners. The UNP clashed with the SLFP in 92, the LSSP in 16, the CP in five, and United Front–supported independents in two of the 119 contested single-member constituencies. The UNP's ally, the MEP, fought the SLFP or the LSSP in the remaining four. In only six of these constituencies did the combined votes of the United Front candidate and the UNP or MEP candidate total less than 90 per cent of the votes cast. The marked polarization of votes which occurred between the UNP-MEP alliance and the United Front suggests that the election, like elections in Britain, assumed the character of a plebiscite on the Government, with voters expressing a desire for a return of the UNP-led Government or its replacement by a United Front Government.

Ceylon's electoral system, like other plurality systems, permits considerable divergence between the proportion of the popular vote a party receives and its relative strength in parliament. In July 1960, the SLFP won 75 of 151 seats in parliament with 34 per cent of the popular vote, whereas the UNP won only 30 seats although it obtained 38 per cent of the votes. A decade later the disparity was even more pronounced. The UNP with 38 per cent of the votes secured only 17 seats in parliament, while the SLFP with 37 per cent of the votes captured no fewer than 91 seats. In 1965, the fortunes of the two major contenders were reversed. The UNP won 44 per cent of the seats with 39 per cent of the votes, while the SLFP obtained only 27 per cent of the seats with 30 per cent of the votes, indicating that the electoral system tends to magnify the margin of victory of the most successful party.[4] Even in the chaotic election of March 1960, when the UNP was the largest single party in parliament with only 50 seats, it secured 33 per cent of the seats with 29 per cent of the votes.

The effects of the electoral system on a party's fortunes are influenced by the territorial concentration of the party's supporters and the number of seats it contests. In 1970, while the UNP with 38 per cent of the popular votes captured only 17 seats, the LSSP with 9 per cent of the votes won 19 seats and the FP with 5 per cent of the votes won 13 seats. This result was possible because of the concentration of the LSSP and FP votes in a small number of constituencies. The LSSP offered only 23 candidates and the FP 19, whereas 130 UNP candidates contested the election. Although the UNP candidates suffered wholesale defeat across the island, almost everywhere they ran a relatively strong second. Not one of the 130 UNP candidates lost his deposit. The SLFP often appears more successful than the UNP in converting popular votes into parliamentary seats as a result of its strength in the less heavily populated interior, where constituencies contain fewer voters, and its propensity to nominate fewer candidates than the UNP. The SLFP has contested

---

[4] If the SLFP, LSSP, and CP alliance is treated as a single electoral entity, the results are not substantially different. In the elections of July 1960 and 1970 in which the alliance was successful, the allied parties combined received 60 per cent of the seats with 44 per cent of the votes and 70 per cent of the seats with 49 per cent of the votes, respectively. In contrast, in their unsuccessful effort in 1965 they obtained only 38 per cent of the seats while receiving 40 per cent of the votes.

between 17 and 30 fewer seats than the UNP in the last four elections.

The single-member electoral districts which return 140 of the 151 elected members of parliament, combined with election by a plurality of votes, have contributed to sharp changes in the parliamentary positions of parties by greatly amplifying the parliamentary consequences of small shifts in votes. The shift of a relatively small proportion of the votes in a single-member constituency can cause the seat to change from one party to another. In contrast, the multimember constituencies have tended to freeze party positions. While the distribution of votes between the leading parties in a multimember constituency may fluctuate, without a drastic shift of votes each is virtually assured of capturing one seat but unlikely to win an additional seat. In each of the four elections since it was created, the two-member Colombo South constituency has returned one UNP and one LSSP candidate. The UNP and the SLFP have usually divided the seats of a second two-member constituency, while the FP has regularly captured one seat in each of the remaining two, usually paired with the SLFP in one and the UNP or an independent in the other. In three of the four elections since the 1959 delimitation, the UNP has won two and the CP one of the three Colombo Central seats.

Reflecting the major and growing role of parties, certain privileges have been given to "recognized" political parties under the election law. The deposit required of each candidate, which is forfeited if he fails to obtain one-eighth of the votes cast in his constituency, has been reduced to Rs. 250 for candidates of recognized parties but is Rs. 1,000 for other candidates. To aid identification of the candidates by illiterate voters, a distinctive symbol is allotted to each candidate in a constituency and is printed on the ballot beside the candidate's name. Recognized parties are allowed to use the same symbol in all constituencies they contest throughout the island (unless, of course, in a multi-member constituency a party has more than one candidate) and are assured of the use of the same symbol from one election to the next. The use of party symbols has had an important consequence in facilitating identification of parties, thereby reinforcing party voting. The major parties have made wide use of their symbols in their literature and campaign materials. The UNP in particular has extensively utilized its symbol, an elephant. The LSSP's symbol is a key, that of the SLFP a hand, the CP a star, and the FP a house (see Figure 6). Independents and ephemeral parties are given one of a host of other symbols such as a bell, umbrella, chair, or lamp.

Sri Lanka
Freedom
Party

United
National
Party

Lanka
Sama Samaja
Party

Communist
Party

Federal
Party

Tamil
Congress

Figure 6. Election symbols of major political parties

The election law was amended in 1964 to provide for the recognition of all parties which contested the July 1960 election and returned at least two members of parliament. Other parties may gain recognition if they contain two persons elected to parliament at the preceding election or can establish that they have been continuously engaged in political activities for at least five years. As a result, eight parties were recognized by virtue of their performance in 1960 and a ninth, the Tamil Congress, by establishing its existence for more than five years.[5] No additional parties were recognized for the 1970 election, although the newly created (and soon to disappear) Sinhala Mahajana Pakshaya entered forty-nine candidates in the contest. The SMP candidates were officially treated as independents, although by administrative arrangement they were allotted the same symbol in each constituency they contested. The criteria for recognition seem sufficiently broad and the advantages of recognition sufficiently slight to provide no serious constraint on the formation and development of new parties.

THE CONDUCT OF ELECTIONS

Responsibility for organizing and conducting elections is vested in a commissioner of elections, who is independent of ministerial control as a protection against partisan pressures. The election-day tasks of conducting the poll and counting the votes are performed by large numbers of public servants drawn from all ministries and departments, who work under the direction of the commissioner of elections and his small staff. Nearly 57,000 public servants were used for polling and counting duties in 1970. The number of polling stations has increased with each election, reducing the distance a voter must travel to cast his ballot and the number of voters served by each station. In the last election there were 5,613 stations, an average of one for each 1,000 registered voters. At the conclusion of the poll, the ballot boxes are delivered to a central location, where ballots from all polling stations in one constituency are mixed together prior to the count to prevent determination of the way a particular polling station

[5] *Report on the Sixth Parliamentary General Election,* p. 7; *Report on the Parliamentary General Elections, 19th March and 20th July, 1960,* Sessional Paper II—1962 (Colombo: Government Press, 1962), p. 92.

voted. Counting continues through the night, and results for most constituencies are announced the following morning. Balloting in the first three elections was spread over several days, but since 1960 the entire poll throughout the island has been conducted on a single day.

To combat impersonation of a legitimate voter by a person who has already voted, the practice of marking each voter's finger with indelible ink was introduced in 1965. The use of private vehicles to transport voters was restricted in 1959 and later virtually all traffic by private vehicles was prohibited on election day in an effort to remove an advantage of wealthy individuals and organizations. Stringent legal restrictions limit the activities of candidates and their authorized agents. An election petition charging campaign improprieties can be brought against a winning candidate, which if successful results in his losing his seat. The number of election petitions filed soared from a modest 13 in 1960 to 43 in 1965 following a tightening of the election law, but settled back to 14 in 1970. Frequent allegations in election petitions include the provision of transportation for voters and the making of false statements against opposing candidates. Until the election results are announced suspicions and tensions abound. Nonetheless, elections have invariably proceeded in an orderly manner, free of major violence, breakdown of administrative machinery, or charges of malfeasance by election officials. In view of the highly charged partisan atmosphere of Ceylonese elections, the absence of serious criticism of the administrative conduct of elections or allegations of fraudulent counting of ballots is striking. That elections are conducted impartially and ballots counted correctly seems generally to be accepted by losers as well as victors.

Voters, Candidates, and Campaigns

A dissolution of parliament must be followed by a general election and, within four months, by the meeting of the newly elected parliament. Simultaneous with the dissolution, dates are announced for the nomination of candidates, the general election, and the meeting of the new parliament. Nomination day follows dissolution by about one month, with the election following between one and two months after nomination day. As the term of parliament is not fixed except to prescribe a maximum life, formerly five and now six years, a parliamentary election may occur at any time. In 1960, two elections were held only four months apart. The cabinet may decide on an election at a time considered favorable to the party in power, as the UNP Government did in 1956. In practice, however, political circumstances have generally left the cabinet little choice. The first election of 1960 followed the prime minister's loss of parliamentary support and the next two elections came after the Government of the day lost a vote of confidence in parliament. The 1970 election came at the end of parliament's maximum term.

THE VOTERS

Virtually every citizen of Ceylon eighteen years of age or over is entitled to vote in the constituency within which he resides. It is the responsibility of the state to compile annually an election register listing every eligible voter by constituency. Disqualifications exist for felons serving in penal institutions, the insane, and persons convicted of certain election offenses or corrupt practices. In 1959, the voting age was lowered from twenty-one to eighteen, although the two elections of 1960 were held before a new election register could be completed so that persons under twenty-one years of age did not cast ballots in a general election until 1965. The approximately one million Indian Tamils who are not citizens of Ceylon make up the only significant element of the adult population unqualified to vote. As British subjects, the Indian Tamils were able to vote in the 1947 election, but prior to the

1952 election Ceylonese citizenship was defined to exclude most of the community and the franchise was restricted to citizens of Ceylon. Indian Tamils of voting age who are Ceylonese citizens constitute under 2 per cent of the electorate.

The Ceylonese electorate is predominantly Sinhalese and Buddhist, overwhelmingly rural, and relatively young. Nearly four-fifths of the eligible voters are Sinhalese and almost three-fourths are Buddhists. Three out of five are under forty years of age. An approximate profile of the electorate[6] appears in Figure 7.

A remarkably high level of popular participation has characterized Ceylonese elections since independence. The proportion of all eligible voters casting ballots has soared to more than 80 per cent in the last two elections (Table 21). This compares with

Table 21.   Participation in parliamentary elections, 1947–1970

Election	Electorate	Voters	Per cent of electorate voting
1947	3,048,145	1,701,150[a]	55.9
1952	2,990,912	2,114,615	70.7
1956	3,464,159	2,391,538	69.0
March 1960	3,724,507	2,889,282	77.6
July 1960	3,724,507	2,827,075	75.9
1965	4,710,887	3,821,918[a]	82.1
1970	5,505,028	4,672,656[a]	85.2

[a] One constituency was not contested.
Source: Report on the Seventh Parliamentary General Election in Ceylon, 27th May, 1970, Sessional Paper VII—1971 (Colombo: Department of Government Printing, 1971), p. 58.

[6] The profile was derived from 1963 census data. In certain cases, figures for Ceylon citizens were not available, necessitating imprecise adjustments of total population figures to exclude noncitizens. Hence, the profile can be considered only an approximation.

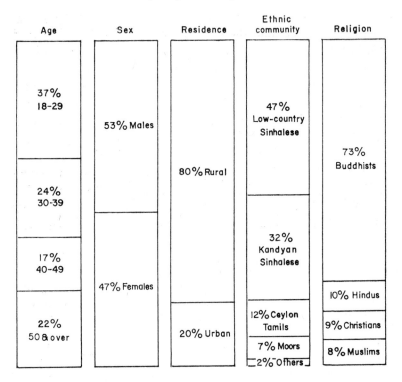

Figure 7. The Ceylonese electorate

turnouts of 58 per cent in the 1967 Indian parliamentary election, 60 per cent in the 1968 American presidential election, and 72 per cent in the 1970 British parliamentary election.[7] The high level of participation is with little doubt related to a marked growth of mass political consciousness in the first decade after independence, stimulated by the official-language issue and the general cumulative effect of political party agitation and propa-

[7] *Report on the Seventh Parliamentary General Election,* p. 54.

ganda. The fact than an apparently firmly entrenched governing party was thrown from office in the 1956 election is thought
to have had a profound psychological impact on the electorate,
transforming the vote from a show of deference or a futile act
of protest to an effective and purposive action which could, in
fact, alter the composition and policies of the Government. The
vigorous competition among parties in most constituencies and
the uncertainty of the election outcome undoubtedly has stimulated awareness of and interest in election contests. Four decades'
experience with the franchise, a high literacy rate, and relatively
wide exposure to mass communications media have presumably
boosted participation in elections. Small constituencies have
helped to bring the contest and the candidates close to the average voter, and a steady increase in the number of polling stations
has contributed to the ease and convenience of voting by reducing the distances voters must travel to cast their ballots.

THE CANDIDATES

More than two candidates contest most seats in parliament.[8]
Except in March 1960, the average number of candidates vying
for each seat at stake has ranged from nearly four in 1947 to
about two and a half in 1956 and July 1960. The March 1960
election, which followed a period of political confusion and a new
delimitation of constituencies, brought forward an astonishing
total of 899 candidates for the 151 seats, an average of about six
candidates per seat. Four months later, however, the number of
candidates plummeted to under 400. The number of candidates

[8] Only three times have candidates been declared elected without a
contest. In 1947, only one candidate sought election from the Puttalam
constituency. Nearly two decades later, in 1965, the sitting M.P.'s from
the two-member Colombo South constituency, each of whom was a nationally prominent leader of his party, were unopposed for re-election. In
1970, an SLFP candidate was declared elected without a contest when a
prospective UNP candidate submitted faulty nomination papers.

nominated by the six durable parties that attract most of the popular votes and win nearly all the seats has tended to stabilize at close to 300, slightly under two per seat, over the last three elections (see Table 22). About one-third of the 140 single-member constituencies were contested by four or more candidates in 1965. In the last election, 53 single-member constituencies were contested by only two candidates, 58 by three candidates, and 28 by four or more candidates (one was not contested).

Candidacy requires only the sponsorship of two persons who are registered voters in the constituency to be contested. To discourage frivolous candidates, a deposit is required which is forfeited if the candidate fails to secure at least one-eighth of the votes cast, or in a multimember constituency one-eighth of the votes polled divided by the number of members elected. Deposits were lost by about one-third of the candidates in the last two elections. Nearly 500 of the 899 candidates who flooded the March 1960 election lost their deposits. Independents and the candidates of a few minor parties have accounted for most lost deposits. Of 135 candidates who lost their deposits in 1970, 121 were independents or candidates of the ephemeral Sinhala Mahajana Pakshaya. Independents and MEP candidates supplied 124 of 172 lost deposits in 1965 and 70 of 84 in July 1960. In contrast, only about one out of twenty-five major party candidates has lost his deposit in the last two elections.[9]

In the major parties, control over the selection of candidates is maintained by the central party organization, providing the leadership with a potential source of disciplinary power over the party's M.P.'s. Often, the leader of the party personally exercises close supervision over the choice of candidates. As an election approaches, a nominations board selects nominees in each constitu-

[9] The UNP, SLFP, LSSP, CP, FP, and TC offered 301 candidates in 1970, of whom only 13 lost their deposits. In 1965, only 10 of these parties' 286 candidates lost their deposits.

Table 22. Candidates in parliamentary elections, 1947–1970

Election	Total candidates	Durable party candidates[a]	Other party candidates	Independent candidates	Average candidates per seat[b]
1947	361	159	21	181	3.8
1952	303	201	17	85	3.2
1956	249	181	4	64	2.6
March 1960	899	416	315	168	6.0
July 1960	393	285	69	39	2.6
1965	495	286	113[c]	96	3.3
1970	441	301	53[d]	87	2.9

[a] Candidates of the UNP, SLFP, LSSP, CP, FP, and TC, including in 1947 candidates of an LSSP faction which contested the election separately but was later reunited with the LSSP, in 1952 candidates of the CP-VLSSP united front, and in 1956 candidates of the MEP coalition.

[b] Ninety-five seats were to be filled in the first three elections and 151 in the last four elections.

[c] Includes four LSSP(R) candidates, three "left" CP candidates, two Eela Thamil Ottumai Munnani candidates, and one United Left Front candidate treated as independents in the official returns.

[d] Includes 49 Sinhala Mahajana Pakshaya candidates treated as independents in the official returns.

Source: See Table 18.

ency the party decides to contest. The opinion of the party's branches in the constituency is ordinarily sought and is frequently of major importance in making the selection. Candidates are not required by law or convention to reside in the constituency they seek to represent and candidates from outside are not unusual, but the tendency has been for local ties to assume increasing importance. Chairmen of village or town councils in the constituency are among those most frequently sought as candidates. Despite the apparent trend toward voting on party lines, the individual candidate's personal appeal to voters in the constituency is still believed capable of gaining or losing significant numbers of votes. With few exceptions, the first consideration in candidate selection is that the nominee be of the same ethnic community, caste, and religion as the majority of the constituency residents. One effective constraint on the party leadership in selecting a candidate is the possibility that a locally influential party member who is denied the nomination will contest the election as an independent and draw support away from the party candidate.

THE ELECTION CAMPAIGN

Few public events in Ceylon can rival the color and excitement of the parliamentary election campaign. The campaign usually begins in earnest after nomination day and runs for the month or more until the day before the balloting occurs. Even earlier, parties prepare their election manifestos, screen prospective candidates, and gird themselves for the contest. The opening of the UNP's campaign in 1970 was announced immediately after the dissolution of parliament, two months before the election. The United Front's campaign was declared to have entered its "final phase" a month prior to the election. The campaign efforts of the major parties are centrally directed by the party leadership, who exercise a strong voice in the selection of candidates, proclaim the principal issues, publish the campaign literature, and organize the major meetings and rallies. The UNP and the SLFP, both of which field a large number of candidates, have adopted the practice of assigning responsibility for a cluster of constituencies to a prominent party figure, usually a minister or ex-minister, who is influential in the region. The major burden of campaigning, however, is borne by the individual candidate and his personal supporters, aided by the party branches and youth leagues in the constituency.

The candidate depends primarily on village-to-village and house-to-house canvassing. Innumerable small gatherings and several major rallies will be arranged through the constituency, at which the candidate, his local supporters, and occasionally a few national party leaders will address the crowds obtained. An appearance by the party leader, who is likely to be either the prime minister or a former prime minister, is in particular demand by candidates. The party leader ordinarily schedules at least one visit in every constituency contested by his party. Leaders of the UNP and the SLFP are required to visit a hundred or more constituencies. In 1965 and 1970, SLFP leader Sirimavo Bandaranike campaigned not only for the SLFP candidates but also for candidates of the allied LSSP and CP. In 1970, canvassing in her own constituency was delegated to her son to free her to work on behalf of other United Front candidates. In a constituency containing a significant ethnic, caste, or religious minority, a party spokesman belonging to the same minority frequently is imported to campaign for the party's nominee.

As in other democratic countries, a bewildering confusion of personalities, policy issues, parochial concerns, and loyalties and prejudices are intertwined in the election campaign. The UNP and the SLFP have placed great stress on the party leader's qualifications to lead the nation and have called upon the voters to make Dudley Senanayake or Sirimavo Bandaranaike prime minister by casting ballots for the party's parliamentary candidate. The larger parties have attacked independent and minor-party candidates on grounds that they could not form a Government if elected. The FP has repeatedly sought votes for its candidates by arguing that the party is the most effective instrument of the Tamil people in resisting Sinhalese domination. Specific policy issues often sharply divide the major contenders and assume a position of prominence in campaigns. The official-language issue and Buddhist discontents largely dominated the 1956 campaign. In 1965, the UNP made a major issue of the SLFP's Marxist alliance and a claimed threat to Buddhism and democracy posed by the Marxists, while the SLFP-Marxist United Front emphasized social justice and equality of status and opportunity, particularly for the Sinhalese Buddhists. Employment, the cost of living, and the ration of subsidized rice provided consumers became the major themes of the 1970 campaign. The national leadership and the individual candidates of a party have ordinarily identified the same issues and have taken consistent positions on them.

The contest within individual constituencies, in addition to repeating national themes and issues, regularly includes a strong emphasis on the services to be rendered to the parochial interests of the locality and its inhabitants. Most candidates frequently and insistently argue that they can obtain more roads, schools, dispensaries, and jobs for the constituency than their opponents can. A deep-seated belief exists—with some reason, at least in the early years of independence—that an area which votes for the winning party will receive more generous treatment in the dissemination of government services than one returning a member of the opposition. A typical crossroads or village speech for a candidate seeking to oust an incumbent includes an assertion that the locality has been neglected in the past due to the failures of the sitting M.P. As his party is certain of victory nationally, the candidate's election will make it possible for him to work for the constituency within the inner councils of the Government (perhaps citing kinship or other ties with a powerful party leader) and to obtain the material improvements previously denied the locality. If the candidate is an incumbent defending his seat, his speech typically points to the many roads, schools, and other facilities the constituency has obtained through his efforts and argues that since his party is certain to be returned to power he must be re-elected to assure continued favorable treatment for the constituency. Where a minority predominates locally, the prospective position of the minority after the election is likely to be the central concern of the campaign. The character of the campaign and the content of appeals to voters reflect a sharp decline in deferential voting and a correspondingly steep rise in instrumental voting over recent decades. Parties and candidates assume the vote is no longer given in deference for superior social status, but is cast in anticipation of the delivery of benefits, material or symbolic, to the voter.

An election manifesto declaring the party's position on major issues and outlining the party's proposed program is drafted by each party and widely circulated during the campaign. In 1970, the UNP issued 750,000 Sinhalese, 300,000 English, and 250,000 Tamil copies of its manifesto.[10] The manifestos have received considerable prominence not only during the campaign but also after the election. Victorious parties have claimed that the election constituted a popular mandate to carry out policies specified in their manifestos. When the United Front came to power in 1970, its election manifesto was reprinted by the Department of Government Printing and circulated by the Information Department and the United Front parties as a blueprint of intended Government action.

[10] Information supplied to the author by the UNP headquarters.

The costs of campaigning in Ceylon are relatively modest. Paid advertising in mass communications media is almost unknown. Constituencies are small and travel expenses are slight. Extensive use is made of posters and leaflets, some provided by the party headquarters and some by the individual candidate. Campaign expenditures reported by candidates in 1970 averaged Rs. 3,443 (about $580).[11] The extent of financial assistance rendered the nominee by the central party organization varies according to the party and the circumstances of the candidate. Every important party attempts to help its nominees, ordinarily by providing copies of party manifestos, posters, and other literature for distribution, possibly the amount of the deposit, and some further financial assistance. It is generally assumed that the UNP has considerably greater funds at its disposal than other parties and is better able to supply candidates who lack personal resources with financial support than opposing parties. During the 1965 campaign, both the UNP and the SLFP distributed large numbers of shirts and caps of the party's color—green for the UNP and blue for the SLFP.

Organizations other than political parties play some role in campaigns, but generally not a central one. The conspicuous part played in 1956 by the Eksath Bhikkhu Peramuna, an organization of bhikkhus (Buddhist monks) created to campaign for the MEP coalition and against the UNP, has had no parallel in subsequent campaigns. The 1956 EBP campaign rivaled that of the opposition parties in zeal and flamboyance. After largely disappearing from the 1960 campaigns, bhikkhus' organizations reappeared in 1965 in both of the major contending camps, but their activities were restrained in comparison with the 1956 EBP effort.[12] In the 1970 campaign, a furious last-minute battle de-

[11] *Report on the Seventh Parliamentary General Election*, p. 35.
[12] On the role of bhikkhus' organizations in politics, see Chapter 5.

veloped over an alleged endorsement of the United Front by the head of a prominent chapter of bhikkhus, with the pro–United Front newspapers featuring the endorsement and the pro-UNP press and Radio Ceylon carrying denials of the statement. Trade unions have provided some assistance to parties, primarily in the form of campaign workers and the sponsorship of rallies. The leadership of the Ceylon Workers' Congress worked for UNP candidates among estate employees in 1965 and 1970, while the head of the CWC's chief rival, the Democratic Workers' Congress, campaigned for the United Front in both elections. University students and faculty staged a large rally to protest actions of the minister of education shortly before the 1970 election, resulting in the closing of the university.

The press is highly partisan, and during a campaign news reporting has commonly reflected the partisan sympathies of the newspapers. The support of the press has gone overwhelmingly to the UNP in each campaign. In 1970, the UNP retained the backing of the two largest newspaper chains, the Associated Newspapers of Ceylon (known as Lakehouse) and the Times group, although the smaller Independent Newspapers group, which had supported the UNP in 1965, shifted to the United Front. In 1965, Lakehouse functioned as a virtual auxiliary of the UNP, printing and distributing UNP campaign materials as well as disseminating news favorable to the party. Lakehouse funds of Rs. 215,000 (about $36,000) were spent directly on UNP campaign activities in 1965, and Lakehouse expenditures for political purposes in the six months preceding the 1965 election may have totaled nearly Rs. 845,000 (about $144,000).[13]

[13] *Report of the Commission Appointed Under the Commissions of Inquiry Act to Inquire into and Report on Certain Matters Affecting the Associated Newspapers of Ceylon Ltd., and Other Connected Companies,* Sessional Paper VIII—1971 (Colombo: Department of Government Printing, 1971), pp. 90–103.

The role of Lakehouse in 1970 was somewhat less conspicuous but seemed scarcely less partisan. On the evening the election results were announced, a crowd of presumed United Front enthusiasts attacked and set fire to the Lakehouse building.

5. *Communal Loyalties and*
Groups in Politics

The division of the peoples of Ceylon into sharply differentiated particularistic groups has left a deep imprint on the island's politics. Sentiments of solidarity within and rivalry between communal groups have generated many political issues and controversies, and notions of communal loyalty or rivalry are often an unspoken influence on the behavior of voters, politicians, and bureaucrats. Three types of particularistic identification exist within the larger social fabric of Ceylon. The most profound and conspicuous is the division of the population into clearly delimited ethnic communities, each of which is distinguished by a common language, a predominant religion, and a sense of constituting a unique and separate group. Intertwined with the ethnic divisions are religious identifications, which almost coincide with and frequently reinforce the ethnic cleavages. Finally, the larger communities are subdivided into castes, forming an additional basis for solidarity and differentiation. Ethnic and religious conflict has appeared in dramatic issues of national politics. Caste emerges as a political factor principally at the local or constituency level. Each identification commonly carries an assumption of the primacy of communal loyalty in social or political action.

Communal groups—whether ethnic, religious, or caste—share the characteristics of mutually exclusive and ascriptive membership.[1] The individual identifies himself and is identified by others as belonging to one and only one ethnic community, religion, or caste. Furthermore, with the possible but infrequent exception of religious conversion, all three types of groups are ascriptive, with membership acquired by birth and lasting throughout an individual's life. It is the exclusive and involuntary character of membership and the persistent consciousness of the sentimental bonds binding the community together that distinguish the communal groups from categories of persons defined by social class, occupation, or region.

The Politics of Ethnic Groups and Language

Of the communal cleavages, the most prominent and politically explosive is the division of the island's population into separate ethnic groups differentiated by a distinctive language, religion, social organization, territorial concentration, and sense of a shared history and ancestry. Even when adoption of the English language or the Christian religion has blurred the lines of separation, identification with the ethnic community has generally remained sharp and clear. The Sinhalese, who constitute 71 per cent of the Ceylonese population, enjoy an overwhelming numerical predominance. Confronting the Sinhalese are two sizable minority communities, the Ceylon Tamils and the Indian Tamils, each including about one-tenth of the island's population, and several smaller minorities. The Ceylon Tamils, politically the most significant minority, have long been prominent in govern-

[1] The term community is most frequently employed in Ceylon in referring to the groups bound together by an ethnic-linguistic identity, although it is also used in connection with religious groups and castes. In each case, community implies a strong consciousness of commonality, solidarity, and distinctiveness. As used here, unless the context indicates explicit reference to ethnic groups, all three types of solidary groups will be considered communities or communal groups.

ment employment and public affairs. The Indian Tamils, although nearly as numerous as the Ceylon Tamils, are largely noncitizens widely viewed as aliens temporarily resident in Ceylon. The Ceylon Moors, about 6 per cent of the population, maintain an identity distinct from either the Sinhalese or the Tamils, based largely on their adherence to Islam. Other ethnic communities—Indian Moors, Malays, and Burghers—are too small to constitute major forces in politics, although their senses of separate identity may be no less strong.

ETHNIC SEPARATION IN POLITICS

Each of the major ethnic communities displays a clear pattern of regional concentration. The Sinhalese predominate throughout the island except in the North and East. Outside of the Northern and Eastern Provinces, Sinhalese made up 80 per cent or more of the population in eleven of sixteen administrative districts, and in only one district did they fail to form a majority of the population at the 1963 census (see Table 23). The Ceylon Tamils have lived for many centuries in and around the Jaffna Peninsula at the northern tip of the island. In 1963, they constituted 95 per cent of the Jaffna district population and formed a majority in the other two Northern Province districts. In the polyglot Eastern Province, they were a majority of the inhabitants of the Batticaloa district and a sizable element of the population in the two remaining districts. More than three-quarters of all Ceylon Tamils lived in the Northern and Eastern Provinces in 1963, with half of the remainder resident in the heavily populated Colombo district.

The Indian Tamils are concentrated in the estate areas of the Kandyan highlands, with 80 per cent of the community enumerated in the five contiguous districts of Kandy, Nuwara Eliya, Badulla, Ratnapura, and Kegalla. The Ceylon Moors

Table 23. Ethnic communities by district, 1963

Province/district	Per cent of district population[a]				
	Sinhalese	Ceylon Tamils	Indian Tamils	Ceylon Moors	Others
Western Province					
Colombo	83	6	3	5	4
Kalutara	87	1	6	6	—
Southern Province					
Galle	94	1	2	3	—
Matara	94	—	3	2	—
Hambantota	97	—	—	1	1
Sabaragamuwa Province					
Ratnapura	78	1	19	1	1
Kegalla	83	1	11	4	1
Central Province					
Kandy	60	3	28	7	1
Matale	72	4	17	6	1
Nuwara Eliya	38	3	57	1	1
Uva Province					
Badulla	55	3	38	3	1
Monaragala	87	1	9	2	1
North-Western Province					
Kurunegala	93	1	1	4	1
Puttalam	80	7	2	9	1
North-Central Province					
Anuradhapura	89	2	1	7	1
Polonnaruwa	87	4	—	8	1
Northern Province					
Jaffna	1	95	2	1	—
Mannar	4	51	16	24	5
Vavuniya	18	63	11	7	1
Eastern Province					
Batticaloa	3	71	1	23	1
Amparai	29	23	1	46	1
Trincomalee	29	37	2	29	2

[a] Some lines do not add to 100 per cent due to rounding.
Source: Ceylon, Department of Census and Statistics, *Statistical Abstract of Ceylon, 1967–1968* (Colombo: Department of Government Printing, 1970), Tables 17–18, pp. 32–33.

constitute a major proportion of the population only on the east coast and in the sparcely populated Mannar district in the North-west, but are found throughout the island. In 1963, nearly 30 per cent of the community resided in the Eastern Province, while one-third inhabited the Western and North-Western Provinces.

As a result of the territorial concentration of ethnic communities, most parliamentary constituencies are relatively homogeneous ethnically. In nearly half of the 140 single-member constituencies, 90 per cent or more of the population is of a single ethnic community and in almost three-quarters one community constitutes at least 75 per cent of the population.[2] Only in the multimember constituencies and a handful of ethnically mixed areas, mostly in the Eastern Province, are serious rivalries at the constituency level likely. Voters almost invariably return candidates of the same ethnic community as the constituency majority. Sinhalese regularly win about 80 per cent of the seats in parliament, all but a small handful of the seats outside the North and East. Ceylon Tamils consistently hold about one-eighth and Ceylon Moors less than one-twelfth of the parliamentary seats.

The trend of politics since independence has been toward a vertical integration of ethnic communities, reducing or blurring internal class, caste, and regional distinctions, but creating a sharper horizontal distinction between communities as each of the major ethnic groups has tended to draw into itself and emphasize its own language, religion, and culture. The division of the Sinhalese community into low-country and Kandyan branches was accentuated by the differential impact of the West and social changes over the last few centuries. The Kandyans remained closer to traditional customs and practices and generally lagged behind the low-country Sinhalese in education, nonagri-

[2] Data on the ethnic and religious composition of constituencies are from *Report of the Delimitation Commission,* Sessional Paper XV—1959 (Colombo: Government Press, 1959).

cultural employment, urbanization, and secularization. Both low-country and Kandyan Sinhalese are primarily Buddhists, but the Sinhalese Christian minority is largely composed of low-country Sinhalese. Recently, with increasing mobility, spreading educational opportunities, and improvements in transportation and communication, the differentiation appears to be of declining significance. Some specifically Kandyan grievances remain and find expression in politics, particularly those resulting from landlessness and the dearth of educational and employment opportunities in the Kandyan areas. The growth of Sinhalese self-awareness and demands for recognition, however, have tended to draw the two branches of the community together in common cause, and the major issues of communal relations have tended to minimize internal Sinhalese divisions by focusing on Sinhalese-minority relations. The Ceylon Tamils are somewhat more vaguely separable into the inhabitants of the Jaffna Peninsula and those of the eastern coast, a division which is also occasionally expressed in politics. However, as among the Sinhalese, the larger issues of majority-minority relations have tended to obscure and reduce the internal cleavages within the Ceylon Tamil community, and Tamil political leaders have made explicit efforts to overcome the lingering sense of divergent interests and loyalties. The most tenacious of the divisions of Ceylon Tamil society, that of caste, has produced widening political ramifications in recent years with uncertain implications for the solidarity of the ethnic community.

The Indian Tamils, descendents of Tamil-speaking South Indians who migrated to Ceylon as estate laborers over the last century, have tended to remain clustered in the estate areas largely isolated from the other communities. Hostility toward the Indian Tamils is particularly marked among the Kandyan Sinhalese in those areas where the estates have crowded the villages and Indian Tamil labor has restricted the employment opportunities of the Sinhalese as population pressure has mounted and landlessness has grown. While the Indian Tamils share a common language and religion with the Ceylon Tamils, a sense of common identity has not developed, inhibited by differences of occupation and economic circumstances, caste, geographical location, and historical experience. Although most Indian Tamils today were born in Ceylon, they are still widely viewed as aliens. On the basis of their lack of indigenous roots or enduring connection with the island, a majority of the community was denied Ceylonese citizenship, and persistent efforts have been made to secure their repatriation to India. By 1964, 134,000 Indian Tamils, about one-eighth of the community, had obtained Ceylonese citizenship. A 1964 agreement between Ceylon and India provided for the return to India of 525,000 and the granting of Ceylonese citizenship to 300,000 Indian Tamils within fifteen years, but by mid-1970 only 12,798 had departed for India and only 7,316 had received Ceylonese citizenship.[3]

The profound sense of separate identity dividing ethnic communities is reflected in a tendency for majority and minority communities to gravitate toward separate organizations. The tendency surfaced half a century ago in the first years of the Ceylon National Congress, founded by both Sinhalese and Tamil leaders in 1919. Two years later, in a dispute over communal representation, most Tamil members withdrew from the Congress to establish a Tamil Maha Jana Sabha. Since independence, most major parties other than the explicitly minority parties have attempted to be multicommunal in membership and base of support, but have found themselves essentially dependent on the Sinhalese community. The only parties which have won substantial political backing from the Ceylon Tamils have been the TC and the FP, both founded explicitly and exclusively to champion

[3] *Ceylon Daily News,* July 23, 1970, p. 5.

the interests of the Tamil community in politics. In launching the party, the FP's founder argued that "as long as there are activities directed against communities and as long as those communities are minority communities, they must for their self-protection bind themselves in a communal way."[4] After 1952 the only candidates of parties other than the TC and FP to capture Ceylon Tamil constituencies were one CP candidate in 1956, one UNP candidate in 1965, and two UNP candidates (one of whom was later unseated) in 1970.

Until their disfranchisement, the Indian Tamils adhered to the Ceylon Indian Congress, an organization formed in 1939 to defend the community in politics. Subsequently, those Indian Tamils possessing Ceylonese citizenship have constituted a marginal electoral influence in about a dozen constituencies in the estate areas, providing the Ceylon Workers' Congress and the Democratic Workers' Congress, the two principal Indian Tamil organizations, with some leverage in bargaining with the major political parties. A political party called the Dravida Munnetra Kazhagam of Ceylon, inspired by the DMK of Tamilnadu state in South India, has existed among the Indian Tamils for a decade but has been only intermittently active and has an uncertain influence. The party's declared intention to contest the 1970 election did not materialize.

The Ceylon Moors have not been represented by a separate party, probably because they are too small in number and too widely scattered to function effectively as a separate organization in a majoritarian and territorial electoral system. Associations of Moors have, however, functioned as interest groups. The All-Ceylon Moors Association and the All-Ceylon Muslim League have been the principal organizations articulating Moor interests in politics.

[4] Ceylon, House of Representatives, *Parliamentary Debates* (*Hansard*), vol. 5, col. 491 (Dec. 10, 1948).

COMMUNAL RIVALRY AND THE LANGUAGE ISSUE

Modern communal rivalry can be traced to a widening of political awareness and the introduction of constitutional reforms in the early decades of the present century. The prospect of political power shifting from the hands of foreign colonial officials to elected Ceylonese politicians produced growing concern with the relative political strength of the various ethnic communities, on the assumption that power possessed by members of one community would be used for the exclusive benefit of that community. In the constitutional debate, the Sinhalese sought an unencumbered majoritarian political system, while the minorities fought to restrict and reduce the political power of the Sinhalese majority by constitutional safeguards and communal representation. In the landmark constitution of 1931 and again in 1946, the constitutional issue was decided in favor of the Sinhalese majority. A dominant legislature was created which was certain to contain a majority of Sinhalese representatives.

The Sinhalese, conscious of being the predominant people of the island for many centuries but feeling themselves deprived of the status and material benefits commensurate with their majority position, began to demand recognition of a special status for their language and their religion and a full measure of opportunities proportionate to their numbers. The growing mood of assertiveness was expressed by Sirimavo Bandaranaike when she warned, "The Tamil people must accept the fact that the Sinhala majority will no longer permit themselves to be cheated of their rights."[5] Although insistent on their position and prerogatives as the majority people of Ceylon, the Sinhalese also display a marked sense of insecurity as an embattled minority relative to the many millions of Tamil- and other Dravidian-speaking peoples in neighboring South India. While the Ceylon Tamils

[5] *Tribune* (Colombo), May 7, 1967, p. 3.

view themselves as a small and unique people with no roots or connections outside the island, the Sinhalese commonly view the Tamils of Ceylon as a branch of a massive Dravidian-speaking nation spreading across South India, through Ceylon, to Malaysia. As one Sinhalese politician asserted: "In this country the problem of the Tamils is not a minority problem. The Sinhalese are the minority in Dravidastan. We are carrying on a struggle for our national existence against the Dravidastan majority."[6]

Majority-minority rivalry after independence increasingly focused on the question of an official language. The language controversy originated in protest against the exclusive privileges enjoyed by a small, multicommunal elite educated in the English language, which monopolized the professions, white-collar public service posts, and virtually all other presitigious and rewarding positions. As education in Sinhalese and Tamil spread rapidly, demands mounted for expanded opportunities for those educated in the indigenous languages, culminating in the demand for "swabhasha" or the people's "own language" as the official language of government and, hence, the language of social and economic opportunity. Among the Sinhalese majority, sentiment swiftly mounted to install Sinhalese, the language of the overwhelming majority of the citizens of Ceylon, as the sole official language. While it did not arise primarily as a communal dispute, the language issue possessed profound communal implications and great potential for mobilizing communal support. Language is one of the most important attributes separating the two major communities and is fundamental to the self-identification of each. As communal solidarity was aroused, the communal distribution of opportunities for government employment and social advance-

---

[6] Ceylon, House of Representatives, *Parliamentary Debates* (*Hansard*), vol. 48, col. 1313 (Sept. 3, 1962).

ment became intertwined with the psychological satisfactions derived from a recognition of a special status for one's own language and a pre-eminent position for one's own people.

An important role in the rise of the demand for Sinhalese as the only official language was played by communal competition for public employment and Sinhalese resentment of disproportionate Tamil representation in the public service. Early opportunities for education in English and a dearth of alternative avenues of employment had led many Ceylon Tamils to enter the public service. With rising education and aspirations and a stagnation of other possibilities, Sinhalese increasingly sought public service appointments, but felt their opportunities restricted by the prior establishment of the Tamils in the public service. The adoption of Sinhalese as the only language of government was seen as a means of correcting the imbalance created under colonial rule and compensating the Sinhalese for past injustices.

The language controversy arose closely associated with the social, political, and ideological changes involved in the process of modernization. With the adoption of universal suffrage and the spread of political consciousness downward to new social strata, the aspirations of the masses of the people received increasing political expression. In a society in which communal identification remained strong, popular aspirations were frequently articulated in communal terms. Egalitarian and populist sentiments were reflected in the demands that access to new opportunities be opened for the broad Sinhalese-speaking masses. Sinhalese was the language of the majority of the common people, who had long suffered from social and economic disadvantages. The triumph of the Sinhalese language could be viewed as a liberation of the underprivileged majority, rather than as an advantage gained by one community over another. Speaking of the Sinhalese-only movement, Prime Minister Sirimavo Bandaranaike claimed:

We have tried to eliminate the wide gap which existed between the Government and the governed, between the elite and the masses. . . . By giving the due and rightful place to the Sinhala language as the Official Language of the country, we have made it possible for those voiceless millions who spoke only that language, to play an effective part in the affairs of the country. As long as English reigned, their freedom was limited.[7]

The State Council had resolved in 1944 that English should be replaced as the official language by both Sinhalese and Tamil, and this objective was accepted by most politicians and political groups in the first years of independence. As sentiment for Sinhalese as the only official language mounted in the early 1950's, SLFP leader S. W. R. D. Bandaranaike took up the issue to attack the governing UNP. Faced with mounting pressure on the language issue, the UNP executed an abrupt reversal of position and declared for Sinhalese only. The 1956 election, which closely followed the UNP conversion, saw the UNP swept from power by a Bandaranaike-led coalition pledged to immediate enactment of Sinhalese-only legislation. It was the first election defeat suffered by a governing party in Ceylon.

With the passage of the Official Language Act, declaring Sinhalese to be the sole official language, communal relations deteriorated rapidly and positions on the language issue hardened. In 1958, the island was swept by brutal communal riots claiming hundreds of lives and sending Tamils living in the South fleeing toward Jaffna and Sinhalese living in the North streaming to the South. For the first time since independence, no Tamil served in the cabinet between 1956 and 1965. In 1963, the LSSP shifted from advocacy of both Sinhalese and Tamil as official languages to acceptance of Sinhalese only, the last party other than the explicitly Tamil parties to do so.

[7] "Sixteenth Anniversary of Independence," *Ceylon Today,* XIII (Feb. 1964), 6.

The 1965 election defeat of the SLFP-LSSP coalition brought to power a self-proclaimed National Government primarily dependent on UNP votes in parliament, but also supported by the FP, the TC, and the CWC. The following year, regulations providing for the use of the Tamil language for certain public purposes were promulgated under an act passed soon after the 1958 riots but not previously implemented. The National Government's alleged concessions to the minorities were immediately attacked by the SLFP-Marxist opposition as a betrayal of Sinhalese interests. The 1966 Tamil language regulations prompted an opposition-sponsored demonstration that culminated in riots in Colombo. By 1970, however, the force of Sinhalese communal assertiveness seemed to have ebbed. Sinhalese was installed and scarcely challenged as the sole official language, and considerable progress had been registered in promoting the use of Sinhalese in government administration and in education. The United Front which came to power in 1970, although deriving its support almost entirely from Sinhalese areas, appeared anxious to avert the hostility of the minorities. The appearance for the first time of several SLFP candidates in the North reflected less a serious expectation of victory than a gesture toward the Tamils. A Tamil was included in the cabinet and minority spokesmen were named appointed M.P.'s. The decline of communal passions was evident in the disasterous 1970 performance of the Sinhala Mahajana Pakshaya, which campaigned with Sinhalese communal appeals but, although it contested nearly one-third of the seats in parliament, captured only 0.4 per cent of the popular votes.

The politically explosive force of language and ethnic sentiments was, nonetheless, starkly demonstrated by the events of 1956–1966. For nearly a decade the political rupture between Sinhalese and Tamils seemed almost complete. The Ceylon Tamils embraced parties dedicated solely to defending Tamil interests, and parties dependent on Sinhalese votes vied with each other to display their more ardent and uncompromising enthusiasm for Sinhalese aspirations. A party that did not support majority aspirations lost popular backing among the Sinhalese, but could not win compensating votes from the Tamil community in competition with the explicitly Tamil parties. Consequently, the rise of a communally divisive issue tended to drive all parties other than the professed Tamil parties into espousal of Sinhalese communal demands. As a Tamil M.P. charged, "though we are supposed to be working on party lines, and though Governments are alleged to be formed on a party basis, yet, in regard to minority rights of language, religion and race, no one party led by a leader of the majority community is different from the other."[8] While communal tension and rivalry are not perpetual, the lingering sense of separate identity and communal solidarity has created the continuing possibility of communal confrontation in politics.

Religious Identifications in Politics

Religion emerged as a major issue in national politics intimately associated with the rivalry between majority and minority ethnic communities, finding expression in similar demands for status and opportunity for the majority. Buddhists constitute about two-thirds of the island's population. Hindus form the largest religious minority, followed by Christians and Muslims (Table 24). Religious affiliations are closely related to ethnic-linguistic identifications. The Sinhalese are overwhelmingly Buddhists, the Ceylon and Indian Tamils are predominately Hindu, and the Moors together with the small Malay community are virtually identical with the island's Muslim population. The correspondence between ethnic and religious groups is indicated in Table 25. The only religious group not identified with an individ-

---

[8] Ceylon, Constituent Assembly, *Official Report*, vol. 1, col. 390 (March 16, 1971).

ual ethnic community is the Christian minority, composed of Sinhalese, Tamils, and Burghers.

DEMANDS OF THE BUDDHIST MAJORITY

The influence of religious identifications in politics closely parallels that of ethnic communal sentiments, involving similar

Table 24.   Religious affiliation, 1963

Religion	Per cent of population
Buddhist	66.2
Hindu	18.5
Christian	8.4
Muslim	6.8
Other	0.1
Total	100.0

Source: Ceylon, Department of Census and Statistics, *Statistical Abstract of Ceylon, 1967–1968* (Colombo: Department of Government Printing, 1970), Table 19, p. 34.

Table 25.   Religion of ethnic communities, 1946

Ethnic community	Per cent of ethnic community			
	Buddhist	Hindu	Muslim	Christian
Sinhalese	92	—	—	8
Ceylon Tamils	3	81	—	16
Indian Tamils	2	89	—	8
Ceylon Moors	1	—	99	—

Source: Ceylon, Department of Census and Statistics, *Census of Ceylon, 1946,* Vol. IV (Colombo: Government Press, 1952), Table 16, p. 275.

feelings of group self-consciousness, exclusiveness, and solidarity. The impact of religion on politics increased dramatically in the first decade after independence with demands by the Sinhalese Buddhist majority for recognition and recompense for felt injustices suffered under colonial rule. The Sinhalese people had been intimately associated with Theravada Buddhism for two millennia, and adherence to Buddhism was an important factor in Sinhalese self-identification and sense of differentiation from the Hindu peoples of Ceylon and India. Early stirrings of national resurgence among the Sinhalese had accompanied a Buddhist revival in the late nineteenth century, which encompassed a reaction against Christian proselytizing, traditionalist attacks on Western cultural influences, and restlessness with colonial political domination. Long-simmering Buddhist discontents and resentment of Christian advantages in education and employment were channeled after independence into insistent demands for expanded opportunities for Buddhists and symbolic recognition of a special status for Buddhism as the religion of the majority.

The Buddhist discontents erupted into political activism in the 1956 election campaign, intermingled with the agitation for Sinhalese as the only official language. The approach of the Buddha Jayanthi, the 2,500th anniversary of the death of the Buddha and by tradition the simultaneous arrival of the Sinhalese in Ceylon, highlighted Buddhist dissatisfaction. Shortly before the election campaign, the All-Ceylon Buddhist Congress, an influential Buddhist lay organization, issued a report stressing the disabilities confronting Buddhism, attributing the plight of Buddhism to persecution and discrimination during colonial rule, and accusing the UNP Government of perpetuating colonial favoritism toward Christianity after independence. The Buddhist discontents and demands for redress were repeated by the opposition political parties and carried across the Sinhalese areas of the island by large numbers of bhikkhus. Among the political changes associated with the 1956 election was the new militancy and virtually unchallengeable political strength of Buddhism.

Buddhist resentment was particularly strong against the Christian hold on education, with its important implications for employment opportunities. Christian denominational schools had maintained a leading position in education, particularly English-language education, since the nineteenth century. While the number of government schools had increased rapidly, a large part of the island's educational institutions remained in the hands of Christian, primarily Roman Catholic, religious organizations. A colonial practice of providing public funds to support religious and other private schools had continued after independence and the expenditure of public funds per student in the private assisted schools was almost double that in the government schools. As the proportion of government grants received by Christian schools was much greater than that received by Buddhist schools, Buddhists came to feel that they were required to support an educational system run by Christians to serve the needs of the Christian community. Although non-Christians were admitted to Christian schools, and in fact often formed a majority of the students, many Buddhists resented the education of Buddhist children in a Christian environment and feared covert Christian influences and attempts at conversion. A major step toward alleviating Buddhist grievances was taken after the SLFP's 1960 election victory. More than 2,500 private schools, all but a small handful of the private schools in existence, were taken over by the government without compensation under a "national system" of education which the minister of education contended was required "to ensure equitable distribution of educational opportunities regardless of class, creed or locality."[9]

Another recurring Buddhist demand, that Poya days, marked

[9] Ceylon, House of Representatives, *Parliamentary Debates (Hansard)*, vol. 39, col. 795 (Aug. 26, 1960).

by the four phases of the moon, be substituted for Sundays as public holidays, was adopted in 1966 but abandoned less than six years later. During the 1965 election campaign, a United Front promise to make the monthly full-moon Poya day a national holiday was countered by a UNP pledge that all four Poya days would become holidays. The Poya holiday was inaugurated at the beginning of 1966 and hailed as a great triumph for Buddhism, but considerable dissatisfaction developed as a result of the irregularity of the lunar calendar. In 1971, after the United Front had replaced the UNP in power, Ceylon abandoned the Poya calendar and returned to the week demarcated by Sundays, but as a gesture toward Buddhist opinion each full-moon Poya day, the principal day of Buddhist religious observance, was designated a national holiday.

Buddhist resentment against Christian educational and employment advantages gained under colonial rule was directed as vehemently against Sinhalese Christians as against Christians of other ethnic communities. The continuing demands for recompense for past wrongs, explicitly for the Buddhist rather than for the Sinhalese population, was illustrated in a controversial recommendation of a National Education Commission shortly after the schools takeover. Claiming that the educational disadvantages of Buddhists would exist for many years, the commission recommended the establishment of quotas for each religion, based on the proportion of Ceylonese citizens represented by each, to control university admissions and recruitment to the public service. The recommendation advocated quotas based on religion rather than ethnic community to compensate members of the Buddhist majority for deprivations suffered under colonial rule "simply because they have stuck to the religion which binds them to their native soil."[10]

[10] *Final Report of the National Education Commission, 1961,* Sessional Paper XVII—1962 (Colombo: Government Press, 1962), pp. 152–153.

The demands made in the name of the Buddhist majority, while often backed by bhikkhus, were largely originated and championed by lay organizations under middle-class, urban leadership such as the All-Ceylon Buddhist Congress. Among the most militant, outspoken, and politically active of the lay organizations championing Buddhist claims was the Bauddha Jathika Balavegaya (Buddhist National Force) founded by L. H. Mettananda, a former principal of a prominent Buddhist school in Colombo. In place of an outlook of world renunciation and detachment commonly attributed to Buddhism, the lay organizations displayed a competitive, activist orientation and a concern for worldly rewards and gratifications for Buddhists. Many of the champions of the Buddhist demands were trained in Christian missionary schools or in Buddhist schools modeled on the Christian schools and, while reacting vigorously against Christian proselytizing, seemingly borrowed or absorbed organizational forms, activist orientations, and concern with worldly conditions from the Christian churches and doctrines.[11] The new militancy and worldliness was more evident among the Buddhists of the low country than among the generally conservative Kandyan Buddhists.

From a universal religion, Buddhism is gradually being adopted as a national symbol for Ceylon and specifically for the Sinhalese. The two-thirds of the Ceylonese who are Buddhists

---

Nine of the twenty commission members, however, dissented from the recommendation for religious quotas and the proposal was not adopted.

[11] Contemporary Ceylonese Buddhism has been termed "Protestant Buddhism," implying both the explicit protest against Christian intrusions it contains and its implicit adoption of the missionary ardor, organizational devices, and strict moral outlook of Protestant Christianity. See Gananath Obeyesekere, "Religious Symbolism and Political Change in Ceylon," *Modern Ceylon Studies,* I (Jan. 1970), 43–63.

(and Sinhalese) seem increasingly to perceive Ceylon as a Buddhist nation and Buddhism as the national religion. An annual conference of the All-Ceylon Buddhist Congress in 1969 was told:

The Buddhists of Ceylon have the biggest stake in the preservation of our nation. Even if this island is wiped off the face of the earth, one cannot visualize the extinction of Hinduism, Islam, or Christianity. But, on the day the Ceylonese nation is no more, Therevada [sic] Buddhism—with all its pristine purity—is lost to the world. It is, therefore, the bounden duty of every Buddhist to prevent the disintegration of his nation.[12]

Buddhism seems to have won the struggle for symbolic status as the pre-eminent religion in Ceylon. Buddhist images and symbols adorn many public offices and buildings, and Buddhist ceremonies regularly mark public occasions. For more than a decade, the SLFP has repeatedly promised to "ensure its proper place to Buddhism, the religion of the majority."[13] The UNP noted in a 1963 restatement of party policy: "In practice, since Independence, Buddhism has gradually been recognised by the State as its official religion and Buddhist ceremonies are performed at the chief State functions."[14] Indicative of the symbolic triumph of Buddhism, the constitution adopted in 1972 contained the declaration: "The Republic of Sri Lanka shall give to Buddhism the foremost place and accordingly it shall be the duty

[12] "51st Session of Ceylon Buddhist Congress," *World Buddhism,* XVIII (Jan. 1970), 163.

[13] *Election Manifesto of the Sri Lanka Freedom Party, 1965* (Colombo: Sri Lanka Freedom Party, 1965), p. 6. Similarly, *Śrī Laṅkā Nidahas Pakshayē Māthivarana Prakāśanaya, 1960* (Colombo: Sri Lanka Freedom Party, 1960), p. 11.

[14] United National Party, *What We Believe* (Colombo: United National Party, 1963), p. 10.

of the State to protect and foster Buddhism while assuring to all religions [freedom of religious belief and practice]."[15]

BHIKKHUS IN POLITICS

Along with the recent changes in Ceylonese Buddhism has come a greater involvement by bhikkhus in worldly affairs, including politics. An argument appeared that historically the sangha (order of bhikkhus) had intervened in politics in times of trial or crisis to protect Buddhism and the Sinhalese nation. As one prominent bhikkhu asserted, "the claim of the Sangha today to be heard in relation to social, political and economic problems and to guide the people is no new demand, but a reassertion of a right universally exercised and equally widely acknowledged, up to the British occupation of the country."[16] The 1956 election saw bhikkhus emerge for the first time as a major, organized political force. Concern for the state of Buddhism, combined with grievances over a decline in their own status and functions, contributed to a rapid politicization of the sangha, particularly among the bhikkhus of the low country. Changes during the colonial period had undermined the ancient social and economic foundations of the sangha, and the growth of secular education had deprived bhikkhus of their traditional educational function. As few bhikkhus had learned English and the Sinhalese language seemed intimately connected with Buddhism and Buddhist village life, many bhikkhus became ardent supporters of demands for Sinhalese as the official language. At the beginning of the 1956 election campaign, an organization called the Eksath Bhikkhu Peramuna (United Front of Bhikkhus) plunged into the contest with great energy, attacking the

[15] *The Constitution of Sri Lanka (Ceylon)* (Colombo: Department of Government Printing, 1972), p. 4.
[16] Pahamune Sri Sumangala, in the foreword to D. C. Vijayavardhana, *The Revolt in the Temple* (Colombo: Sinha Publications, 1953), p. 19.

UNP and mobilizing support for the rival SLFP-led coalition in the name of Buddhism. The activities of the EBP are often credited with playing a major role in the defeat of the UNP.

The EBP continued its aggressive political activism after the 1956 election, bringing the organization into increasing conflict with the Government it had helped to install. EBP spokesmen conducted political rallies and demonstrations, engaged in political propaganda, and issued threats and orders to the Government. The EBP spearheaded efforts to prevent concessions to the Tamils on the language issue. The Government dropped provisions for the use of Tamil from the Official Language Act in 1956 because of strident opposition in which the EBP played a conspicuous role. In 1958, a large group of bhikkhus demonstrated at the residence of Prime Minister S. W. R. D. Bandaranaike in protest against an agreement on language and other communal issues the prime minister had reached with the Federal Party leaders. Bandaranaike publicly repudiated the agreement. EBP leader Mapitigama Buddharakkita loomed briefly as one of the most powerful figures in Ceylonese politics. A principal founder and joint secretary of the EBP, Buddharakkita was also an SLFP vice president and had been deeply immersed in partisan activities and struggles for power within the SLFP. He was believed to have sought to oust Bandaranaike from the leadership of the SLFP in early 1959. Later in the year, Bandaranaike was assassinated by a bhikkhu belonging to the EBP. Buddharakkita was convicted of conspiracy in the assassination and described as the chief architect of the plot. The arrest of Buddharakkita ended the kind of overt partisanship and unrestrained pressure tactics which had characterized EBP activities since 1956. The EBP had come to symbolize the cynical manipulation of religious and linguistic passions for personal gain. A Buddha Sasana Commission, appointed in response to Buddhist demands for a government commission to make recommendations for the reform of the sangha, issued its report shortly after Bandaranaike's death. Among the recommendations was a declaration that bhikkhus should remain out of partisan politics.[17]

After largely withdrawing from the campaign scene in 1960, bhikkhus returned to politics in 1965. No single organization emerged as the principal instrument of bhikkhu activity, however, and both major political camps received support from bhikkhus. The UNP appeared to enjoy the backing of a preponderance of the politically active bhikkhus, including individual bhikkhus who had energetically opposed the UNP nine years earlier, but bhikkhus also worked for the SLFP-Marxist United Front. Pro–United Front bhikkhus, many of whom were associated with Vidyalankara University and from the low-country Ramanya and Amarapura sects, formed an organization called the Sri Lanka Eksath Bhikkhu Mandalaya. Among the groups of bhikkhus working for the UNP were the Maha Sangha Peramuna and the Tri-Nikaya Maha Sangha Sabha. The pro-UNP bhikkhus concentrated their attack on Marxist inclusion in the United Front and charged that a United Front victory would endanger Buddhism. In his initial statement on becoming prime minister, UNP leader Dudley Senanayake declared that "my first duty is to thank the people and particularly the venerable members of the Maha Sangha for the help and support they have given me."[18] The Tri-Nikaya Maha Sangha Sabha claimed that its 12,000 members "were responsible for the creation of the present National Government."[19]

A United Front–sponsored demonstration against Tamil lan-

[17] *Buddha Sāsana Komishan Vārthāva,* Sessional Paper XVIII—1959 (Colombo: Government Press, 1959), p. 278.

[18] "Ceylon's New Government," *Ceylon Today,* XIV (March-April 1965), 3.

[19] "New Ceylon Prime Minister's Pledge," *World Buddhism,* XIII (April 1965), 13.

guage regulations, which were proposed by the Government in 1966, was led by bhikkhus, and one bhikkhu was killed in a clash between demonstrators and police. United Front charges that Prime Minister Senanayake was responsible for the bhikkhu's death were repeated through the 1970 election, and after the United Front victory in that year a monument was erected in memory of the bhikkhu at the spot on which he was slain. Although individual bhikkhus were found working for several parties, activities by bhikkhus again generally subsided in the 1970 campaign.

A section of the sangha seems to have become highly politicized over the last two decades, and some partisan activities by bhikkhus, particularly in election campaigns, have become a regular feature of politics. Political activism and a tendency to support the radical or reformist parties is most pronounced among the younger bhikkhus of all three sects or *nikāyas* into which the sangha is divided. However, the kind of unrestrained aggressiveness associated with EBP activities has not recurred. Furthermore, since 1956 the sangha has been sharply divided politically. Since the demise of the EBP, bhikkhus have not constituted an independent, united, or powerful political force, but have played a marginal role in both major political camps contesting for the support of Sinhalese Buddhists.

THE RELIGIOUS MINORITIES

The major conflict of religious communities on the national level has been between Buddhists and Christians, the majority of whom are Sinhalese. Although a few incidents of temple desecration occurred during the 1958 communal riots, ethnic and linguistic rather than religious rivalry has characterized relations between Buddhist Sinhalese and Hindu Tamils. While Tamil society contains a significant Christian minority, little conflict has appeared between Tamil Christians and Hindus, perhaps because both have felt themselves threatened by the demands of the Sinhalese Buddhist majority. The Federal Party, the self-professed defender of the predominantly Hindu Ceylon Tamils, has contained several prominent leaders who were Christians, including FP founder S. J. V. Chelvanayakam. Hinduism has appeared in politics only as it is involved in caste conflict within Ceylon Tamil society.

The Muslim population, as a relatively small and geographically dispersed minority internally divided by ancestry and sense of commonality into Moors and Malays, has not functioned as a cohesive group in national politics. At the constituency level, the major political parties regularly direct specific appeals to Muslim voters where they constitute a significant proportion of the population. In Colombo and other areas containing Muslim concentrations, both the UNP and the SLFP have regularly nominated Muslim candidates for local and national office. In 1959, a Muslim UNP member was chosen as mayor of Colombo for the first time. Irrespective of the party in power, one Muslim is perennially included within the cabinet. The All-Ceylon Muslim League, although not functioning as a political party, has served since before independence as a spokesman for Muslim interests in public affairs. The league has been led by wealthy Muslim merchants and professionals, largely from Colombo, most of whom have been associated with the UNP. The Islamic Socialist Front was formed after 1965 by a Muslim SLFP leader to mobilize Muslim political support for the SLFP.

Roman Catholics constitute 87 per cent of Ceylonese Christians. The principal concentration of Catholics, mostly members of the Karāva caste traditionally involved in fishing, is found on the island's west coast from Colombo north to Negombo. At least until 1965, the Catholic church was openly hostile to the Marxist parties, cool to the SLFP, and generally considered to be pro-UNP. Prior to the 1952 election, the archbishop of Colombo issued a pastoral letter warning Catholics against voting for candidates holding political views banned by the church or hostile to the church. The letter stirred wide controversy and served to identify the church with the UNP, as the missive appeared to be aimed at the UNP's opponents. In an environment of mounting Buddhist militancy after 1952, the Catholic hierarchy became cautious of open partisan involvement, but reports persisted that the influence of the Catholic clergy was used in the parish to back UNP candidates. Among Buddhist militants, severe resentment developed against a Catholic lay organization, Catholic Action, which was claimed to operate within government offices, private business firms, and the armed forces to secure preferential recruitment and promotion for Catholics. In 1960–1961, the Catholic hierarchy and community clashed bitterly with the SLFP Government over the state takeover of private schools, the majority of which had been operated by the Catholic church. Catholics attempted to obstruct the schools takeover by staging demonstrations and occupying the school buildings. In early 1962, a planned coup d'etat involving a handful of military and police officers, most of whom were Catholics, increased public and government hostility toward the Catholics and other Christians and led to a reshuffling of senior military officers to end the predominance of Christians at the higher ranks.

Voters in seven parliamentary constituencies north of Colombo are predominantly Catholic. The UNP captured six of these seats in both 1960 elections and all seven in 1965. After 1965, however, Catholic support of the UNP appears to have eroded. Four of the seven predominantly Catholic seats were won by the SLFP in 1970. Disillusionment with the UNP apparently followed the UNP-dominated National Government's substitution of Poya days for Sundays as the weekly holiday and failure to alter the state control of schools. Catholics also reportedly resented the absence of a Catholic in the cabinet from 1965 to 1968. The shift away from the UNP probably also reflected the Catholic population's response to the same nonreligious issues, particularly unemployment and rising living costs, which produced the 1970 United Front landslide.

The Role of Caste in Politics

While ethnic and religious identities have been sources of major and unambiguous political claims and controversies, the role of caste in politics has been muted. With the exception of recent agitation by Tamil "untouchables," caste has generated no major national political issues. Seldom does any direct reference to Sinhalese caste appear in the public pronouncements of any political party. Yet, informal conversations on politics tend to focus on caste more than on any other single factor except political parties. Caste identification indeed remains strong, despite the disclaimers of polite society, and caste is a factor of major significance in politics. Seldom, however, is it articulated in terms of explicit caste issues or demands. The occupational and ritual functions of caste have almost vanished, and the social disabilities based on caste are generally slight, particularly in Sinhalese society, but the ethos of caste remains as a sense of solidarity and mutual obligation.

Intracaste solidarity and intercaste rivalry are most prominent in election behavior, although caste considerations may also influence appointments to government posts and the dispensing of government benefits such as the allotment of land in government-sponsored colonization schemes. Suspicion and mistrust of those not of one's own caste encourages caste solidarity in voting, and the typical voter is presumed to support a candidate of his own caste if one is available. In contrast with India, where an intricate and atomized caste pattern and extremely large constituencies generally prevent a single caste from constituting an absolute majority in a parliamentary constituency, the considerably less intricate caste structure and much smaller constituencies of Ceylon make it likely that many constituencies, particularly in the Sinhalese areas, contain a majority of one caste, and in most constituencies a single caste is predominant. All major parties commonly nominate candidates of the dominant caste in the constituency. Caste divisions, unlike ethnic divisions, do not generally coincide with lines of partisan cleavage.

CASTE AND POLITICS IN SINHALESE SOCIETY

The caste system among the Sinhalese has developed with markedly different characteristics from those typically encountered in Hindu societies. Caste distinctions and disabilities are much less marked, and the status hierarchy is not as steep as among Hindus in Ceylon or India.[20] As the Sinhalese caste system has evolved in a Buddhist society, no caste possesses a monopoly of priestly functions, and caste separateness is based on traditional social practice rather than on religious sanction. Although castes of low status suffer from some disadvantages and discrimination, there is no true untouchability in the Sinhalese caste system. Because of the much less rigid character of caste relationships, the influences of universalistic attitudes and alternative identifications have probably been able to gain greater headway and further erode the effective significance of caste in many social and political circumstances.

Several distinctive features of the Sinhalese caste system influence the political role of caste. The number of castes is relatively small. The highest in status, the Goyigama, is also the most numerous and includes about half of the entire Sinhalese population.[21] The Karāva, Salāgama, and Durāva castes are also con-

[20] The following description of the Sinhalese caste system has drawn heavily from Bryce Ryan, *Caste in Modern Ceylon* (New Brunswick, N.J.: Rutgers University Press, 1953).

[21] There has been no caste census in modern times and never an island-

sidered to possess high status, immediately below the Goyigama in the ritual hierarchy. These three castes and the Goyigama caste together probably include some two-thirds or more of the Sinhalese, and the hierarchical differences among them are slight. Consequently, the pattern of numerous members of lower castes attacking the prerogatives of a small high-caste elite has never appeared. The remaining third or less of the Sinhalese population is distributed among about twenty separate castes of lower status, including the Vahumpura, Batgam (also called Padu), Hēna, Hunu, Beravā, and Hinnā.

Members of the Goyigama caste are found throughout the Sinhalese parts of the island, and except for a narrow belt along the west and south coasts there are few areas in which the Goyigama is not either a majority or the single most numerous caste. Hence, in most areas away from the coast, numerical predominance, reinforced in some localities by economic strength or vestiges of deferential behavior, leaves the Goyigama caste almost unchallenged politically. Here, each competing political party normally nominates a Goyigama candidate and caste tensions or interests seldom erupt in election contests. Goyigama political dominance is starkly illustrated by the caste composition of recent parliaments.[22] Nearly three-quarters of the Sinhalese M.P.'s returned in the last two elections were Goyigama. About half of all non-Goyigama Sinhalese M.P.'s were elected from constituencies along the west and south coasts in 1970. Elsewhere in the Sinhalese areas, Goyigama candidates captured seven out of every eight constituencies.

---

wide caste census, so that precise data on the size and distribution of castes is unobtainable.

[22] Data on the caste of the M.P.'s elected in 1965 and 1970 were obtained by the author from a number of informed persons associated with parliament or political parties at the time and is likely to be accurate, although no authoritative tabulation of the caste of M.P.'s exists.

The narrow coastal belt extending roughly from Chilaw on the west coast to Tangalla in the South is heavily non-Goyigama, populated principally by the Karāva, Salāgama, and Durāva castes. In southeastern seaboard constituencies, twelve candidates of the Karāva caste, two of the Salāgama caste, and two of the Durāva caste were victorious in the 1970 election. These coastal castes have tended to be articulate and aggressive and to resent Goyigama presumptions of superiority. It is among the non-Goyigama high castes that the most important political role is attributed to caste and on the coast that the most conspicuous eruptions of caste rivalry appear. The Karāva and Salāgama castes have been engaged in rivalry with the Goyigama caste and with each other for decades, and caste consciousness and solidarity in politics is probably at its strongest among these castes, especially in the South.

Lack of territorial concentration has been a serious obstacle to the electoral strength of the lower castes, already handicapped by low social esteem and frequently unfavorable economic circumstances. Although collectively the lower castes contain perhaps one-third of the Sinhalese population, only a few pockets such as the Rumbakkana constituency in Sabaragamuwa Province and areas around Kurunegala in the North-Western Province are clearly identifiable as concentrations of one of these castes. Prior to 1959, the election of a lower-caste candidate to parliament was rare. A substantial reduction in the size of constituencies accompanied a new delimitation in 1959. In the smaller constituencies local concentrations of lower-caste voters assumed greater electoral significance and in a few cases were numerically predominant. About ten parliamentary seats have been won by lower-caste candidates in recent elections, principally by members of the Vahumpura and Batgam castes. The Vahumpura caste is regarded as among the largest, possibly the largest, Sinhalese caste excluding the Goyigama, with a membership claimed to exceed one million. The caste's members are widely scattered through the low country and the Kandyan interior. The Batgam caste, although fairly numerous in the Kandyan provinces, is of very low traditional status and economically depressed. In 1958, a member of the Batgam caste became the first Sinhalese to be named an appointed M.P.; subsequently the practice of naming one appointed M.P. from one of the Sinhalese lower castes became established. The appointments presumably were intended to attract to the governing party support from the sizable but widely scattered castes.

While few parliamentary constituencies can be won by appeal to the lower castes, frivolous candidates may be encouraged to draw lower-caste votes away from an opposing party. Such calculations were thought to have figured in the apparent massive debacle of the MEP in 1965. The MEP offered a total of sixty-one candidates, of whom only one was elected and fifty-five lost their deposits for failing to poll at least one-eighth of the vote in the constituency. The MEP entered the election informally allied with the UNP, and where MEP candidates had a serious chance they were not opposed by the UNP. However, the majority of MEP candidates contested constituencies in which the UNP was pitted against a candidate of the United Front. A large number of the MEP candidates were from lower castes, and it is thought that they were intended to attract low-caste votes on the basis of caste solidarity which were otherwise likely to go to one of the United Front parties on the basis of social and economic issues, thus enhancing the prospects of a UNP victory in the constituency.

Broad trends in voting by non-Goyigama castes are often claimed, but are elusive. It is widely believed that the non-Goyigama voters in the low country have generally been anti-UNP, as the UNP was considered to be Goyigama dominated. In the Southwest, non-Goyigama votes frequently went to the Marxists, the first organized opponents of the UNP, and much of the electoral strength of the Marxist parties continues to be concentrated in the non-Goyigama coastal constituencies south of Colombo and along the south coast. S. W. R. D. Bandaranaike was thought to have attracted a considerable proportion of the non-Goyigama vote, both low-country and Kandyan, to the SLFP in the 1950's. Although himself of an aristocratic Goyigama family, Bandaranaike seemed more solicitous of the minority castes and receptive to their interests. After 1960, SLFP support among the non-Goyigama castes seemed to decline. Asoka Karunaratne's split with the SLFP in 1963 is thought to have resulted in the erosion of SLFP support among the low-status and disadvantaged castes of the interior. Karunaratne, a member of the Batgam caste, resigned as a parliamentary secretary with an angry blast at the SLFP Government for caste bias and subsequently fought the 1965 election allied with the UNP. Following the election, Karunaratne was named a cabinet minister and eventually joined the UNP. Sweeping UNP gains and SLFP losses in the Central Province in 1965 may in part have reflected shifts in the votes of the Batgam and other depressed castes which are relatively numerous in the province. In the United Front landslide five years later, however, the SLFP won heavily in the Central Province, and in adjacent Sabaragamuwa Province Karunaratne was defeated by an SLFP candidate also belonging to a lower caste.

While caste is one of the most compelling considerations for any political party in selecting a candidate for a particular constituency, other intervening factors can neutralize or weaken the influence of caste solidarity. The conservative Goyigama landowner may vote for a non-Goyigama UNP candidate in preference to a Goyigama Marxist. Examples can be cited of M.P.'s representing constituencies in which their own caste is numerically insignificant. This has been particularly evident in certain Kandyan constituencies represented by members of the low-country Karāva or Salāgama castes who had migrated to the interior as traders or public servants. The frequent ambiguity of the impact of caste in election contests is illustrated by a 1966 by-election. The constituency was overwhelmingly Goyigama and had been an LSSP stronghold for a decade. When the seat fell vacant, Colvin R. de Silva, a nationally prominent LSSP leader, was given his party's nomination. Dr. de Silva, a member of the Salāgama caste, was pitted against a Goyigama candidate of the UNP. Dr. de Silva captured the seat, but the LSSP's margin was cut from 5,200 votes in 1965 to less than 350. The fall in the LSSP vote could be interpreted as reflecting the unwillingness of Goyigama voters to support a non-Goyigama candidate. Conversely, the fact that Dr. de Silva did win the election although belonging to a caste with very few members in the constituency and not a local resident suggests that caste and parochial factors may be less decisive than party loyalty and secular issues. In 1970, the constituency returned Dr. de Silva with a restored 5,200-vote majority.

Every political party seriously concerned with elective office must seek a share of the Goyigama vote, as the size and distribution of the caste inevitably leads to Goyigama control of most constituencies. No significant party has emerged as a caste party and no major party has failed to collect some support from a relatively wide range of castes. It is indicative of the interaction of castes and parties that victorious Sinhalese candidates of the SLFP in 1970, although three-quarters Goyigama, included Karāva, Salāgama, Vahumpura, and Batgam members. Five Sinhalese castes were represented in the LSSP parliamentary contingent and three in that of the UNP. All prime ministers and most of the more powerful cabinet ministers have been Goyigama. While members of other castes are found within the top circles of party leaders, it is generally assumed that Goyigama status is an unspoken prerequisite for the premiership. C. P. de Silva, a member of the Salāgama caste, became president of the SLFP in early 1960 and headed the party in the March election that year. Many politicians believe that the SLFP lost votes because it was not led by a Goyigama, and this is said to have been a major factor which led de Silva to relinquish party leadership prior to the July 1960 election. While the Karāva and Salāgama castes are invariably represented in cabinets, occasionally holding important portfolios, members of the lower castes holding cabinet posts have been few and their ministries have not been the large and powerful ones.

A new and startling dimension to the interaction of caste and politics could be glimpsed in the 1971 insurrection of rural Sinhalese youths. Although across the island no clear caste pattern emerged, in certain districts the insurgency found strong support among youths belonging to socially and economically disadvantaged lower castes. In these districts, at least, it seemed that frustration with the circumstances of the lower castes reinforced the frustrations of thwarted aspirations felt by many educated village youths, resulting in a rejection of the legitimate political process based on elections and representative institutions and a resort to armed violence.

CASTE AND POLITICS IN CEYLON TAMIL SOCIETY

Among the predominantly Hindu Ceylon Tamils, caste distinctions are more rigorous and hierarchical than among the largely Buddhist Sinhalese. Although Brahmins have never been numerous nor held economic or political power, the Vellala, the traditional landowning and cultivating caste, has dominated public life in the North. The seventeen Ceylon Tamil M.P.'s elected in 1965 included thirteen Vallalas. The Karayar caste, which is particularly strong in the Point Pedro constituency and a few other coastal constituencies, and the related Mukkuvar caste of the east coast have also secured representation in parliament in recent elections.

A major segment of Tamil society, generally estimated at one-fourth of the entire community, belongs to "untouchable" castes, euphemistically called the "depressed classes" or "minority Tamils." Social disabilities and economic disadvantages have continued to fetter the untouchables to the present day. In the mid-1960's smoldering resentment flared into vigorous and aggressive protest among the untouchable castes of the North, and a number of organizations claiming to speak for the untouchables sprang up. The All-Ceylon Minority Tamils' Mahasabha had existed for a number of years to promote the interests of a least a section of the untouchables. Among other organizations to appear were an All-Ceylon Hindu Congress and an All-Ceylon Underprivileged Tamil Uplift Movement. A few "minority Tamils" have sought to escape the rigors of the Hindu caste system by conversion to Buddhism, leading to the formation of an All-Ceylon Tamil Buddhist Association. The untouchable castes are themselves stratified and separated by caste distinctions, and often organizations working for the removal of caste disabilities are in practice virtually limited to a single untouchable caste.

A Prevention of Social Disabilities Act, passed in 1957, provided for fine or imprisonment of "any person who imposes any social disability on any other person by reason of such other person's caste."[23] The first prosecution under the act, however, did not occur until 1967, a decade after its passage. The untouchable caste organizations and the political parties supporting them sought to obtain admission to public eating places, the services of barbers, and access to wells. The greatest efforts and most intense

[23] Prevention of Social Disabilities Act, No. 21 of 1957, sec. 2.

controversy, however, focused on demands for entry into Hindu temples. One 1967 report claimed that of 1,309 Hindu temples in the North, only 226 were open to the "minority Tamils."[24] Tamil society apparently became deeply divided between those demanding an end to caste disabilities and those upholding the age-old practices of caste. The most dramatic confrontation occurred in 1968, when more than five hundred untouchables attempted through a satyagraha campaign to gain entry into the ancient Maviddapuram Kandasamy temple, a stronghold of saivite orthodoxy. Entry was refused by the temple authorities and physically barred by a "volunteer force" of caste Hindus. After a week of tension punctuated by clashes between the "volunteer force" and the satyagrahis, the campaign was broken off without achieving its objective.

In an attempt to bolster the unity of the Tamil-speaking people, the Federal Party has denounced the existence of untouchability and sought to reduce caste disabilities through campaigns to secure the right of temple entry and to open eating places and barber shops to the untouchable castes. The Federalists also elected to the Senate a member of the "minority Tamils" in 1957. The FP president in 1966 declared it to be "imperative and urgent for us to remove the curse of untouchability and other caste humiliations and injustices."[25] Some observers believe that the Federal Party has lost support among the conservative dominant castes by speaking out on the side of the untouchables, but has failed to win support among the low castes because of its own high-caste leadership and alleged lack of militancy in attacking caste disabilities. One "minority Tamil" organization, the All-Ceylon Underprivileged Tamil Uplift Movement, claimed

[24] *Ceylon Observer,* Sept. 26, 1967, p. 11.

[25] E. M. V. Naganathan, *Ilankai Tamil Arasu Kadchi 10th National Convention, Kalmunai: Presidential Address* (Colombo: Ilankai Tamil Arasu Kadchi, 1966), p. 6.

in a petition to the minister of education that the disadvantaged castes were neglected "because our representatives in Parliament, all of whom belong to the so-called high castes, have never brought our problems to the attention of the Government."[26] FP spokesmen have charged that the grievances of the untouchables were being exploited by Sinhalese politicians to divide and weaken the Tamils.

During 1967 the "left" Communists commenced vigorously and conspicuously to champion the mounting caste protest, and other parties began to involve themselves in the agitation. The following year, the secretaries of the three United Front parties paid a joint visit to Jaffna to investigate the caste situation. The eruption of caste protest, after generations of untouchable submissiveness, jolted the conservative Tamil society of the North and seemed certain to alter the established patterns of politics in Jaffna. By 1970, however, the caste protest had abated, at least temporarily, and its political impact was not apparent in the election results. After the election, a leader of the "minority Tamils" was named an appointed M.P. by the United Front Government, which had been brought to power by the Sinhalese South. Whether political activism by the Tamil untouchables would create an effective new political force in the North, perhaps in association with predominantly Sinhalese political parties, remained unclear.

[26] *Times of Ceylon,* Sept. 8, 1967, p. 3.

6. Challenges to the Political Order

The Ceylonese political system has exhibited an impressive capacity to adapt to the transformations of the past quarter of a century and to retain the effective forms and processes of parliamentary democracy. Yet, agonizing challenges remain. The central problem of political development in Ceylon stems from the swift rise in popular aspirations and expectations, combined with severely limited resources for their fulfillment. The rapid growth of social mobilization, political participation, and demands threatens to outrun the capacity of the political system to absorb the changes and satisfy the demands. A failure to satisfy rising aspirations creates a danger of mounting popular frustration and alienation, which could lead to instability and disorder. The trials of the political system can be observed most vividly in the eruptions of coercive protest and political violence and in the struggles to improve economic conditions and opportunities through government action. The future course of politics in Ceylon may well be determined by the response of the political system to these two often interrelated challenges.

Coercive Protest and Political Violence

It is a significant commentary on the character of the Ceylonese political system that a Government has never been forced from power by violence or coercion, whereas Governments have repeatedly been displaced by the operation of the constitutional elective process. Nonetheless, extraparliamentary pressures, civil disorder, and violence do play a role in the politics of the island. "Direct-action" techniques assume a wide variety of forms ranging from attempts to seize power by force to orderly demonstrations of protest. A basic distinction can be made between actions intended to displace those in power by assassination, coup d'etat, or insurrection and actions intended to force authorities into some course they would not otherwise take but without seeking to drive them from office or to overturn the constitutional order. Serious disorders may occur which are not explicitly directed against the Government or the holders of political office, but nonetheless quickly involve the Government when the authorities attempt to restore order. Thus, the brutal communal riots of 1958, although not directed against the Government, were eventually suppressed by police and military force.

COERCIVE PROTEST AND THE POLITICAL PROCESS

Protest rallies and demonstrations are a part of the accepted and customary behavior of opposition groups in Ceylon. Often, their aim is to dramatize disagreement with an action or policy of the Government or to mobilize public sentiment against the party in power. In such cases, they reflect the vitality of party competition. All parties seek to organize huge rallies and demonstrations, which tend to be viewed as symbolic representations of the party's strength and wide popular support and, hence, as lending legitimacy to the party's claims. At times, however, the objective of demonstrations and other "direct-action" techniques is to coerce the Government by threatening or causing civil disorder or the disruption of governmental activities. Even if avowedly peaceful, rallies and demonstrations often carry an implicit threat of disorder.

Political strikes, hartals, and satyagraha campaigns are coercive in intent, but are usually non-violent and accepted forms of dissent. Political strikes generally last one day and are viewed as symbolic acts of protest rather than as serious efforts to undermine the Government. The hartal, like the political strike, involves the disruption of economic activities as a sign of political dissent, but in addition to a work stoppage it includes the closing of shops and schools and the suspension of all normal activities. Black flags are usually displayed as a symbol of protest and mourning. The satyagraha is the Gandhian technique of nonviolent resistance. Participants stand or sit in a roadway, building entrance, or other public place as a demonstration of protest, often disrupting activities by blocking movement on a street or access to a building.

In 1953, a major hartal was called by the Marxist parties and the Federal Party to protest a cabinet decision to abolish a subsidy on rice which produced a sharp rise in the price of rice to consumers. In addition to closing businesses and public offices and disrupting transportation and communication, violent disorders spread through the southwestern corner of the island, resulting in at least ten deaths and extensive property damage. Although disorders continued for several days, the hartal had been planned for only a single day and was officially terminated by the sponsoring parties after the first day. The resignation from office of Prime Minister Dudley Senanayake two months later is generally attributed to the hartal. A "left" Communist labor publication later said of the episode:

The Hartal was a tremendous success. Transport was completely paralysed. Workers stayed away from work. Shops remained closed. Road blocks had been laid across most roads and even the Police could not move about. In the Western and Southern Provinces and particularly in the City of Colombo life practically came to a stop. Huge crowds had collected all over and Govt. could not enforce law and order. Before 12 noon the riot act had been read in several places. . . . But in some places the crowds refused to disperse and the Police were forced to shoot—killing and wounding several. The total number of those killed ultimately rose to 12 Martyrs to Dudley Senanayake's UNP Police bullets.[1]

Subsequent resorts to coercive protest techniques have been considerably smaller in scope and impact. Several hartals were staged by the FP between 1956 and 1964 in protest against the adoption of Sinhalese as the sole official language. Amid the language and communal tensions after 1956, satyagraha was employed by both Sinhalese and Tamil militants. A political strike was called by the LSSP in 1959 to protest an amendment strengthening the Public Security Ordinance. In 1962, the LSSP, CP, and MEP joined in sponsoring a one-day general strike intended to force withdrawal from the Colombo harbor of military personnel who were performing essential harbor operations during a prolonged dock workers' strike. The SLFP, LSSP, and CP called political strikes in 1964 to protest the defeat in parliament of the SLFP-LSSP Government and in 1966 as a demonstration against proposed official-language regulations. The latter demonstration resulted in disorders in Colombo which claimed one life.

Demonstrations, rallies, and political strikes are largely a phenomenon of the cities, where potential participants are massed and a maximum political impact can be achieved. The political strength of urban populations outside the electoral process was suggested in the complaint of one rural representative:

Why do you spend all the money in the towns? Because the people in the towns are vociferous, they can get together and shout and their demands are met. But the poor peasant and the poor villager, who always supported this Government, cannot get together. They

[1] *The History of 25 Years of Proud Service to the Working Class by the Ceylon Trade Union Federation* (Colombo: Ceylon Trade Union Federation, 1965), p. 17. Government sources claimed a death toll of only ten in the hartal.

cannot shout. They cannot strike. . . . [Their] demands go unheeded.[2]

Coercive techniques are sometimes the weapons of a minority, frustrated and helpless before the parliamentary strength of a determined or unsympathetic majority. Shortly after passage of the Official Language Act in 1956, the FP resolved to undertake "direct action by non-violent means" to secure its language and other objectives.[3] After repeated threats, the party launched a satyagraha and civil disobedience movement throughout the Tamil-speaking areas of the North and East in early 1961. The campaign was intended to force concessions from the SLFP Government by disrupting and bringing to a standstill the normal functioning of public agencies in the Tamil areas. Satyagrahis sat on the pavement blocking entrance to government offices, and the party appealed to Tamil public servants to remain away from work. After the campaign had dragged on for two months, the Federalists decided as an act of civil disobedience to defy the postal laws by establishing their own post office and issuing their own stamps. The Government responded by declaring an emergency, arresting the FP leaders, and proscribing the party. The campaign produced extensive disruption of administration in the Northern and Eastern Provinces for two months but failed to extract any concession from the Government.

Over the years, government leaders seem to have adopted increasingly stern responses to threats of disorder. Dudley Senanayake resigned as prime minister shortly after he had been forced to declare an emergency and order police action which produced a number of deaths in 1953. In 1966, however, after returning to the premiership, he responded to disorders growing out of a

[2] Ceylon, House of Representatives, *Parliamentary Debates* (*Hansard*), vol. 30, col. 1581 (Nov. 28, 1957).

[3] *Ceylon Faces Crisis* (Colombo: Federal Party, 1957), p. 32.

demonstration on the language issue by declaring: "This Government is responsible for the safety of the subjects, for the preservation of law and order. . . . And if it is necessary to shoot to preserve law and order we will shoot."[4] Prime Minister S. W. R. D. Bandaranaike delayed for four terror-filled days after the outbreak of the 1958 communal riots before he declared an emergency and sanctioned military suppression of the riots. His widow, on assuming the premiership, adamantly refused to make concessions when threatened with disruption of government activities or disorder during the 1960–1961 schools takeover, the Federalist satyagraha of 1961, and a series of strikes in 1962–1963. At the outbreak of the 1971 insurgency, she proclaimed: "No Government worth its name can succumb to criminal force. No Government can bow down to thuggery and intimidation."[5]

Resort to declarations of emergency has tended to mount until periods of "emergency" have become as common as "normal" periods. During the five years after the declaration of an emergency in April 1958, emergency rule spanned a total of thirty-six months. Half of the fourteen-year period 1958–1972 was spent under states of emergency. The 1970 United Front election manifesto denounced the UNP-led National Government for ruling under emergency powers for 1,086 of its 1,825 days in office.[6] But less than a year later, in March 1971, the United Front Government imposed an emergency in the face of growing evidence of a planned insurrection. The Public Security Ordinance gives the authorities extensive powers during a state of emer-

[4] Ceylon, House of Representatives, *Parliamentary Debates (Hansard)*, vol. 64, col. 165 (Jan. 8, 1966).

[5] "A Broadcast Message to the Nation by the Hon. Prime Minister" (mimeographed; Department of Information press release, April 9, 1971), p. 2.

[6] *Joint Election Menifesto* [sic] *of the S.L.F.P.-L.S.S.P.-C.P. United Front, 1970* (leaflet; Colombo, n.d.), p. 1.

gency, and in the serious crises of the 1958 communal riots or the 1971 insurrection sweeping powers were assumed and exercised with vigor. Between these severe trials, however, the frequent states of emergency had only limited practical significance. The FP leaders were held under house arrest for a year following the 1961 satyagraha. The pro–United Front newspaper *Jana Dina* was banned for more than five months in 1967 for publishing an article allegedly defaming the prime minister. Nonetheless, political activity by opposition parties and individuals generally proceeds without evident inhibition and the state of emergency often produces slight manifestation of crisis or extraordinary government actions.

ASSASSINATION AND COUP D'ETAT

The only assassination of a Ceylonese political leader to occur in modern history was the murder of Prime Minister S. W. R. D. Bandaranaike in 1959. Bandaranaike's death followed a period of great turbulence and rising political and communal passions. The Eksath Bhikkhu Peramuna leader Mapitigama Buddharakkita, who was convicted of plotting the assassination, had been involved in an unsuccessful attempt to remove Bandaranaike from leadership of the SLFP a few months earlier.[7] He was also connected with a shipping venture which had failed to obtain an expected government contract. Although rumors of complicity by other political figures circulated for a time, it appears that the plot was limited to a small group surrounding Buddharakkita and was motivated by personal ambitions and grievances. A commission of judges investigating the assassination concluded that no organization had been involved in the plot.[8]

[7] On the political activities of the EBP and Buddharakkita, see Chapter 5.

[8] *Report to His Excellency the Governor-General by the Commission Appointed in Terms of the Commissions of Inquiry Act to Inquire into*

Twice during the 1960's plots to seize power by coup d'etat were charged. Neither was carried to execution and in both cases the alleged conspirators were eventually released. In January 1962, a dramatic announcement was made that a planned coup d'etat had been discovered and foiled at the last moment. According to an official statement, a group of military and police officers and former officers planned to arrest cabinet ministers, the commanders of the armed forces, and certain other public officials and political leaders and to establish an emergency regime, presumably under military control, for which they hoped to secure the sanction of the governor-general.[9] Following by a few years a successful military coup in Pakistan, the plot was formulated during a series of major strikes and about a year after the religious and communal crises created by the FP-sponsored satyagraha in the North and the government takeover of Christian and other private schools. The belief that political leadership dependent on popular support through elections was incapable of maintaining stability and facing difficult decisions reportedly contributed to the plan. Originally, twenty-four defendants were named; the number was eventually reduced to sixteen. After long legal battles, the special legislation under which they were tried was invalidated on appeal to the Privy Council and all were released. Most of the suspects were Roman Catholics, and several were from prominent and wealthy Colombo families, leading to allegations that they were motivated by hostility toward the egalitarian and pro-Buddhist positions of the SLFP Government and

---

and Report on Certain Matters Connected with the Assassination of the Late Prime Minister Solomon West Ridgeway Dias Bandaranaike, Sessional Paper III—1965 (Colombo: Government Press, 1965), p. 11.

[9] *Coup d'Etat: Statement Read on Behalf of the Government by Felix R. Dias Bandaranaike, Parliamentary Secretary for Defence and External Affairs, in the House of Representatives on 13.2.62* (Colombo: Government Press, 1962).

wished to re-establish the advantages of the privileged classes and the Christians. The plot, however, appeared to lack any semblance of broad support or political backing.

Four years later, allegations of a second plot to seize power by coup d'etat were made. In this case, the alleged plot was claimed to be directed at a conservative UNP-dominated Government, with the plotters described as SLFP sympathizers. In 1970, all twelve defendants were acquitted by the Supreme Court. Among those arrested was the recently resigned army commander, Major-General Richard Udugama. He had been appointed to command of the army in the aftermath of the 1962 coup plot, in what was interpreted as a move to replace Christians with Buddhists in military command posts and to assure the loyalty of the armed forces to the SLFP Government. Following the 1965 change in Government, the army commander and the inspector-general of police both resigned when security arrangements for the opposition-sponsored political strike and demonstration in January 1966 were held to have been inadequate.[10] Government supporters suspected that the disturbances had been mishandled intentionally to discredit the Government. Shortly thereafter, the alleged coup plan was reported and Udugama was detained along with a handful of junior officers and enlisted men. Soon after his release, Udugama was elected to parliament as an SLFP candidate in the 1970 general election.

Rumors of other coup plots have occasionally circulated, but have proved to be without foundation. In view of the high level

---

[10] A committee of senior public servants investigating arrangements for the anticipated disturbances concluded that army and police officials had been lax in their preparations. *Report of the Special Committee Appointed to Inquire into and Report on the Police Arrangements on the 8th January, 1966, in Connection with the Motion in the House of Representatives on the Regulations under the Tamil Language (Special Provisions) Act,* Sessional Paper V—1966 (Colombo: Government Press, 1966).

of popular political consciousness prevailing in Ceylon, it seems extremely unlikely that a military coup d'etat could be successful unless in addition to military officers it had relatively strong political backing or some base of popular support. While the nature, seriousness, and even existence of the alleged coup d'etat plots of the 1960's remain subject to controversy, little evidence of sympathy for a military takeover has appeared among politicians or the public in Ceylon.

THE 1971 INSURRECTION

The insurrection which erupted in April 1971 constituted the most dramatic bid to seize power by force and the most agonizing test of the political order in modern times. Insurgents armed primarily with shotguns and homemade hand bombs launched simultaneous nighttime attacks on seventy-four police stations across the island and reportedly planned to kidnap or assassinate the prime minister. The earlier discovery of caches of weapons and explosives and a raid on the American embassy had alerted the authorities, who had declared an emergency a few weeks previously. The premature attack on one police station a day before the general uprising further signaled the insurgents' intentions. After a few anxious weeks, the armed forces were able to assume the initiative and drive the rebels into a few jungle areas. The last insurgent bands were not destroyed or scattered for nearly three months. About 14,000 suspected insurgents surrendered or were captured. The death toll was officially estimated in July at 1,200, of whom 60 were military and police personnel.[11] The number of fatalities was widely believed to be much higher, however, and unofficial but informed estimates were seldom below 6,000. All reports agreed that an overwhelming

[11] "The Statement on Insurgency Made in Parliament on 20.7.71 by the Honourable Prime Minister" (mimeographed; Department of Information press release, n.d.), p. 5.

proportion of the casualties were among insurgents or suspected insurgents. In summarizing the economic toll of the uprising, Finance Minister N. M. Perera noted:

Not only the Governmental machine, but the whole economy came to a grinding halt. Departments ceased to function; industrial establishments closed down; factories were damaged; paddy crops remained unreaped. . . . Police Stations, Co-operative Stores and Post Offices were demolished and ransacked. Motor vehicles, including buses and lorries, were destroyed and many houses were gutted. This is the dreary path of counter-revolution that ravaged the country for 3 to 4 months.[12]

The uprising was planned and executed by a semiclandestine organization called the Janatha Vimukthi Peramuna (People's Liberation Front). Labeled a "Che Guevarist" movement by the press, the JVP professed to be Marxist and seems to have been inspired by Guevarist and Maoist ideas on the role of violent revolution and reliance on a rural base, but its ideological perspective did not appear to be carefully formulated or articulated. The organization apparently had existed since about 1964 but made its first public appearance during the 1970 election campaign when JVP spokesmen campaigned for the United Front.[13] In contrast with the "Naxalite" movement in India, which engaged in a protracted series of scattered terrorist attacks on police and landlords, the Ceylonese insurgents apparently hoped to overturn the political order by a single swift blow—a strategy of

[12] *Budget Speech, 1971–72, by the Hon. Dr. N. M. Perera, M. P., Minister of Finance* (Colombo: Department of Government Printing, 1971), p. 9.

[13] Some reports claimed that the JVP contained two factions, one of which worked for the United Front while the other ignored the contest as a meaningless exercise between indistinguishable groups of nonrevolutionary politicians. The latter faction is said to have led the insurrection against the United Front Government less than a year later.

"one-night revolution." Their tactics evidently were heavily dependent on surprise and they did not appear to possess contingency plans or alternative tactics for the loss of surprise or the failure of their initial assault. Some rural police stations were overrun, two small urban areas were held for a time, and several major roads were cut, including the main highway linking Colombo with Kandy. No major town or city was captured, and no significant victory was scored over government forces. Although reports of the rebels' relations with villagers conflict, the insurrectionary movement evidently received little assistance or encouragement from outside its own ranks. The armed forces, police, and civil bureaucracy all stood firmly behind the Government. The major labor organizations condemned the uprising and aided in the operations against it.

Rumors of foreign instigation or assistance were rampant, but were firmly denied by official spokesmen. Prime Minister Sirimavo Bandaranaike contended:

The designing and ambitious leaders of this movement had led their supporters to believe that arms, supplies and moral support would be forthcoming from certain foreign powers, and their supporters seem to have believed this. I am satisfied that these terrorist leaders made these false claims to rally support to their cause and there seems to have been no basis for any such claim.[14]

A short time after the insurgency broke out, however, the North Korean embassy was closed and its staff ordered from the country. Ceylon had established diplomatic relations with North Korea only after the United Front had come to power less than a year earlier. The North Koreans, Mrs. Bandaranaike related, were informed that "the effect of certain activities carried on by

[14] "Text of Broadcast to the Nation by the Hon. Sirimavo Bandaranaike, Prime Minister, on April 24, 1971" (mimeographed; Department of Information press release, April 24, 1971), p. 3.

them was giving strength and support to these terrorists." As they failed to comply with her request that these activities cease, the embassy was closed and they were ordered to depart.[15] The North Koreans' objectionable activities were not specified, but they had been energetically engaged in disseminating propaganda extolling the virtues of violent revolution and outlining revolutionary techniques. Other rumors centered on a possible Chinese role, stimulated by the presence of a Chinese ship in the Colombo harbor at the time of the uprising. Within the Marxist parties, arguments appeared that the insurrection was a plot of the American CIA, intended as a provocation to justify a right-wing coup. No foreign-made arms were reported found, although the Indian navy's patrol of the island's coast at the request of the Ceylon government suggested apprehension that foreign supplies might be landed. In response to its appeals, the government received arms, ammunition, and equipment from India, Pakistan, the United States, the Soviet Union, Britain, Yugoslavia, and Egypt.

The insurgents were primarily youths between sixteen and twenty-five years of age, almost exclusively Sinhalese, and principally of village backgrounds, and they included a number of girls. Some members of the youth leagues of most political parties were thought to have been involved but the insurgents could not generally be identified with any of the legal parties. Mrs. Bandaranaike described them as "a group of disgruntled and designing persons drawn from the rejects and the unwanted of practically every recognized political party, motivated by overweening personal ambitions, personal frustrations, and disappointments and ready for instant solutions to all ills of the world."[16] Many were reported to have been members of a "land army" formed in 1967 to provide employment for young men in reclamation and irrigation projects and abolished in 1970. The self-declared leader of

[15] *Ibid.*
[16] *Ibid.*

the JVP, who was under detention at the time of the insurrection, had once studied medicine at Lumumba University in Moscow and claimed to have been refused readmission, apparently for voicing Maoist ideas. For a time, he was active in the "left" Communist youth league. A thirty-one-year-old Samasamajist M.P. who was first elected to parliament in 1970 was the only M.P. detained in connection with the insurrection. Another LSSP M.P. was gravely wounded while participating in a military expedition against the insurgents. CP leader Pieter Keuneman described the JVP as "a potentially fascist and terroristic movement" which advocated "an infantile form of negative nihilism."[17] The tiny LSSP(R) and "left" CP were the only established parties which did not vigorously condemn the insurgency.

Indications existed of long planning and considerable organization. For some months, identical posters and slogans had been appearing simultaneously at scattered locations across the island, presumably indicating communications exercises. Weapons and explosives had been laboriously assembled and bombs manufactured at several secret locations. The insurgents were organized in small cells and were outfitted with homemade blue cotton uniforms. Activists were indoctrinated through a series of five lectures entitled (1) "The Economic Situation in Ceylon," (2) "Indian Expansionism," (3) "The History of the Left Movement in Ceylon," (4) "Is Ceylon Really Independent?" and (5) "The Need for Revolution," the latter being given only to selected persons. The texts of the lectures have not been made public. Reportedly, they contained harsh criticism of the existing Marxist parties, hostility and distrust toward India, and an unsophisticated outlook on economic, political, and social questions.

[17] "Radio Speech of Hon. Pieter Keuneman" (mimeographed; Department of Information press release, April 8, 1971), p. 2.

Economic improvement was to be sought through diversification of agricultural crops and partition of the estates, with the land distributed among small cultivators. The movement appeared to contain significant elements of heroic romanticism. Insurgents took oaths of austerity and self-denial. Imposing titles ranging from judge to prime minister were assumed by local insurgent leaders.

Suggestions of growing restlessness, frustration, and alienation had been evident among youths for several years, rooted in the drastic failure of employment opportunities to keep pace with an explosive expansion of education and soaring aspirations and expectations. The annual output of university graduates increased more than sevenfold between 1960 and 1970.[18] Between 1952 and 1970, the number of persons leaving school after completing the ninth or tenth year of education rose from about 22,000 to 130,000, and those completing the eleventh or twelfth year but not going on to university studies soared from about 2,000 to 40,000.[19] The flood of educated youths, for the most part educated in the Sinhalese language and heavily concentrated in "arts" curricula, overwhelmingly sought white-collar employment as government servants or schoolteachers. However, employment opportunities for educated persons fell woefully behind the spiraling output of the nation's schools. In 1969/1970, the rate of unemployment among persons aged fifteen to twenty-four with

[18] Ceylon, Department of Census and Statistics, *Statistical Abstract of Ceylon, 1964* (Colombo: Government Press, 1965), Table 239, p. 340; Ceylon, Department of Census and Statistics, *Statistical Pocket Book of Ceylon, 1970* (Colombo: Department of Government Printing, 1970), Table 34, p. 51.

[19] *Matching Employment Opportunities and Expectations: A Programme of Action for Ceylon,* Vol. I: *The Report of an Inter-Agency Team Organised by the International Labour Office* (Geneva: International Labour Office, 1971), pp. 16–17.

secondary educations was about 70 per cent.[20] Many of the educated youths remained without employment for extended periods, supported by their families. Perhaps scarcely less frustrating than idleness was the frequent necessity to take jobs which fell starkly short of their expectations and hopes. Most of the insurgents came from the ranks of the educated village youths. While government spokesmen argued that many of the captured insurgents were in fact employed, it is probable that the type of employment often failed to match the youths' expectations. Also, the high level of unemployment, the long and idle wait for employment, and the frequent disappointment with eventual jobs may well have created a wave of disillusionment and alienation among youths, including those who had found employment.

Compounding the explosive problem of inadequate employment opportunities, the swift educational expansion opened a yawning generational gulf in the villages, undermining parental and family control and blocking intergenerational communication. Many of the educated youths were the sons and daughters of village cultivators, craftsmen, and small traders, the first members of their families ever to receive an education beyond the most elementary level. One elder was quoted as explaining: "Brother, these young people are educated while we are not. We do not even understand some of the words they use, which they have learned at the University. We cannot argue with them."[21] In certain areas, particularly the Kegalla district, the insurgents reportedly were largely youths belonging to the low-status Batgam caste, and in these localities elements of caste conflict appeared in the uprising. Over most of the island, however, caste did not seem to be a major factor in the insurrection, despite some reported JVP leadership rivalries between members of the

[20] *Ibid.*, pp. 3–4, 21–33.
[21] *Nation* (Colombo), July 13, 1971, p. 8.

Karāva and the Goyigama castes. At least half of the suspected insurgents held in detention were said to belong to the Goyigama caste, approximating the Goyigama proportion of the Sinhalese population.

It is unlikely that the consequences of the 1971 insurgency will be fully evident for some years. The significance of the military in politics, which was previously slight, may have been abruptly enhanced by the insurrection. The popularly elected, self-styled "People's Government" was required to rely on the military for its survival in office and for the preservation of the entire political order. Considerations of the military's intentions and desires may figure in future political calculations as they had not before. Furthermore, an expansion of the small armed forces and modernization of their outmoded arms and equipment have been promised. The insurgency brought unprecedented violence and death to the usually placid villages of Ceylon. The experience could heighten the expectation and perhaps the acceptance of violence as a means of resolving political and social conflicts. The extent of alienation and hostility toward the political order following in the wake of the insurgency, not only among the young but among the thousands of parents left with dead or imprisoned sons and daughters, is impossible to estimate. A legend of heroism and martyrdom quickly sprang up around the insurrection. Many persons who were repelled by the movement's goals and horrified by the means employed seem to have been awed by the appearance of reckless bravery. Almost miraculous courage, skill, and cunning have often been attributed to the insurgents. In a nation which enjoys relatively few heroic legends, it is possible that the legend of heroism and sacrifice will be preserved and embellished long after the JVP objectives, tactics, and accomplishments are forgotten.

Problems of Economic Development

The major challenge of politics in Ceylon during the 1970's may well be to balance the great popular gains in education, health, and social services with economic growth and employment opportunities. By 1970, Ceylonese society could look back on a record of remarkable achievement in education and literacy, public health, and welfare, increasingly shared by the broad masses of the population. Between 1950/1951 and 1969/1970, school enrollments more than doubled, and government expenditure on education increased almost fivefold. Life expectancy at birth climbed from forty-four years for males and forty-two years for females in 1946 to sixty-five years for males and sixty-seven years for females in 1968.[22] The Ceylonese population had access to free education from primary through university levels and free out-patient medical services. They enjoyed heavy subsidies on staple foods, textiles, and transportation. The great strides in welfare and equality, however, were increasingly accompanied by rising prices, unemployment and underemployment, shortages and black-marketeering, severe pressures on customary living standards for the middle class and white-collar employees, and a general atmosphere of stagnation and futility.

Economic growth had failed to keep pace with a rapidly increasing population and spiraling aspirations and expectations. Gross national product at constant prices grew at an annual rate of 4.5 per cent in the decade 1960–1969.[23] Per capita growth, however, was much smaller due to the rapid rise in population.

[22] Ceylon, Ministry of Planning and Employment, *The Five Year Plan, 1972–1976* (Colombo: Department of Government Printing, 1971), pp. 109, 113.

[23] Central Bank of Ceylon, *Annual Report of the Monetary Board to the Minister of Finance for the Year 1970* (Colombo: Central Bank of Ceylon, 1971), p. 1.

Per capita gross national product at constant (1959) prices climbed from Rs. 635 in 1960 to Rs. 773 in 1970, an annual average rate of growth of about 2.2 per cent (see Table 26). An accelerating rate of growth in per capita gross national product during the period 1965–1970—about double the 1960–1965 growth rate—was accompanied by sharp increases in the cost of living. The number of unemployed climbed from about 340,000 (10.5 per cent of the labor force) in 1959/1960 to 550,000 (14 per cent of the labor force) in 1969/1970.[24] The basic problem was a common one among the economically underdeveloped, low-income countries: the nation had been consuming its output, leaving little available for the capital investment needed for economic expansion. Particularly critical have been chronic shortages of foreign exchange, which sharply restricted the acquisition of foreign equipment and materials necessary for the expansion of productive capacity. Indeed, Ceylon has for a number of years exported less than it has imported, with the deficit in its international trade met by aid and loans. The foreign exchange problem, exacerbated by declining world market prices for the island's principal exports, stems in part from the need to import huge quantities of food and other consumption goods, particularly rice, which are passed to consumers under heavy subsidy. Although successive Governments repeatedly committed themselves to economic development objectives, in the final allocation of priorities their decisions have generally been for widening consumption. Sirimavo Bandaranaike acknowledged in 1971: "Hitherto, we have been emphasizing mainly the welfare aspects of socialism to the neglect of development activity. While our policies have

[24] "A Survey of Employment, Unemployment and Underemployment in Ceylon," *International Labour Review*, LXXXVII (March 1963), 251; *Matching Employment Opportunities and Expectations*, p. 25. The accuracy and comparability of unemployment statistics are, however, uncertain.

Table 26. Economic trends, 1960–1970

| Year | Gross national product at 1959 prices | | Per capita gross national product at 1959 prices | | Cost of living index for Colombo Town |
	Million rupees	Per cent increase over preceding year	Rupees	Per cent increase (or decrease) from preceding year	(1952 = 100.0)
1960	6,289		635		103.5
1961	6,425	2.2	632	(−0.5)	104.8
1962	6,710	4.4	643	1.7	106.3
1963	6,900	2.8	648	0.8	108.8
1964	7,363	6.7	675	4.2	112.2
1965	7,551	2.6	676	0.1	112.5
1966	7,818	3.5	683	1.0	112.3
1967	8,210	5.0	702	2.8	114.8
1968	8,862	7.9	739	5.3	121.5
1969	9,316	5.1	759	2.7	130.5
1970	9,695	4.1	773	1.8	138.2

Source: Central Bank of Ceylon, *Annual Report of the Monetary Board to the Minister of Finance* for 1969 and 1970 (Colombo: Central Bank of Ceylon, 1970–1971).

solved certain problems such as illiteracy and extreme poverty, they have allowed other problems such as unemployment to develop."[25]

DEVELOPMENT PLANNING AND IMPLEMENTATION

Aspirations for economic development were occasionally proclaimed in the early years of independence, but with little apparent sense of urgency or direction. Aggregate statistics showed a per capita national income in Ceylon about double that of neighboring countries and the poorer sections of society were only beginning to find an effective voice in politics. An international trade boom coinciding with the Korean War, which momentarily created high prices for Ceylon's exports, postponed the emergence of stark economic problems. In addition, during the first decade of independence, the political leadership was largely preoccupied with the establishment of new political structures and processes and distracted by questions of national integration. Development efforts were concentrated on irrigation and the clearing of jungle areas for peasant colonization.

After the 1956 election, a National Planning Council headed by the prime minister was created and the first comprehensive development plan was formulated, emphasizing industrial rather than agricultural growth and assigning a dominant role in development activities to public agencies. Implementation, however, was virtually forgotten in the political and communal turmoil of the following years. The destruction of privilege and the equalization of status and opportunity were the dominant themes of politics for almost a decade after 1956. Concern focused on the equitable distribution of existing resources, rather

[25] "Statement by the Hon. Prime Minister in the House of Representatives on 9th November, 1971: Socio-Economic Measures" (mimeographed; Department of Information press release, n.d.), p. 5.

than on the expansion of the resources available. After 1960, the National Planning Council effectively ceased to function and its secretariat was converted into a National Planning Department, which appeared to lack strong political support or effective access to the top levels of governmental decision making. Although some development efforts were made, particularly in the establishment of state-owned industrial corporations, few coordinated or comprehensive efforts at economic expansion were pursued between 1960 and 1965.

By 1965, the long-neglected economic difficulties had reached a state of undeniable urgency. On formation of the National Government in 1965, steps were taken to strengthen planning machinery, improve the access of planning officials to the top governmental leadership, and monitor progress toward plan goals. A separate Ministry of Planning and Economic Affairs was established directly under the prime minister. Cabinet subcommittees, one concerned with planning and a second with food production, were created and assumed a significant role in policy making. A committee of permanent secretaries of ministries concerned with development was formed to facilitate implementation of development policies. Under the National Government, emphasis shifted to the expansion of agricultural production, particularly of food crops for domestic consumption to reduce food imports. A widely heralded "grow-more-food campaign" became a major focus of development efforts. Also, greater scope was given to private business, with provision of tax incentives and the allocation of scarce foreign exchange for capital equipment and raw materials to private firms. Prime Minister Dudley Senanayake frequently linked his official-language policy and his cooperation with the minorities to economic development, claiming that communal harmony was essential for development to occur. Some notable successes were scored in raising food production, but other problems, including inflation and unemployment, had worsened by 1970, and the net economic achievements of the 1965–1970 Government remain a matter of controversy.

The United Front Government came to power in 1970 promising to solve the acute problems of unemployment and soaring living costs while maintaining the high level of subsidies and welfare services. Before new economic programs could be formulated, the 1971 insurrection erupted, dramatically underlining the grim social and political implications of economic stagnation. Seven months after the insurrection, a five-year development plan was issued, in what was described as "a time of social and economic crisis unparalleled in the history of modern Ceylon."[26] Emphasis again shifted to heavy reliance on public agencies and initiatives and to industrial growth. The plan noted that "when the country is faced with an unemployment problem of the present magnitude all other considerations must necessarily be subordinate."[27] Even if 810,000 new jobs were created by 1976, it was conceded that some 290,000 persons would remain unemployed at the end of the plan period.[28] In addition to seeking to attack the problem of unemployment and to generate long-term growth, the plan proposed to promote the egalitarian goals of the United Front by ameliorating the distress of the underprivileged segments of society and by limiting the holdings of agricultural land and residential property, which constituted the major source of inequitable distribution of wealth.

The inability to implement plans and to achieve designated goals has long been viewed as the most serious weakness of government development efforts. Some of the failures of implementation can be attributed to political decisions and leadership. Political officeholders have frequently seemed to lack clear understanding of the requirements of economic growth and have often appeared

[26] *The Five Year Plan*, p. 1.

[27] *Ibid.*, p. 11.

[28] *Ibid.*, p. 31.

to subordinate development policies to considerations of immediate political advantage. In addition, responsibility for inadequate implementation has regularly been charged to the public service. Despite increasingly heavy development duties, the bureaucracy has been slow to abandon a structure and ethos reflecting its earlier functions of preserving law and order and gathering taxes. The conventional outlook of public servants has been that theirs was essentially a regulatory function, applying regulations and precedents to applications and petitions placed before them. They have displayed little aptitude for duties requiring initiative, innovation, and dispatch. A complaint of the 1966 administrative reforms committee depicted one type of problem encountered:

The gravest defect in the public sector projects is the inability of departments to carry out a programme of work within the period of time they themselves prescribe. . . . The tradition has grown for departments to promise fulfillment of a programme by a specified date and make no determined effort to fulfill the programme by that date. In the past there was no deterrent penalty enforced by Government for such failure. . . . There is no known case of any officer having been called upon to explain failure to keep to a target as a personal dereliction of duty.[29]

In recent years, increasing efforts have been made to align administrative organization and roles more closely to the performance of development functions. The post of government agent was progressively transformed from an administrative and regulatory one to a largely developmental one, particularly after 1965, when government agents were given responsibility for the program of expanding food production. A committee of permanent secretaries argued in 1967 that "the Government Agent's

[29] *Report of the Committee on Administrative Reforms,* Sessional Paper IX—1966 (Colombo: Government Press, 1966), p. 13.

office is no longer administrative in the sense it was twenty years ago. It is now essentially a development assignment."[30] The 1971 five-year plan described the district administration headed by the government agent as the "focal point" of implementation for the major projects, with responsibility for coordinating departmental development activities.[31] Since 1970, plans have been advanced to increase the number of divisional revenue officers and to assign to them responsibility for small-scale development projects (with a suitable change in title). District development committees and divisional development councils were created in 1971 as a link between the administrative apparatus of government and the public.

In addition to the changing functions in field administration, attention has been given to improving the performance of public servants engaged in development tasks. Little interest had been shown in training in the public service until 1967, when an Academy of Administrative Studies was founded to provide in-service training and to serve as a catalyst for administrative reform. Although the need for technical expertise had grown with the bureaucracy's expanding development functions, the public service had tended to cling to the notion of the "generalist" administrator who is able to direct any department or project without benefit of specialized knowledge or training. Complaints against the subordinate status and ineffective use of specialists mounted within the bureaucracy and eventually spilled over into partisan politics. In 1970, the United Front promised to give enhanced status and authority to technicians, and after coming to power appointed engineers as permanent secretaries to two ministries. But whether the recent alterations will markedly im-

[30] "Report of the Committee of Permanent Secretaries on District Organization for Agricultural Development Work" (mimeographed; Colombo, Feb. 10, 1967), p. 6.

[31] *The Five Year Plan,* p. 130.

prove the capability of the public service in development activities is uncertain. Bureaucratic performance in achieving stipulated goals and meeting scheduled targets seems likely to remain a major problem area of economic development efforts.

THE POLITICS OF ECONOMIC DEVELOPMENT

Costly subsidies on rice, sugar, textiles, and other basic consumption goods have consistently been condemned by economists for years. Even politicians have often admitted privately that the high level of subsidization was detrimental to the economic vitality and development of the nation. Yet, the political experience of two decades suggests a public unwillingness to permit abandonment or curtailment of the subsidies.

The most expensive and most sensitive of the subsidies is the consumer's subsidy on rice, begun as a temporary measure during the Second World War, by which a rationed quantity of rice is provided to the public at far below the market price. As a considerable proportion of the rice consumed is imported, the subsidy has not only contributed to large budget deficits but has consumed critically scarce foreign exchange. In 1953, financial pressures led the UNP Government to accept a Central Bank recommendation that the subsidy be discontinued. A resulting rise in the price of rice led to the outburst of protest and violence of the 1953 hartal. The rice cut became an issue in the 1956 election, and when the UNP was defeated the new Government restored the ration of subsidized rice. Faced with serious foreign exchange problems and increasingly large budget deficits, the SLFP minister of finance in 1962 proposed a reduction in the weekly ration of rice from two to one and one-half measures per person. The proposal produced a storm of protest and eventually was withdrawn. In announcing abandonment of the rice cut, the finance minister explained, "if . . . I am given a directive and told that as far as hon. Members of Parliament are concerned we cannot make this cut even for a single day as the result would be politically ruinous for us, then I am constrained to accept their verdict and accede to their wishes."[32]

Four years later, as the cost of rice imports continued to mount, the National Government then in power announced a reduction in the ration of rice from two measures to one. However, whereas the rationed rice had formerly been sold for one-fourth of a rupee a measure, the single measure was made available to the public free of charge. The rice ration reduction loomed as a major issue in the 1970 election. A circular addressed to United Front candidates and campaigners proclaimed the rice cut to be the main issue of the campaign and described it as "the issue on which the masses respond most instinctively."[33] After the United Front victory the second measure was restored at a subsidized price, while the first measure continued to be provided free.

In introducing the 1969/1970 budget of the National Government, the minister of finance noted that efforts at economic growth had necessitated "decisions which were bound to be politically unpopular in the short run."[34] Less than a year later, the National Government had suffered a devastating election defeat. Economic issues probably played a more conspicuous and unambiguous role in 1970 than in previous elections. The UNP and its allies had entered the contest claiming that government policies since 1965 had produced substantial economic gains. While admitting a steep rise in the cost of living, UNP campaigners insisted that incomes of agricultural producers had

[32] Ceylon, House of Representatives, *Parliamentary Debates (Hansard)*, vol. 47, col. 3605 (Aug. 24, 1962).

[33] "United Front Election Bulletin" (mimeographed; Colombo, n.d.), p. 1.

[34] *Budget Speech, 1969–70, by the Hon. U. B. Wanninayake, M.P., Minister of Finance* (Colombo: Department of Government Printing, 1969), p. 6.

also gone up, acute shortages of goods had been reduced, and significant gains in real output had occurred. The United Front countered with accusations that the food drive had benefited only the affluent, and that the masses had suffered from inflation, unemployment, and the reduction in the ration of subsidized rice. Postelection evaluations tended to conclude that substantial gains in food production had been realized, but that few benefits had filtered down to the small cultivators or wage laborers and that the food drive had failed to curb mounting inflation or unemployment.

The 1970 election results were interpreted by some as indicating that the public was not prepared to accept constraints on immediate consumption in the interest of long-range economic development. In a nation such as Ceylon, where the political system is responsive to mass sentiments and resources are woefully inadequate to satisfy immediate demands, long-term development programs are bound to encounter strong political resistance. It is also possible, however, to attribute the National Government's defeat to its failure to check conspicuous privilege and assure a just and equitable distribution of benefits and costs. The regular appearance of farm vehicles, imported to augment the food drive, at the exclusive schools, fashionable weddings, and English-language theaters of Colombo symbolized an important political failing of the 1965–1970 development efforts. Repeated public reaction against curtailment of consumer subsidies and other curbs on immediate consumption may reflect a popular refusal to accept sacrifices for future development, but they may also indicate a lack of confidence that burdens and benefits will be apportioned equitably or that the promised gains will be realized.

A harsh political dilemma had materialized by the early 1970's. For years, requirements of long-range economic expansion had been postponed as political leaders faced the prospect of demonstrations, disorders, and election defeats if they failed to respond to immediate demands. Population growth, as well as rising aspirations, made economic progress appear imperative in order to avoid future massive privation and despair. Yet, failure to achieve rapid improvement in employment opportunities and to ameliorate other pressing problems could generate social and political tensions and explosions which would stifle all prospect of economic development. The 1971 insurrection graphically underscored the immediacy of the crisis of rising hopes and expectations unaccompanied by improved opportunities. The time apparently had passed when political leaders could ignore the requirements of long-term development, but neither could they neglect urgent immediate wants and needs without risking turmoil and instability, which could quickly reverse any economic gains.

Conclusion: Political Development, Performance, and Prospects of the Ceylonese Polity

On the promulgation of the new Ceylonese constitution in May 1972, an impressive political record could be claimed for the island. Forty-one years earlier, Ceylon had been the first nation in Asia to introduce universal adult suffrage. Elections had been held regularly and had assumed an effective role in determining the personnel and policies of government. Orderly transfers of power between opposing political parties had been effected five times in the twenty-four years since independence. Vigorous competition between coherent and durable parties had emerged as one of the most striking features of Ceylonese politics. An experienced and rationally organized bureaucracy had withstood the postindependence changes and reforms as a skilled, functioning, and fairly adaptable instrument of public purposes. While many other newly independent countries were experiencing severe instability or adopting authoritarian regimes, the Ceylonese political order had survived intact the stresses of a major sociopolitical change involving the entry of new and broader social groups into purposeful and effective political participation, an eruption of communal tensions and rivalry, and mounting problems associated with sluggish economic growth, inflation, and unemployment.

Yet, despite the indications of the strength, vigor, and durability of political institutions, by 1972 concern and uncertainty abounded. A year earlier, the political order had faced an attack of unprecedented severity and destructiveness, which left deep wounds on the society and polity. Economic performance remained disappointing. Demands generated by swiftly rising mass aspirations and expectations, compounded by rapid population growth, strained the nation's resources and appeared to pose a renewed threat to political stability and continuity. A senior cabinet minister in late 1971 warned that "the alternatives we face are either total fulfillment of government's economic development plans, or complete disruption of the social order."[35]

Several alternative views of political development have appeared in recent years.[36] By most definitions, Ceylon had experi-

[35] Maithripala Senanayake, "Text of the Address to Participants of the Management Development Course Held at the Academy of Administrative Studies—October, 1971," *Journal of Development Administration* (Colombo), II (Nov. 1971), 1.

[36] Gabriel A. Almond and G. Bingham Powell, Jr., *Comparative Politics: A Developmental Approach* (Boston: Little, Brown and Co., 1966), pp. 299–332; Karl W. Deutsch, "Social Mobilization and Political Development," *American Political Science Review*, LV (Sept. 1961), 493–514; Alfred Diamant, "Political Development: Approaches to Theory and Strategy," in John D. Montgomery and William J. Siffin (eds.), *Approaches to Development: Politics, Administration and Change* (New York: McGraw-Hill Book Co., 1966), pp. 15–47; S. N. Eisenstadt, *Modernization: Protest and Change* (Englewood Cliffs, N.J.: Prentice-Hall, Inc., 1966); Lucian W. Pye, *Aspects of Political Development* (Bos-

enced substantial development by 1972. If political modernization or development is linked with a broader process of socio-
economic modernization and conceived as involving rapid social
mobilization, widening political participation, and penetration of
the society by political agencies and activities, Ceylon has un-
questionably been undergoing swift and extensive political development over the past two or three decades. Social mobilization
is suggested by the steadily climbing levels of literacy and education and by the wide exposure to mass communications media.
A high and rising level of popular participation is most readily
observable in the remarkably large proportion of the electorate
casting ballots in parliamentary elections. A number of indications
ranging from the evolving pattern of relations between M.P.'s
and constituents to the programs and campaign styles of parties,
imply a marked growth in the responsiveness of the political
system to the demands of a mobilized mass public. Similarly,
political development defined as the emergence of numerous differentiated, functionally specific, autonomous political structures
is evident in the multiplication of specialized government agencies
at the national and local levels, the growth of political parties,
and the appearance of associational groups representing a variety
of specific occupational, communal, and other interests and
identifications. A more ambiguous conclusion is reached if political development is equated with the capacity of the political
system to process the demands and resolve the issues by which it
is confronted. The sheer survival of the system without breakdown or cataclysmic upheaval presumably is evidence of relative
success in handling demands and issues to the present time. The
striking advances in education and social services over the last

ton: Little, Brown and Co., 1966), pp. 31–48; and Fred W. Riggs, *Administration in Developing Countries: The Theory of Prismatic Society*
(Boston: Houghton Mifflin Co., 1964), pp. 3–49.

few decades suggest the capacity of the system to respond to certain popular demands. Comparable performance has not, however, been registered in improving employment opportunities and economic circumstances. Sustained capacity to satisfy the demands and achieve the goals of the society is undoubtedly of paramount importance to the survival of the existing political system and presumably is essential for further development.

From another perspective, political development has been distinguished from modernization and viewed as the growth of political institutions characterized by adaptibility, complexity, autonomy, and organizational coherence. The processes of modernization are seen as potentially disruptive to the political order. Swift social mobilization followed by growing popular demands and rising political participation may widen the gap between aspirations and satisfactions, producing social frustration, which in turn may lead to political unrest and instability. If institutionalization has not progressed sufficiently to allow the political system to withstand the stresses of rapidly rising participation and new and growing demands, the result may be turbulence, upheaval, and political "decay" rather than development.[37]

In Ceylon, the institutionalization of representative, executive, and administrative organizations appears to have advanced steadily over a period of many decades. The bureaucracy has evolved continuously since the early nineteenth century, and a legislature elected by universal suffrage has been in existence without interruption for more than four decades. Although the time span is relatively short, about a quarter of a century, institutionalization of the political party system also seems advanced. Elections have become party contests and candidates of parties

[37] Samuel P. Huntington, "Political Development and Political Decay," *World Politics,* XVII (April 1965), 386–430; and the same author's *Political Order in Changing Societies* (New Haven, Conn.: Yale University Press, 1968), pp. 1–92.

that have been continuously active since shortly after independence have received at least 90 per cent of all votes cast in recent elections. The adjustment of parties to the abrupt rise of purposive mass participation in the 1950's, creating new demands and styles of mobilizing support, suggests adaptability and durability. The ability of the UNP to survive its 1956 defeat and subsequent change in program and leadership, of the SLFP to outlive the 1959 assassination of its founder-leader and later to adjust to its Marxist alliance, and of the LSSP to shelve its millennial goals for incremental advances suggests that institutionalization has occurred on a significant scale. Party penetration of the ubiquitous local government councils and the swift growth and consolidation of the labor movement over the past twenty years are among the additional signs of institutionalization. The institutional growth which had occurred in Ceylon by the 1950's may explain the political system's ability to weather the shocks of the post independence participation revolution without breakdown or overthrow.

Ceylon has also experienced swift mass mobilization and mounting participation. Demands have been soaring. Some indications of growing social frustration have appeared, most starkly in the 1971 insurrection. Pressures of steeply rising aspirations and demands, stimulated by the explosive expansion of education, are likely to persist or increase. Despite the seemingly high level of institutionalization, hopes and expectations threaten to outrun the capacity of the political system to provide acceptable satisfactions. If the island's political institutions prove unable to respond to the spiraling demands, the consequence could be rising social frustration, leading to instability and turbulence which could undermine or demolish the political order.

An evaluation of the performance of Ceylon's political system must note the existence of areas of marked stability and sophistication. The constitution was neither abrogated nor suspended in a quarter of a century following independence, and, except for the period 1959–1960, legislatures and cabinets have served for reasonable terms without major or repeated changes of personnel or policies. In a world in which relatively few regimes tolerate a strong and uninhibited opposition, the ability of the opposition to function with few constraints in Ceylon and, indeed, to be repeatedly handed control of the government suggests a high level of political sophistication and a firm commitment to the norms of liberal democracy. It could hardly be claimed, however, that the politics of the island have been untroubled or that the political system has been fully successful in resolving the issues and problems which have confronted it. While political parties and representative institutions have displayed adaptibility and resilience in responding to the social mobilization and populist upsurge of the past two decades, the new relationships and processes have yet to be fully developed and tested. The survival and adaptation of institutions has frequently been accompanied by the triumph of short-run expediency and the sacrifice of the vision and determination required for economic growth, social cohesion, or other presumed long-range objectives of the society.

Through much of the period since independence, the political system has been concerned with questions of vertical integration involving a narrowing of the psychological and material gulf between the elite and the masses, and major strides toward satisfying emerging egalitarian sentiments have been made without severe disruption or upheaval. Problems of the horizontal integration of ethnic and religious groups, however, have remained largely unresolved. Although communal passions have not returned to the levels of 1956–1958, the satisfaction of majority demands for recognition and preference has left the minorities resentful and insecure. The FP greeted the 1972 constitution by proclaiming a period of mourning for the Tamil people. While the constitution's provisions designating Sinhalese as the official language and conferring a special status on the Buddhist religion did little more than confirm the previously established situation, they served to remind nearly one-third of the island's population of their uncertain position within the polity. The days of mourning declared by the Federalists symbolized both the continued resentment and the helplessness of the minorities in the face of the Sinhalese Buddhist majority's drive for pre-eminent status within the nation.

As the 1970's began, public concern was increasingly focused on the intractable problem of inadequate economic performance. A debate has long raged in Ceylon over the respective roles of public and private enterprise in the economy. Although the emphasis has shifted from one sector to the other, each recent Government has accepted the principle of a mixed economy, with contributions toward economic expansion sought from both sectors. The stark fact, however, is that few signs of dynamism have appeared in either sector. The nation has not succeeded in creating a framework for the vigorous and self-sustaining growth of either public or private economic activity. Time appears to be running precariously short. Increasingly, political protest and social unrest have appeared directly traceable to the frustrations and disappointments of lagging economic growth. A marked and rapid improvement in economic performance—whether initiated by public or private agencies—seems essential to forestall mounting social frustration and a spreading popular sense of deprivation, with their grim implications for the social and political order. Furthermore, the economic stringencies could sharpen other social tensions as communal loyalties are mobilized in the competition for the insufficient resources and opportunities, further taxing the ability of the nation's political institutions to provide order and progress.

Ceylon can look back on an uncommon record of social advancement and political stability. The nation's political future, however, appears uncertain and perilous. The immediate and inescapable public problem of the early 1970's is the need to generate economic expansion which can offer new benefits and opportunities and alleviate the mounting frustrations of thwarted hopes and unfulfilled expectations. Other challenges and perils may lie beyond the immediately compelling economic and employment crisis. Profound and rapid changes in social and political patterns, relationships, values, and attitudes are likely to occur for many years. The dislocations, tensions, and uncertainties of a rapidly changing social environment are bound to create situations that are politically volatile. The Ceylonese polity surmounted earlier stresses and challenges, and the political structures and processes which have developed over the past few decades seem impressively sturdy and sophisticated. The 1970's will almost certainly be a time of trial, testing the capacity of the island's political system to withstand the stresses produced by rising popular wants and expectations and to respond to the steadily mounting demands of a mobilized mass public with severely limited material resources.

Selected Readings
on Modern Ceylon

For further inquiry into modern Ceylon, a brief selection of readings which are generally accessible outside Ceylon appears below. A recent and impressively comprehensive bibliography is contained in H. A. I. Goonetileke, *A Bibliography of Ceylon* (2 vols.; Zug, Switzerland: Inter Documentation Company, [1970]). In addition to the general histories, the remarkable descriptive account of Robert Knox, *An Historical Relation of Ceylon* (Glasgow: James Mac-Lehouse & Sons, 1911), first published in 1681, deserves mention.

General and Modern History

Arasaratnam, S. *Ceylon*. Englewood Cliffs, N.J.: Prentice-Hall, Inc., 1964.

De Silva, K. M. "The Formation and Character of the Ceylon National Congress, 1917–1919," *Ceylon Journal of Historical and Social Studies,* X (Jan.–Dec. 1967 [published Aug. 1970]), 70–102.

Jayawardena, Visakha Kumari. *The Rise of the Labor Movement in Ceylon*. Durham, N.C.: Duke University Press, 1972.

Ludowyk, E. F. C. *The Modern History of Ceylon*. New York: Frederick A. Praeger, 1966.

Mendis, G. C. *Ceylon Today and Yesterday,* 2nd ed. Colombo: Associated Newspapers of Ceylon, Ltd., 1963.

———. *Ceylon Under the British,* 2nd ed. Colombo: Colombo Apothecaries Co., Ltd., 1948.

Pakeman, S. A. *Ceylon*. New York: Frederick A. Praeger, 1964.

Tennent, Sir James Emerson. *Ceylon: An Account of the Island.* 2 vols. 3rd ed. London: Longman, Green, Longman, and Roberts, 1859.

Society and Economy

Corea, Gamani. "Ceylon," in Cranley Onslow (ed.), *Asian Economic Development.* New York: Federick A. Praeger, 1965, pp. 29–65.

Karunatilake, H. N. S. *Economic Development in Ceylon.* New York: Frederick A. Praeger, 1971.

Matching Employment Opportunities and Expectations: A Programme of Action for Ceylon. 2 vols. Geneva: International Labour Office, 1971.

Obeyesekere, Gananath. *Land Tenure in Village Ceylon.* Cambridge, England: Cambridge University Press, 1967.

Ryan, Bryce. *Caste in Modern Ceylon.* New Brunswick, N.J.: Rutgers University Press, 1953.

Snodgrass, Donald R. *Ceylon: An Export Economy in Transition.* Homewood, Ill.: Richard D. Irwin, Inc., 1966.

Straus, Murray A. "Westernization, Insecurity, and Sinhalese Social Structure," *International Journal of Social Psychiatry,* XII (Spring 1966), 130–138.

Tambiah, S. J. "Ceylon," in Richard D. Lambert and Bert F. Hoselitz (eds.), *The Role of Savings and Wealth in Southern Asia and the West.* Paris: UNESCO, 1963, pp. 44–125.

Yalman, Nur. *Under the Bo Tree.* Berkeley: University of California Press, 1967.

Politics and Government

Jupp, James. "Constitutional Development in Ceylon Since Independence," *Public Affairs,* XLI (Summer 1968), 169–183.

Kearney, Robert N. *Communalism and Language in the Politics of Ceylon.* Durham, N.C.: Duke University Press, 1967.

——. "The Marxist Parties of Ceylon," in Paul R. Brass and Marcus

F. Franda (eds.), *Radical Politics in South Asia*. Cambridge, Mass.: M.I.T. Press, 1973.

———. *Trade Unions and Politics in Ceylon*. Berkeley: University of California Press, 1971.

LaPorte, Robert, Jr. "Administrative, Political, and Social Constraints on Economic Development in Ceylon," *International Review of Administrative Sciences*, XXXVI, no. 2 (1970), 1–14.

Lerski, George J."The Twilight of Ceylonese Trotskyism," *Pacific Affairs*, XLIII (Fall 1970), 382–393.

Politicus (pseud.). "The April Revolt in Ceylon," *Asian Survey*, XII (March 1972), 259–274.

Smith, Donald E. (ed.). *South Asian Politics and Religion*. Princeton, N.J.: Princeton University Press, 1966, Part IV.

Van der Kroef, Justus M. "Ceylon's Political Left: Its Development and Aspirations," *Pacific Affairs*, XL (Fall-Winter 1967–1968), 250–278.

Wilson, A. Jeyaratnam. "The Tamil Federal Party in Ceylon Politics," *Journal of Commonwealth Political Studies*, IV (July 1966), 117–137.

Wriggins, W. Howard. *Ceylon: Dilemmas of a New Nation*. Princeton, N.J.: Princeton University Press, 1960.

An Introductory Guide to Research
on Contemporary Politics in Ceylon

The sources and materials described below are recommended to the scholar commencing research into contemporary Ceylonese politics. An effort has been made to select chiefly recent materials in the English language. The use of Sinhalese for indispensable political publications has been growing rapidly for more than a decade, however, and the number of fields within which fruitful research is possible without use of Sinhalese-language materials is rapidly shrinking.

Ceylon Government Publications

The government of Ceylon is a prolific publisher, and government documents and reports are invaluable for political and other social science research. Basic economic and social data are available in the reports on the decennial census issued by the Department of Census and Statistics. The first census of the island was conducted in 1871 and censuses were repeated each decade thereafter through 1921. Of particular note is the classic report by E. B. Denham, *Ceylon at the Census of 1911* (Colombo: Government Printer, 1912). In 1931 only a partial census was conducted, and the next enumeration was delayed until 1946. Subsequent censuses were held in 1953, in 1963, and, for population, in 1971, with a census of agriculture and industry to follow in 1973. Unfortunately, the published reports are often many years in appearing, and the gap between the enumeration and publication of the results seems to be widening. The full results of the 1963 census had not been published nine years after the census was held. The Department of Census and

Statistics released a *Statistical Abstract of Ceylon* and a *Ceylon Year Book* annually for many years, but recently publication has lagged and may have ceased, at least on a regular basis. A less comprehensive *Statistical Pocket Book of Ceylon* has been issued since 1966.

The *Annual Report of the Monetary Board to the Minister of Finance,* prepared by the Central Bank of Ceylon, is the most valuable single source for economic data. The finance minister's annual *Budget Speech* is issued as a pamphlet by the Ministry of Finance. *Administration Reports,* submitted annually by heads of departments and government agents, contain useful information not only on department and kachcheri operations but also on substantive areas of departmental responsibility such as labor, education, local government, or law enforcement. *The Acts of Ceylon,* published annually, contains statutes enacted during the year.

The *Parliamentary Debates (Hansard)* of the House of Representatives from 1947 until the chamber's replacement by the National State Assembly in 1972 and of the Senate from 1947 to 1971, together with the *Official Report* of Constituent Assembly debates in 1970–1972, are invaluable storehouses of information and opinion. The debates are published in the language in which a speech or comment is delivered. Members may speak in Sinhalese, Tamil, or English, and over the past fifteen years the proportion of speeches in Sinhalese has increased considerably, while the use of English has steadily declined. Regular reports of the auditor-general and the public accounts committee are published in a Parliamentary Series, along with a few special reports to parliament such as *The Reports of the Parliamentary Bribery Commission, 1959–60,* Parliamentary Series no. 1 of the Fifth Parliament, First Session, 1960 (Colombo: Government Press, 1960), and *Report on the Incidents in Colombo on 1st May, 1965,* Parliamentary Series no. 6 of the Sixth Parliament, First Session, 1965–66 (Colombo: Government Press, 1966).

A great variety of reports on innumerable subjects are published as Sessional Papers each year. A selection of Sessional Papers of particular interest to the political scientist follows.

Final Report of the Press Commission. Sessional Paper XI—1964. Colombo: Government Press, 1964.

Interim Report of the Salaries and Cadres Commission, 1969. Sessional Paper VII—1969. Colombo: Department of Government Printing, 1969.

Report of the Commission Appointed under the Commissions of Inquiry Act to Inquire into and Report on Certain Matters Affecting the Associated Newspapers of Ceylon Ltd., and Other Connected Companies. Sessional Paper VIII—1971. Colombo: Department of Government Printing, 1971.

Report of the Commission on Local Government. Sessional Paper XXXIII—1955. Colombo: Government Press, 1955.

Report of the Committee Appointed to Report on the Ceylon Administrative Service. Sessional Paper VI—1966. Colombo: Government Press, 1966.

Report of the Committee on Administrative Reforms. Sessional Paper IX—1966. Colombo: Government Press, 1966.

Report of the Delimitation Commission. Sessional Paper XV—1959. Colombo: Government Press, 1959.

Report of the First Delimitation Commission Appointed in Accordance with Sub-section (1) of Section 76 of the Ceylon (Constitution) Order in Council, 1946. Sessional Paper XIII—1946. Colombo: Government Press, 1946.

Report of the National Wage Policy Commission. Sessional Paper VIII—1961. Colombo: Government Press, 1961.

Report of the Salaries and Cadre Commission, 1961. Part I: Sessional Paper III—1961. Part II: Sessional Paper IV—1961. Colombo: Government Press, 1961.

Report on the Parliamentary General Elections, 19th March and 20th July, 1960. Sessional Paper II—1962. Colombo: Government Press, 1962.

Report on the Seventh Parliamentary General Election in Ceylon, 27th May, 1970. Sessional Paper VII—1971. Colombo: Department of Government Printing, 1971.

Report on the Sixth Parliamentary General Election of Ceylon, 22nd March, 1965. Sessional Paper XX—1966. Colombo: Government Press, 1966.

Report to His Excellency the Governor-General by the Commission Appointed in Terms of the Commissions of Inquiry Act to Inquire into and Report on Certain Matters Connected with the Assassination of the Late Prime Minister Solomon West Ridgeway Dias Bandaranaike. Sessional Paper III—1965. Colombo: Government Press, 1965.

A few periodicals are published by government agencies. The *Ceylon Government Gazette* contains official notices and proclamations. A monthly periodical, *Ceylon Today,* has been published by the Department of Information since 1952, although delays in publication and combined issues have been common in recent years. The *Ceylon Labour Gazette* has been issued monthly by the Department of Labour for more than twenty years. The Central Bank of Ceylon publishes a monthly *Bulletin.* The Academy of Administrative Studies began publication of a quarterly *Training Digest* in 1968, which was replaced in 1970 by a biannual *Journal of Development Administration.*

Among the notable nonserial government publications are the following:

Central Bank of Ceylon. Department of Economic Research. *Survey of Ceylon's Consumer Finances, 1963.* Colombo: Central Bank of Ceylon, 1964.

The Ceylon Government Manual of Procedure, 4th ed. Colombo: Government Press, 1957 (updated by periodic correction slips).

The Constitution of Sri Lanka (Ceylon). Colombo: Department of Government Printing, 1972.

Department of Elections. *Results of Parliamentary General Elections in Ceylon, 1947–1970.* Colombo: Department of Government Printing, 1971.

Department of National Planning. *The Development Programme, 1964–1965.* Colombo: Government Press, 1964.

Ministry of Finance. *Economic and Social Development of Ceylon (A Survey), 1926–1954.* Colombo: Government Press, 1955.

——. *Economic and Social Progress, 1965–1969.* Colombo: Department of Government Printing, 1969.

Ministry of Planning and Economic Affairs. *The Development Programme, 1966–67.* Colombo: Government Press, 1966.

Ministry of Planning and Employment. *The Five Year Plan, 1972–1976.* Colombo: Department of Government Printing, 1971.

National Planning Council. *The Ten-Year Plan.* Colombo: Government Press, 1959.

Political Party Publications

Most publications of Ceylonese political parties are ephemeral leaflets, pamphlets, and handbills related to a particular occasion and intended to be persuasive rather than informative. During each parliamentary election campaign, election manifestos are widely circulated by virtually all active parties. Resolutions of party conferences and/or speeches by the party president have been issued intermittently by the UNP, the FP, and the CP, and occasionally by additional parties. Since the 1950's, the SLFP has been somewhat irregularly issuing a publication containing brief articles by party leaders and functionaries, mostly in Sinhalese, under the title—with slight variations from year to year—of *Śrī Laṅkā Nidahas Pakshayē Saṅvathsara Kalāpaya* (Sri Lanka Freedom Party's Anniversary Volume). The major parties publish newspapers weekly or intermittently, but they are generally of marginal value to the scholar. The CP's weekly *Forward* is one of the few remaining party newspapers published regularly in English. *Siṅhalē* and *Siyarata* are published by the SLFP and the UNP, respectively. Below are listed a few of the party publications of more enduring value, excluding election manifestos and periodical or serial publications.

The Case for a Federal Constitution for Ceylon: Resolutions Passed at the First National Convention of the Ilankai Tamil Arasu Kadchi. Colombo: Ilankai Tamil Arasu Kadchi, 1951.

Ceylon Faces Crisis. Colombo: Federal Party, 1957.

For a People's Government: The Common Programme of the Sri Lanka Freedom Party, the Lanka Samasamaja Party and the Ceylon Communist Party. Colombo, n.d.

Goonewardene, Leslie. *The Differences Between Trotskyism and Stalinism.* Colombo: Lanka Sama Samaja Publication, 1954.

——. *A Short History of the Lanka Sama Samaja Party.* Colombo: Lanka Sama Samaja Party, 1960.

——. *What We Stand For.* Colombo: Lanka Sama Samaja Party, 1959.

Keuneman, Pieter. *Twenty Years of the Ceylon Communist Party.* Colombo: Ceylon Communist Party, n.d.

——. *Under the Banner of Unity: Report of Pieter Keuneman, General Secretary, on Behalf of the Central Committee.* Colombo: Ceylon Communist Party, 1964.

Laṅkā Samasamāja Pakshayē Vyavasthāva [Lanka Sama Samaja Party's Constitution]. Colombo: Lanka Sama Samaja Party, n.d.

Lanka Sama Samaja Party. *Programme of Action, Adopted at the Unity Conference, June 4th, 1950.* Colombo: Lanka Sama Samaja Party, 1950.

On Questions of the International Communist Movement: Statement of the Central Committee of the Ceylon Communist Party. Colombo: Ceylon Communist Party, 1963.

Perera, Basil. *Pieter Keuneman: A Profile.* Colombo: Ceylon Communist Party, 1967.

Reply to the Central Committee of the Ceylon Communist Party. Colombo: Worker Publication, n.d.

Śrī Laṅkā Nidahas Pakshayē Vyavasthā [Sri Lanka Freedom Party's Constitution]. Colombo: Sri Lanka Freedom Party, 1958.

Tampoe, Bala. "Open Letter to the Members of the Lanka Sama Samaja Party from the Lanka Sama Samaja Party (Revolutionary)." (Mimeographed.) Colombo, Aug. 9, 1969.

25 Years of the Ceylon Communist Party. Colombo: People's Publishing House, 1968.

United National Party Constitution. Colombo: United National Party, 1962.

United National Party. *Progress Through Stability: United National Party Manifesto.* Colombo: United National Party, 1958.

———. *What We Believe.* Colombo: United National Party, 1963.
Why Lake House Seeks to Destroy the Coalition. Colombo, n.d.

Publications of Labor and Business Organizations

A number of the major labor organizations issue annual or biennial reports or speeches of officers, usually coinciding with their
general membership meetings or delegates' conferences. Among the
most regularly issued and informative are those of the Ceylon
Mercantile Union, Ceylon Workers' Congress, Democratic Workers'
Congress, and Government Clerical Service Union. *Bank Worker,
CMU Bulletin, Congress News,* and *Red Tape* are newspapers issued
on a fairly regular monthly or bimonthly basis by the Ceylon Bank
Employees' Union, Ceylon Mercantile Union, Ceylon Workers'
Congress, and Government Clerical Service Union, respectively.
The Employers' Federation of Ceylon, Ceylon Estates Employers'
Federation, and the Ceylon Chamber of Commerce have issued
speeches and reports annually. In addition to the periodic speeches
and reports, the following publications have appeared:

Ceylon Chamber of Commerce. *125 Years of Service, 1839–1964.*
Colombo: Ceylon Chamber of Commerce, 1964.

The C.F.T.U. and the Working Class Movement. Colombo: Ceylon Federation of Trade Unions, 1966.

Employers' Federation of Ceylon. *Rules (Revised 1964).* Colombo:
Employers' Federation of Ceylon, n.d.

Government Clerical Service Union. *Golden Jubilee Souvenir, 1920–
1970.* Colombo: Government Clerical Service Union, 1971.

*The History of 25 Years of Proud Service to the Working Class by
the Ceylon Trade Union Federation.* Colombo: Ceylon Trade
Union Federation, 1965.

Tampoe, P. B. *The Ports Strike and Its Gains.* Colombo: Ceylon
Mercantile Union, 1970.

Newspapers and Periodicals

General-circulation newspapers are a disappointing but unavoidable source. Political reporting in the press is spotty, sometimes in-

accurate, and often partisan. There are three large newspaper chains, Associated Newspapers of Ceylon (known as Lakehouse), the Times of Ceylon group, and the Independent Newspapers group (also called the Davasa group). The most prominent English-language newspaper is the *Ceylon Daily News,* which also probably carries the largest volume of political news of any newspaper. Its coverage, however, is sharply skewed to the interests of the urban, Westernized, affluent classes, and its publisher, Lakehouse, has been politically controversial. Other Lakehouse dailies are the *Ceylon Observer* in English, *Dinamina* and *Janata* in Sinhalese, and *Thinakaran* in Tamil. The Sinhalese-language *Silumina* has the largest circulation of several Lakehouse weekly newspapers. The Times group publishes the *Ceylon Daily Mirror* and the *Times of Ceylon* in English and *Lankādipa* in Sinhalese daily, along with several weekly newspapers. The dailies *Davasa* in Sinhalese and *Sun* in English, the Sinhalese weekly *Rividina,* and several smaller newspapers are published by the Independent Newspapers group. A few significant newspapers unaffiliated with the three major chains have been founded during the past decade. The pro-CP Sinhalese daily *Aththa* and the pro-LSSP Sinhalese daily *Jana Dina* and English weekly *Nation* present political perspectives which contrast sharply with those of the chain newspapers, but they contain relatively limited quantities of factual political reporting. *Virakesari* is an older independently published Tamil-language daily. *Tribune,* published in English as a weekly newspaper for many years, was converted into a news magazine in 1971. All the previously mentioned newspapers are published in Colombo. *Elanadu,* a Tamil daily, and *Morning Star,* an English weekly, are published in Jaffna.

Serious periodicals in Ceylon have a short life expectancy, with many publication delays and lapses. The principal scholarly journals in the last few decades have been the *University of Ceylon Review,* the *Ceylon Journal of Historical and Social Studies,* and the newly established *Modern Ceylon Studies.* The *Ceylon Historical Journal* for a number of years has been devoted to reprinting old historical and descriptive works on Ceylon. In 1971, a journal called *Marga* was launched to promote discussion of public issues surrounding economic and social development with an impressive array of early contributors. The pro-LSSP periodical *Young Socialist* has appeared fairly regularly since 1961. *Ferguson's Ceylon Directory,* published annually by Lakehouse for more than a century, is a thick collection of miscellaneous information.

Secondary Sources

While it is impossible to list all published works of potential value to the study of contemporary Ceylonese politics, a selection of specialized studies, mostly published within the last decade, appears below. Articles largely devoted to reporting on current political events are not included. Each year since 1963, the February issue of *Asian Survey* has contained an article on political developments in Ceylon during the preceding year.

Abhayavardhana, Hector. "Categories of Left Thinking in Ceylon," *A Miscellany: Community Pamphlet No. 4.* Colombo: Community Institute, n.d., pp. 31–57.

Ames, Michael. "Ideological and Social Change in Ceylon," *Human Organization,* XXII (Spring 1963), 45–53.

Blackton, Charles S. "The Ceylon Insurgency, 1971," *Australia's Neighbours* (publication of the Australian Institute of International Affairs), 4th series, no. 76 (July–Aug. 1971), pp. 4–7.

Ceylon Daily News. *Parliament of Ceylon* for 1947, 1956, 1960, 1965, and 1970. Colombo: Associated Newspapers of Ceylon, Ltd., n.d.

Cooray, Joseph A. L. *Constitutional Government and Human Rights in a Developing Society.* Colombo: Colombo Apothecaries Co., Ltd., 1969.

Fernando, J. L. *Three Prime Ministers of Ceylon: An 'Inside Story.'* Colombo: M. D. Gunasena & Co., Ltd., 1963.

Gunatilleke, Godfrey. "Commitments to Development," *Marga* (Colombo), I, no. 1 (1971), 92–124.

Hulugalle, H. A. J. *Centenary Volume of the Colombo Municipal Council, 1865–1965.* Colombo: Colombo Municipal Council, 1965.

Jayasuriya, J. E. *Education in Ceylon Before and After Independence, 1939–1968.* Colombo: Associated Educational Publishers, 1969.

Jeffries, Sir Charles. *'O.E.G.': A Biography of Sir Oliver Ernest Goonetilleke.* London: Pall Mall Press, 1969.

Kearney, Robert N. "Ceylon: The Contemporary Bureaucracy," in Ralph Braibanti and associates, *Asian Bureaucratic Systems Emergent from the British Imperial Tradition.* Durham, N.C.: Duke University Press, 1966, pp. 485–549.

——. "The Communist Parties of Ceylon: Rivalry and Alliance," in Robert A. Scalapino (ed.), *The Communist Revolution in Asia,* 2nd ed. Englewood Cliffs, N.J.: Prentice-Hall, Inc., 1969, pp. 391–416.

——. "Militant Public Service Trade Unionism in a New State: The Case of Ceylon," *Journal of Asian Studies,* XXV (May 1966), 397–412.

——. "The Partisan Involvement of Trade Unions in Ceylon," *Asian Survey,* VIII (July 1968), 576–588.

——. "Sinhalese Nationalism and Social Conflict in Ceylon," *Pacific Affairs,* XXXVII (Summer 1964), 125–136.

Kodikara, S. U. "Communalism and Political Modernisation in Ceylon," *Modern Ceylon Studies,* I (Jan. 1970), 94–114.

——. *Indo-Ceylon Relations Since Independence.* Colombo: Ceylon Institute of World Affairs, 1965.

Lerski, George J. *Origins of Trotskyism in Ceylon: A Documentary History of the Lanka Sama Samaja Party, 1935–1942.* Stanford, California.: Hoover Institution on War, Revolution and Peace, 1968.

Obeyesekere, Gananath. "Religious Symbolism and Political Change in Ceylon," *Modern Ceylon Studies,* I (Jan. 1970), 43–63.

Phadnis, Urmila. "The Problem of the People of Indian Origin in Ceylon: Issues and Possible Solutions," *International Studies* (New Delhi), V (April 1964), 424–434.

——. "Sri Lanka: The New Constitution," *Economic and Political Weekly* (Bombay), VII (June 10, 1972), 1139–1141.

Pieris, Ralph. "Universities, Politics and Public Opinion in Ceylon," *Minerva,* II (Summer 1964), 435–454.

Wanasinghe, Shelton. "New Perspectives in Management," *Marga* (Colombo), I, no. 1 (1971), 55–71.

Weerawardana, I. D. S. *Ceylon General Election, 1956.* Colombo: M. D. Gunasena & Co., Ltd., 1960.

Wilson, A. Jeyaratnam. "Factors in the Working of Parliamentary Institutions in Ceylon," *Young Socialist* (Colombo), no. 16 (Aug. 1966), pp. 13–23.

——. "The Public Services in Ceylon," in C. R. Hensmen (ed.), *The Public Services and the People: Community Pamphlet No. 3.* Colombo: Community Institute, 1963, pp. 9–37.

Wiswawarnapala, W. A. "Composition of Cabinets, 1948–1960," *Young Socialist* (Colombo), no. 10 (Sept. 1963), pp. 267–272.

——. "Kachcheri System of District Administration in Ceylon," *Indian Journal of Public Administration,* XVI (Oct.–Dec. 1970), 541–556.

Woodward, Calvin A. *Growth of a Party System in Ceylon.* Providence, R.I.: Brown University Press, 1969.

Index

THE POLITICS OF CEYLON (SRI LANKA)

Designed by R. E. Rosenbaum.
Composed by York Composition Co., Inc.,
in 11 point Intertype Baskerville, 2 points leaded,
with display lines in Palatino italic.
Printed letterpress from type by York Composition Co.
on Warren's 1854 text, 60 pound basis,
with the Cornell University Press watermark.
Bound by Vail-Ballou Press
in Columbia book cloth
and stamped in All Purpose foil.

Library of Congress Cataloging in Publication Data
(For library cataloging purposes only)

Kearney, Robert N
  The politics of Ceylon (Sri Lanka)

  (South Asian political systems)
  Bibliography: p.
  1. Ceylon—Politics and government.
I. Title. II. Series.
JQ653 1973.K4   320.4'549'3   73-8702
ISBN 0-8014-0798-2